BEST BOOK OF
HEROES AND HEROINES

George Washington: Leader of the People

The Story of Albert Schweitze

BEST BOOK OF HEROES AND HEROINES

Edited by

PAULINE RUSH EVANS

Color Illustrations by

CHARLES McCURRY

Line Illustrations by

RAPHAEL BUSONI

Doubleday & Company, Inc., Garden City, New York

for

J. G. Ferguson Publishing Company, Chicago

Library of Congress Catalog Card Number 64-16232

Printed in the United States of America

Introducing—

Preface

I have watched the *Best Book Series* in the making—and over and over again I have wished that such books had been available when my children were growing up. It seems to me that arranging stories by subject matter will be most appealing to children. And certainly there is something here for every child. . . . Each volume contains weeks and months of fine reading.

What I particularly like is that this is a series of books for *reading*—not for looking. Every book is illustrated, and handsomely illustrated, but the emphasis is where it should be—on the stories themselves. Today, as always, children want and need reading that they can really get their teeth into.

The child who has this series to grow on is fortunate indeed. It comes too late for my own children, but my younger grandchildren will be able to enjoy the *Best Book Series*—every one of them.

SIDONIE M. GRUENBERG
Former Director, Child Study Association of America

The Story-Time Library

BEST BOOK OF ANIMAL STORIES

BEST BOOK OF MYSTERY STORIES

BEST BOOK OF DOG STORIES

BEST BOOK OF ADVENTURE STORIES

BEST BOOK OF HORSE STORIES

BEST BOOK OF HEROES AND HEROINES

Acknowledgments

Thanks are due to the following authors, publishers, publications and agents for permission to use the material indicated.

Abelard-Schuman, Limited for "The Chicken-House Hospital" and "The Hospital Established" from THE STORY OF ALBERT SCHWEITZER by Jo Manton, copyright 1955 by Abelard-Schuman, Inc. Abingdon Press for "Plant Wizard: George Washington Carver" from ARMED WITH COURAGE by May McNeer and Lynd Ward, copyright © 1957 by Abingdon Press. J. M. Dent & Sons, Ltd. for "Pasteur" and "Florence Nightingale" from THE ROLL CALL OF HONOR by Sir Arthur T. Quiller-Couch. Doubleday & Company, Inc., for "In the Beginning," "First Words," and "Opening World" from THE STORY OF MY LIFE by Helen Keller, copyright, 1903, 1931, by Helen Keller. Follett Publishing Company for "A Young Surveyor" from GEORGE WASHINGTON: LEADER OF THE PEOPLE by Clara Ingram Judson, copyright 1951 by Follett Publishing Company. Hermann Hagedorn for "Lindbergh" from THE BOOK OF COURAGE by Hermann Hagedorn. Harcourt, Brace and Company, Inc., for "Gentryville's Strong Boy" and "A Good Stepmother" from ABE LINCOLN GROWS UP by Carl Sandburg, copyright, 1926, 1928, by Harcourt, Brace and Company, Inc.; renewed by Carl Sandburg; for "Going West" from NARCISSA WHITMAN: PIONEER OF OREGON by Jeanette Eaton, copyright, 1941, by Harcourt, Brace and Company, Inc. J. B. Lippincott Company for "Damien the Leper" from MAN OF MOLOKAI by Ann Roos, copyright, 1943, by Ann Roos. Little, Brown & Company for "Ferdinand Magellan" from MAP MAKERS by Joseph Cottler and Haym Jaffe, copyright, 1931, by Joseph Cottler and Haym Jaffe. Lothrop, Lee and Shepard Co., Inc., for "Columbus and the Queen" from CHRISTOPHER COLUMBUS AND HIS BROTHERS by Amy Hogeboom, copyright, 1951, by Lothrop, Lee & Shepard Co., Inc. The Macmillan Company for "At the Court of Charles VII" and "The Maid Prepares for War" from THE GIRL IN WHITE ARMOR by Albert Bigelow Paine. Julian Messner, Inc., for "The Conquest of Yellow Fever" from WALTER REED, DOCTOR IN UNIFORM by L. N. Wood, copyright date June 11, 1943 by Julian Messner, Inc.; for "Lone Atlantic Flight" from AMELIA EARHART, HEROINE OF THE SKIES by Shannon Garst, copyright date March 23, 1947 by Shannon Garst. Methuen & Co., Ltd., for "The Chicken-House Hospital" and "The Hospital Established" from THE STORY OF ALBERT SCHWEITZER by Jo Manton. Random House, Inc., for "An Eventful Sunday," "Captured by the Shawnees," and "Chief Blackfish's 'Son'" from DANIEL BOONE, by John Mason Brown, copyright 1952 by John Mason Brown; for "The Two Lanterns" and "On Moonlit Roads" from PAUL REVERE AND THE MINUTE MEN, by Dorothy Canfield Fisher, copyright 1950 by Dorothy Canfield Fisher; for "Learning from Mother," "Get It Right on Paper," and "The Flying Machine" from THE WRIGHT BROTHERS by Quentin Reynolds, copyright 1950 by

Quentin Reynolds. Roy Publishers for "A Light in the Dark" and "Not for Sale" from THE RADIUM WOMAN by Eleanor Doorly. The Westminster Press for "Destiny Fulfilled" from YOUNG NATHAN by Marion Marsh Brown, copyright, 1949, by Marion Marsh Brown.

The editor and publisher have made diligent efforts to trace the ownership of all copyright material in this volumn, and believe that all necessary permissions have been secured. If any errors have inadvertently been made, proper corrections will gladly be made in future editions.

Introduction

It's an odd thing, but young people almost always seem to think that the age of heroes ended in their grandfather's day. They've been feeling that way for centuries. And yet, of course, each new generation goes on to produce new heroes, just as each generation did in the past.

Does the idea of heroism today seem old-fashioned to you? How you feel about it depends a good deal, I suppose, on what you think of as heroic. If your idea of a hero is only a person who became famous because of some great and daring deed, then I imagine that heroism could seem pretty remote today. But if you feel, as I do, that a lifetime of great accomplishment and devoted service to others can be as truly heroic as an act of physical bravery, then you find real heroism everywhere in the world today.

Certainly you won't find anything remote about the twenty people in this book. They are modern heroes—not so much because there are no legendary figures among them, but because what they were and what they did has real meaning for us today. These men and women lived and worked all over the world and under all sorts of circumstances—on the battlefield and on the frontier, in ill-equipped laboratories, in crowded, pest-ridden hospitals, and alone in the endless sky. But whenever and wherever they lived, they accomplished something that was important not only to the people of their own time but to all of us today.

I would have liked to have included many others in this book—scientists, ministers, doctors, teachers—scores of people who have lived truly great lives. But there wasn't room.

That's one of the great and encouraging things about our world. No book will ever be big enough to include all of the real heroes and heroines who deserve a place in it.

Danbury, Conn. P.R.E.

Contents

FROM

The Girl in White Armor: The True Story of Joan of Arc

ALBERT BIGELOW PAINE

The wonder and mystery of the life of Joan of Arc is something that has fascinated people for hundreds of years. Even if you don't believe any of the innumerable legends about her, there are still actual historical records that sound miraculous. How, for one thing, could a 17-year-old peasant girl—who could not even read or write—command an army and lead it to victory? Some explain it as a miracle, done with the guidance of heavenly voices. Others say it was because Joan herself had such absolute faith that she was able to transmit it to the weary defeated French forces. But that too was a kind of miracle. We see the Maid here in her first audience with King Charles. Her friend de Baudricourt has warned her that she will be mocked by the courtiers. But Joan proceeds, directly and fearlessly, as she does throughout her life—knowing all the time that death will come to her shortly.

At the Court of Charles VII

JOAN was never one to delay, and a messenger was promptly sent to the castle asking for an audience. The King may, or may not, have been told of this request.

Charles's rule was a mockery, his court a sham. He was the victim of parasites, who were jealous and suspicious of any influence from the outside and made it a point to keep from him anything that might interfere with their pleasure or profit. Chief among them was Georges de La Trémouille, a greedy traitor that stopped at no crime which would serve his ends, and Regnault de Chartres, Archbishop of Reims, who though a churchman of high rank, honored religion only as a form and had neither charity nor human pity in his heart. These two dominated Charles, and ruled such of his kingdom as remained to him. The archbishop bore the title of Chancellor, and La Trémouille that of Chief Counselor; Joan's message naturally fell into their hands.

Their first thought was as to how Joan could be used to their own advantage. The King's prestige was waning; La Trémouille, who traded on it with the English and Burgundians, could not afford to see the kingdom of France entirely a ruin, its King in exile. He had read de Baudricourt's letter about Joan, and, if the girl was what she claimed, it seemed worth while to encourage her. On the other hand, she might prove to be a witch, and dangerous. Whatever she was, she could influence the King against his advisers; one must move cautiously.

So the King's counselors deliberated as to whether he should hear this girl, who came as she said with messages from God. Later in the day a sort of committee came down from the castle to question her.

"Why have you come?" they demanded.

"That I will tell only to the King."

"But it is in the name of the King that you are asked this question."

Joan then answered: "I have been commanded to do two things on the part of the King of Heaven: one to raise the siege of Orleans; the other, to conduct the King to Reims for sacrament and his coronation."

The committee returned and the Council debated. Some were in favor of letting the King see Joan, others not. The matter had been noised through the castle by this time, arousing the interest and curiosity of the courtiers. Many of the idlers, wishing to see this strange girl who claimed to be sent from God, were in favor of her coming. Furthermore, not all of those about the King were evil. Some, like the King's secretary, Alain de Chartier, a gentle poet, were stirred by sympathy for the maid; likewise the Queen, Marie of Anjou, and her mother, Yolande of Aragon, Queen of Sicily, two good women, were favorable to Joan from the beginning.

The timid King, by this time aware of what was going on asked that this girl, before he saw her, be questioned by men of the Church. Messengers claiming to be sent by Heaven with revelations and warnings, were not uncommon. She was probably no more than a fortune teller. She might even be a witch. Nevertheless, if the priests found her harmless he would see her.

Charles was in the depths of despair. The month following the Battle of Rouvray had been his darkest hour. Poor in spirit and purse, surrounded by his tawdry, time-serving court, he had become childish and querulous. How could he guess that to a little girl dreaming over her spinning he had seemed all that was fine and noble—that listening to illumined beings she had come with messages that would lift him up and give him back his kingdom?

The groups of priests who called upon Joan must have found her answers satisfactory, for she was told that the King would receive her that same evening—this being the day of her arrival at Chinon. Yet in the very moment of her coming, the irresolute Charles, prompted by certain of his counselors, would have sent her away. He was reminded—perhaps by Queens Marie and Yolande—that this girl, commended to him by de Baudricourt, had been conducted across provinces occupied by the enemy and had miraculously forded rivers, to come to him. On this he consented to see her.

Being early March (the sixth), it was dark "after dinner" when, by Joan's statement, she went to the castle. One may picture her with her two knights, mounted, preceded by torches, climbing the steep, stony way that winds up to the entrance, crossing the drawbridge and passing under the arch of the lofty *tour de l'horloge,* a clock-tower to this day. A space of court to cross, a stair to mount, then a blaze of light, a dazzle of silk and cloth of gold, and facing it all a peasant girl who claimed to have brought messages to the King.

At the farther end of the room a fire was roaring up the great chimney. Also, according to Joan, there were "fifty *flambeaux,* and three hundred men at arms." At all events there was a great assembly of both men and women. Any diversion was welcome; a novelty like Joan would bring out every member of the castle.

There was a moment of expectant silence. Those idle, simpering people were curious to see how she looked, what she would do first. What they saw was a lithe, rather slender, fairly tall youth, with cropped hair—Joan in the page's costume she had worn from Vaucouleurs, the suit in which she had forded rivers and slept on the frozen ground; surely a curious figure before that tinsel throng.

If they had expected her to be dazed and awed they were quickly undeceived. Led forward by the Count of Vendôme, what she did was to go immediately to Charles, who occupied no special place, but had "retired behind some others," and falling on her knees make him reverence, saying:

"Very illustrious Lord Dauphin, I am come, being sent on the part of God, to give succor to the kingdom, and to you."

Joan never revealed by what sign she knew the King. Her statement: "I recognized him by the counsel and revelation of my Voices," is as far as she ever went on the subject.

The King led her apart—perhaps to the small tower embrasure at the left of the fireplace, where they spoke together. Making reverence, Joan said:

"Noble King, I am called Joan the Maid, and I tell thee on the part of Messire [God] that thou art the true heritor of France, son of the King, and He sends me to conduct thee to

The King led her apart.

Reims, in order that thou receivest there thy coronation and thy sacrament, if such be thy wish."

Charles asked her:

"How am I to know that you come from God?" Joan's answer to this was another secret that died with her; but long after, the King himself, near death, declared that a little before Joan's coming he had made a secret prayer of which no one else could know. He had prayed, he said, that if he was the true heir to the kingdom, God would defend him, or at the worst grant him the grace to escape without death or prison, allowing him to take refuge in Spain or Scotland, ancient brothers in arms, allies of the kings of France. Joan, the King said, repeated to him this prayer, known only to himself and God, thus gaining his confidence.

Returning now to the others, all saw the joy in the King's face. The poet secretary, Alain Chartier, wrote: "It was most manifest the King was greatly encouraged, as if by the Spirit."

Joan's own story of the royal audience was no more than a few words: "When I entered the presence of the King I recognized him by the revelation and counsel of my Voices. I told him I wanted to make war on the English." That was all; she had arrived "without interference"; the long days and longer nights were behind her. She told the King she wanted to make war on the English. It was as when on the road to Burey she had said to Durand Laxart that she wanted him to tell Sire Robert de Baudricourt to have her taken to the King. That was Joan's simple and direct way. She had no use for the roundabout. She traveled in a straight line to the point in view.

The Maid Prepares for War

Charles did not waste time waiting for the written report but at once ordered that soldiers and supplies be collected for the march on Orleans. Queen Yolande, a woman of much ability, went to Tours and Blois to begin preparations, being presently joined by the Duke of Alençon, sent by the King to assist her.

Joan was now, in fact, *chef de guerre*, chief of war. It was the royal decree that captains and all others of whatever rank must follow her leadership. Those hardened old warriors—many of them Armagnac raiders and captains of "free companies"—would not always be easy to handle, which is no wonder when we remember that for years they had been little more than bandits, obeying nobody, not even the King. What they really thought of the King's order, and of Joan, we shall never know. Probably it seemed to them a great new adventure led by a kind of mascot, or enchantress, who was going to give them victory. Whatever they thought they began arriving at Tours, and were sent on to Blois where Queen Yolande and Alençon had organized their camp.

Joan with her page had also come to Tours, conducted by Jean d'Aulon, called "one of the best men in the kingdom," named by the King as chief of her personal staff. They rode with Queen Yolande, who provided them with lodgings in the luxurious home of an old friend and former maid of honor, Eleanore de Paul, now married to a distinguished citizen, Jean du Puy.

At Tours it must have seemed to Joan that her troubles had come to an end. The people thronged about her, wearing small medals struck in her honor. Soldiers marched through the streets, her soldiers to be, breaking into cheers when she appeared among them. In all this she found a divine assurance of victory. She was humbly grateful for having been chosen to save France.

The Maid's military household received important additions at Tours. A second page, a youth called Raymond, was assigned to her; also a priest, Father Pasquerel, as almoner and confessor. Furthermore, she was joined by two of her brothers, Jean and Pierre, who, hearing the astonishing reports, had followed their sister to war. How proud they were of her, and how eagerly she listened to their news! Her devout mother had undertaken a pilgrimage to a distant shrine, to pray for her soldier daughter.

The people thronged about Joan.

The King commanded that armor be constructed for Joan, and for each of her two brothers. Tours was famous for its armorers —there was a whole street of them—but the master workman to whom was given the task of fashioning a suit of steel for the Maid must have found himself somewhat puzzled. He had never made armor before for a young girl, and to get it gracefully shaped, and adjusted and comfortable to the wearer was something of a task.

It was what is known as "white armor," of polished, unbrowned steel, and very beautiful. It gave the wearer an unearthly look, and probably no one better than Joan realized the effect this would have on her followers, and upon the enemy. It was such armor as this that Saint Michael had worn in her visions of him—the armor of the holy pictures, the armor of Heaven.

By an ancient record of the city of Tours Joan's armor cost the sum of one hundred francs, the equal of a thousand dollars, today. A strong horse in that day could be had for twelve francs, so Joan's armor cost the value of eight horses. Her two knights were likewise provided with new armor. Everywhere was preparation for the great campaign—busy days for the armorers of Tours.

Joan still had the sword presented to her by Robert de Baudricourt. She now learned that her heavenly Council wished her to have something different, a blade consecrated by knightly deeds. At Ste. Catherine de Fierbois, the Voices said, there was buried near the altar a sword upon which were stamped five crosses. They told her to send for it.

Joan sent an armorer of Tours with a letter to the clergy at Fierbois, telling them of this and asking them to send the sword, provided that it was their wish that she should have it. They searched as she directed and found the sword with the five crosses on it, buried not very deeply in the earth, but covered with rust. The priests who reverently undertook to remove the rust, reported that it fell away at their touch. Afterward, with those of Tours, they had two sheaths made for it, one of red velvet, and one of cloth of gold. But these were not for service. Joan herself had another made, a strong sheath of leather. This sword Joan especially loved. Her Voices had directed her to it, and it had been found near the altar of Saint Catherine, one of her Voices. The sword had belonged to some brave knight—tradition said to Charles Martel, who had offered it on the altar of Saint Catherine, after his victory over the Saracens, in 732.

Even more than her sword Joan prized her banner. It was made for her in Tours, by commandment, as she said, of Saint Catherine and Saint Margaret. The material of this banner was white linen or fustian, and it was fringed with silk. On it was the figure of God holding the world, at each side a kneeling angel. Inscribed upon it were the words JESUS MARIA, and the field of it was "sown with lilies."

Joan also had a pennon, on which was pictured the Annunciation, with an angel holding a lily. The work on the banner and on the pennon was done by a man named Hauves Poulvoir who had a daughter named Héliote, of about Joan's age. During the days when the work was in progress Joan and pretty Héliote Poulvoir became close friends. Joan was a soldier, getting ready for battle, but amid all the warlike preparations she found joy in the friendship of this young girl. It is easy to imagine the awe in which little Héliote would hold the Maid, who communed with Voices that were sending her to war.

"Joan, Joan, won't you be afraid when you face the cannons and the arrows, and the poised spears?"

"I may be—that is with God. It is certain that I am to be wounded—my blood will flow."

"Joan!"

"Yes, it has been revealed to me."

"And you will still go?"

"I must go, though it be to my death."

We know that Joan at Tours spoke of the wound she would receive at Orleans, for it is mentioned in a letter written a full two weeks before the event. Yet in spite of the prospect of battle and the knowledge that she must suffer, her month there could hardly have been less than a happy one. For the moment she had to face neither conspiracy nor bloodshed. Wherever she turned there was love, faith, and friendliness. The blessings of the cathedral were conferred upon her, her banner, and her arms. Her lodgings were sought by those who regarded her as the hope of France. She was on the way to do the work for which she was born.

FROM

Christopher Columbus and His Brothers

AMY HOGEBOOM

It took courage for Columbus to decide to be the first to sail into unknown waters. But it also took terrible patience. So many times his hopes had been raised, then dashed again. He had to cool his heels in Spain for seven long years, until the war with the Moors was over, and Queen Isabella could again become interested in his plans. Through all these trials, his great dream of discovery had been shared and strengthened by his brothers. Especially Bartholomew, who went to Portugal, then England and France to try to interest the Kings there in outfitting his brother's ships. "Never," wrote Columbus, "have I found better friends to right or left than my own brothers."

Columbus and the Queen

A FEW weeks later, on a hot sultry day in August, Christopher Columbus came striding along a dusty road outside the city of Palos. He was carrying his small son, Diego, on his shoulders. Here, in Spain, he had decided he would surely find aid for his adventure.

With Diego, he had come by ship from Lisbon to Palos, and,

since there was no money to spare, even to hire a mule, they had traveled on foot five long miles from the city.

Diego, who was now nearly five years old, was tired and half asleep when his father stopped in front of the gate of the Monastery of La Rabida. A bell hung in the archway overhead. Columbus hesitated a moment before he pulled the rope to ring it, for he knew he had something difficult to do.

"Would it be too much trouble to bring a cup of water for my boy?" he asked the porter who opened the gate.

It was not too much trouble for the kindly man, and he brought a cup of milk and a slice of bread as well. While Diego munched hungrily, one of the friars came to talk to Columbus and then, since it could be postponed no longer, Columbus was obliged to ask for charity.

"I can pay little or nothing," he said to the friar who led them into the cool shade of the garden, "and I have to go to Cordova on an important matter. In the meantime I have no place to leave my little son, for my wife died not long ago. I hope that I can pay you when . . ."

It was all quickly arranged by the warmhearted friars. They took the boy in at once and urged his father also to rest with them a few days before continuing his journey.

After a hearty supper in the refectory, Father Perez, the Prior, took Columbus to the library to see some books and maps of which they had been speaking. Columbus spoke of the map-making business he and his brother had started in Portugal. Soon it seemed quite natural to be telling also of his reasons for coming to Spain. As he talked of his great enterprise and described so clearly and confidently his plans to reach China and India by a short sea route, the monks listened spellbound. For this *Señor* Columbus, they could see, was an intelligent and a remarkable man such as they seldom met. One by one they began to catch his enthusiasm.

"Yes, yes!" Father Perez broke in, "what you say must surely be true! We also believe that the earth is round, and we do not teach that it is flat as some of the brothers do in their schools."

He talked of his great enterprise.

And what was more, Father Perez went on to say, there were other people in Palos besides the monks who shared his views. Martin Pinzon, the wealthy shipbuilder, was one of them. A bold and experienced mariner, he would be sure to have some valuable suggestions and influence at Court; and Father Perez felt, too, that he could be counted on for support.

It was a wonderful evening, and when Columbus went to bed he was happier than he had been for a long time. Never would he forget the kindness and hospitality of the Monks of La Rabida.

The next morning not only Martin Pinzon and his brother but also the Nino brothers came to see Columbus. They talked a long time together in the monastery garden with Father Perez beaming and nodding his head and exclaiming, "*Si, si!*" whenever there was an opening in the conversation.

"I will let you know," Columbus told the Pinzon and Nino brothers, "as soon as the voyage is certain."

Then he said good-by to Diego and started back to Palos. Now he was free to begin his journey to Cordova where King Ferdinand and Queen Isabella had their residence. As he started off he was full of confidence. Hadn't Father Perez said that the Spanish Court would be glad to listen to him, that Spain would be almost forced to support his plan? He knew on good authority that the Spanish war against the Moors had been far more costly than either Ferdinand or Isabella had expected. The possibility of discovering a short route to the wealth of the Indies would be an enticing one to them, especially now that the Pope had given Portugal exclusive rights to explore along the coast of Africa, and forbidden Spanish ships to sail in that direction.

But when Columbus arrived in Cordova, his hopes faded away once more. It had not been as easy to reach the King and Queen as he had expected, and it was many months before he was granted an audience and permitted to tell his story in Court.

When the time came he dressed carefully in the handsome, richly embroidered suit he had been hopefully saving for that day, and threw over his shoulders a cape of crimson velvet. Then he hastened to the palace.

The long council chamber was half-filled when he entered, and a guard conducted him to a seat in the rear and asked him to wait for his turn. He sat alone in the shadows and watched with interest everything that was taking place, observing especially the men and women close to the dais on which the King and Queen were seated, and the larger group of councilmen seated around the table below.

When his name was called he walked with great dignity to the dais and knelt before the throne. At the royal command he rose and began speaking. He had told his story so often that now it came easily. He explained once more about the narrowness of the ocean which he supposed was all that lay between Spain and China.

"Not far beyond the Azores our ships would come upon Japan," he said. And then he added something which he thought might especially please Queen Isabella, who, he knew, was very religious.

"If the expedition succeeds as I hope," he suggested, "it would not only increase the prestige of Spain by great wealth, but also it might do great good."

"And how is that?" asked Isabella.

"The people of those lands, Your Majesty, can all be taught the Christian religion and be baptized in our faith."

The Queen's face lighted at this, but King Ferdinand nodded a little dubiously.

"Is it true, *Señor* Columbus," he asked, "that you have already made this same proposal to Portugal?"

"It is true, Your Majesty."

"And King John has rejected it?"

"On the contrary," Columbus replied, "King John secretly attempted to carry out the plan, but it failed for lack of a commander with sufficient courage."

The faintest smile on the Queen's face softened her reproof

as she said, "You have supreme confidence in your own courage, *Señor* Columbus?"

"Yes, Your Majesty."

The Queen looked at the King, and the King asked the opinion of the Court advisers.

"It is not a narrow sea, as this gentleman seems to imagine," one of them said positively. "It is so wide no ship could ever hope to cross it. Provisions and fresh water would not last and storms would wreck the ships before they were halfway across. And besides," he concluded scornfully, "probably there is no island of Japan."

This was almost the same thing that King John's advisers in Portugal had reported, and King Ferdinand, who was not in favor of the voyage, was pleased. After a little more discussion Columbus was dismissed abruptly without the slightest encouragement.

It was a bitter disappointment, but a few days later when Columbus had decided that his case was hopeless and he might as well leave Cordova, Queen Isabella sent for him to come privately and talk with her. Isabella was not only a religious woman but she had a strong imagination, and was eager to hear more about those fabulous countries in Asia.

Now as Columbus spoke, she could see the flashing gold roofs on the temples in Japan, and the great throngs of worshipers forsaking their heathen gods and kneeling on the steps of their pagan temples to be baptized in the Christian faith. When he told of India she could see the gorgeous robes and enormous jewels worn by the great Khan of India. She saw the royal banner of Castile flying over the rich new lands. Realizing the extravagance of her own fancies, but impressed nonetheless, she said with a little smile,

"I see you are a poet as well as a dreamer, *Señor* Columbus."

Columbus returned the smile. They understood each other, these two—the Queen of Spain and the tall handsome man from Genoa. And now that he was talking to Isabella alone, Colum-

They understood each other, these two.

bus knew that he was much more eloquent than he had been before the Court.

When he had finished speaking and the spell was broken, Isabella was still convinced that the adventure was worth trying. But Spain was at war with the Moors, who had invaded the southern part of the country.

"Come back when the war is over," Isabella said. In the meantime she granted Columbus a small allowance to enable him to remain in Cordova. He felt encouraged, and for a while waited patiently. But unfortunately the war with the Moors dragged on year after year. For a time Columbus lived with the Duke of Medina, who had become his friend, and who did everything he could to aid him.

Then Bartholomew came from Portugal. He was impatient over the continued delays and thought it was time for his brother to appeal to some other country. "I don't like to leave Spain," Christopher told him. "Every day I hear that the war may end soon. Who can tell? But in the meantime you might be able to interest the King of England."

"It's worth a try," Bartholomew agreed. "I'll start at once."

Bartholomew went not only to England, but also to France. The King of England was too careful of his money to spend it on a doubtful venture, or to risk two or three ships which might never return.

The King of France was not interested in explorations. But he liked the gay and lively Bartholomew, so he decided to keep him around Court, suggesting that he make charts of places nearer home.

"I shall stay here as long as there is work for me," Bartholomew wrote his brother. "In the meantime, perhaps the King will change his mind."

It must have been at about this time that Columbus met his second wife, although no record of the marriage ceremony has ever been found. The lady's name was Beatriz de Harana, and she was the sister of one of Columbus' best friends.

A year or so later a handsome boy was born. "Small as he is, he looks like Bartholomew," said his father with a happy smile.

But he named him Ferdinand as a compliment to the King.

These new family ties helped Columbus keep up his spirits during the next few years when it seemed as though King Ferdinand and Queen Isabella had forgotten him. The war with the Moors still dragged on and people began to laugh at Columbus when he wanted to explain his beliefs concerning the narrow Western Ocean. Some of them made stupid jokes about his "miracle voyage." Only a few good friends stood by him, among them the brothers at the monastery at Palos, where he went often to see Diego.

Columbus had been in Spain nearly seven years when suddenly the war with the Moors was over. Spain was victorious. Columbus hurried to Granada where the final victory had been won. There he joined the crowds which surged up and down the streets, shouting loudly at every glimpse of the King or Queen, and joyously acclaiming the generals.

That night the Duke of Medina gave a great dinner to celebrate the historic moment, and Christopher was given a place of honor. "It's your turn now, Columbus," said the Duke, and drank a toast to his success.

The Duke was right. The next day Queen Isabella sent for him to come to Court. She thoughtfully enclosed a generous sum of money so that he might appear suitably dressed. He bought a handsome green suit, a black cape, and had enough money left over to buy a mule.

The Queen received him warmly, but King Ferdinand was still dubious about the voyage, so after a short discussion he was abruptly dismissed.

Angry and bitter at such treatment, he mounted his mule and rode away from the city. Any man with less courage and faith in himself might now have given up in despair. Not so Columbus!

With his head held high, and his eyes flashing like blue sparks struck from steel, he set out for France. Bartholomew had made many friends at Court and they might be able to help him.

He had jogged scarcely six miles from the city when he was overtaken by a messenger from the Court commanding him to return. The Keeper of the Treasury had reminded the King that the long war had emptied the nation's purse. He said, "Without much cost this might be a good chance to refill it." The King saw his mistake and ordered Columbus back.

Columbus was still burning with resentment when he reappeared in Court. He had been made to feel small and unimportant on his previous visits, but that had only made him more determined. This time he asked for higher profits for himself from the adventure, and he also insisted upon being given the title of "Admiral General," and the promise that he be made governor of any lands that he might discover and Christianize.

The Court hemmed and hawed. "What! An Admiral General who was a foreigner!" No Spaniard would agree to that!

But Columbus calmly explained his side of the question, "If I do not have a title higher than my captains, how can I command them and make them respect my authority?" he said.

Finally King Ferdinand was won over. When all was agreed by both sides, the royal order was made out and signed: "I, the King . . . I, the Queen."

Columbus was jubilant until he realized that Bartholomew would not be able to get to Spain in time to sail with him. "You will not even have received this letter by the time that I leave," he wrote, "for all is to be ready in two weeks."

Ferdinand Magellan

JOSEPH COTTLER AND HAYM JAFFE

FERDINAND MAGELLAN, Portuguese sea captain and adventurer, received a letter from his friend, Francisco Serrano. Magellan had left his friend prowling around somewhere in the Indian Ocean, while he had sailed back to Lisbon.

"I have discovered," said the letter, "a new world, larger and richer than that found by Vasco da Gama, the Spice Islands! I shall remain here, for the native king has made me his captain-general . . ."

The Spice Islands, about which such strange tales had reached Portugal! Here were supposed to live men with spurs on their ankles, hogs with horns, hens that laid their eggs nine feet underground, boiling rivers, poisonous crabs, giant oysters, pearls as large as rocks, and tons of spices.

Since he had renounced his nationality, Magellan went to young Charles V, King of Spain.

"Fit me out a fleet," offered Magellan, "and the Spiceries are yours."

Like Columbus, he explained, he would sail west. On the other side of South America stretched a new ocean which Balboa had seen a few years before. There must be a strait, held Magellan, cleaving through the continent from the east to this ocean. "And westward on this ocean must be the Spice Islands and my friend Francisco." He wanted as much to see his friend Serrano as to blaze the westward way across the world. They had been shipmates together, had starved and made merry together, and were bosom friends. So Magellan would risk danger to come to his friend.

Charles was willing enough that this great adventurer should strike out to the Spiceries in this new way. But the old trouble again appeared in mustering a crew. Who was foolhardy enough to throw his life away? Brave men are not easy to find.

Magellan himself did not think twice about the danger, for his heroism was famous. Everybody knew how he had saved the lives of an entire crew, and how he never seemed to care much for his own skin.

From here and from there at length a crew was chosen. Nearly three hundred men, all sizes, shapes, and nationalities. Five old ships there were, with ribs said to be as soft as butter.

"A week at sea," people warned Magellan, "and the rotten boards will split asunder and leave you drowning like rats."

Magellan listened politely, thanked them all for the sound advice, and went about his business firmly. One of his ships was called *Victoria*—"Victory." This was the motto he would wave around the world.

Colder and colder it grew, and fearfully stormy. The fleet was tossing about helplessly in a gale so fierce that it blew all the forecastles away. Magellan saw he could not go on. He must seek a harbor in which to take shelter for the winter. Suddenly a pleasant coast came into view and toward it Magellan steered.

At once a cry arose, "Back to Spain! Back to Spain!"

"No, my men," declared Magellan, "we shall not go back. Never until we have done what we set out to do—reached the Spice Islands. Here, in this new land, we stay until spring thaws the ice. But already we are farther south than any other navigator has sailed. Courage!"

"But where are we? The country seems uninhabited by man or beast."

Even as the sailors said this, a strange and beautiful animal appeared on a slope. It was about four feet high with a gracefully curved neck, and long slender legs. Above, its silky hair was fawn-colored; below, pure white.

A strange animal appeared on a slope.

"What is it?" asked the wondering sailors. Europeans had never seen such an animal. Later they named it guanaco.

The animal bounded away and a human figure appeared on the slope. He stopped, stared at the strangers, and then approaching, struck up acquaintance. Presently he went to bring his people down. As he strode away, someone whispered to Magellan, "Hasn't he enormous feet?"

He had. It was the country of big feet. Big-feeters, Magellan called the inhabitants—Patagones—and the name has remained.

The big-feeters were equally startled at meeting the small-feeters who stood no higher than their waists, and had strange, bearded faces. What must "John," the Patagonian, have thought of the vanity of these pale pygmies who used a thing which they called a mirror, and into which they liked to gaze at their own faces? John was too polite to say.

They were a club of happy giants, these Patagonians, singing and dancing the day long, living on herbs and the flesh of the guanaco. But what an appetite! Magellan invited two of them for a snack, a mere nibble, that they might talk or make signs at each other about the straits the adventurer was seeking. That was a great mistake, and a calamity to the crew, who were running short of food. For, while Magellan munched on two or three biscuits, the two guests ate up a basketful, and daintily washed it down with half a bucket of water.

"We know nothing of any straits around here," the Patagonians signaled.

So, when the season grew milder, Magellan sailed away from Patagonia. He had not gone far south when suddenly they came upon a vast inlet. As they explored these new waters, it dawned on them that they were in the long-sought strait—the Strait of Magellan, as it is now known.

Fortune was smiling now, thought Magellan, but his men were flinching.

"No one has ever sailed that ocean on the other side of this strait," they argued. "Who knows its perils or its extent or its course? Our provisions are low. We can go no farther. Let us turn back."

Magellan faced them. "My men," he said, "you are right. The voyage will be long and dangerous. Our provisions are wasted. But believe that you are heroes, that the world will never forget you if you succeed in your adventure. For myself, I would rather have to eat the leather on our ships' yards, than turn back. Will you continue with me, or return?"

"On! On! We will go on!" cheered the men. "We will sail with you to the other side of the globe!"

As they sailed westward through the strait, Magellan gave names to all the capes, bays, inlets, mountains, and harbors. To the south lay a land of mountains on whose tops were seen burning fires. Land of Fire, Magellan called it—Tierra del Fuego.

All at once before his hungry eyes lay the waters of the great ocean, seen by Balboa seven years before. With tears of joy and salutes from his cannon, Magellan greeted it.

As the ships swung into the new ocean, the fierce winds died down into a gentle breeze, the heaving waters became peaceful. Thus it continued. Magellan was overjoyed at the change. "A pacific ocean!" he exclaimed.

His joy was short-lived; the food supply was dwindling fast. The faces of the crew became pinched, their eyes watery. And in the starved company broke out the scurvy. Weak with hunger, they offered no resistance to the terrible disease. By dozens the crew perished.

The survivors envied the dead. Food! It was a nightmare with them, with Magellan as well as the rest. No fish could be caught, and no more meat was left. There were no more mealtimes. Each man caught a rat if he could or devoured a biscuit which swarmed with worms.

"I would rather have to eat leather than turn back." Magellan remembered these words. Alas, they had been prophetic. He ordered the crew to cut the hides from the main yards and boil them. When they had no more leather, they would eat sawdust.

One morning the half-dead crew awoke to a strange sound on the water—human voices! They looked out, spellbound. There on the shining waters were swarms of canoes filled with brown men holding aloft stalks of bananas and clusters of nuts. With a cry, the famished crew fell upon the fruits and nuts while their visitors looked on amazed.

In the distance Magellan saw one of the most beautiful sights in the world—island mountains. Forests rose up before him, of bamboos and palms. As he gazed, one of his officers ran up, saying, "Those rascals have stolen our small boat."

"Ah we are among thieves," said Magellan. "Let us call these lands the Robber Islands—Ladrones."

At one of these islands, Guam, he landed and refreshed his men, although he stayed but two days. The Spiceries must be somewhere in these waters, and he must be off to seek them. His bosom friend Francisco awaited him there, and he longed to embrace him, and to say to him that the sight of his dear Francisco was worth all the suffering he had endured.

A week more on the sea and land loomed up. His heart leaped, but in a vain joy, for this new group of islands was not the Spiceries at all. What were they? Magellan took out his map of the world, but he did not find them on it. So he sketched in his new discovery—and the Philippines became a part of the globe. The islands were beautiful with palm trees and clear springs. "Here," thought Magellan, "I can help the sick among my crew to recover." With his own hands he proceeded to tend them.

For a whole day not a human being appeared on the horizon. Magellan was becoming curious when, from one of the neighboring islands, a boat, manned by nine natives, pushed off. Were they friends? The doubt lasted only until the boat touched the shore of Magellan's camp. The native leader stepped forward with joyous greeting and gifts were exchanged between the East and the West. Red caps, and bells, and looking glasses were the gifts of the men of the West. The East was more practical. It supplied the famished adventurers with fish, bananas, and a strange fruit at which Magellan marveled, for it was bread, milk, and oil all in one, he thought—the coconut!

"Come to dinner," invited the native hosts cordially in sign language.

Food was what most interested men who had just come through a starvation period.

"Since we were not prepared for your visit," gesticulated the native king, "you will have to do with our usual simple food."

The first course was an enormous portion of roast pork. The service was entirely of gold—platters and cups of solid gold—and golden plaques and panels blazed brilliantly from the walls, dazzling the eyes and hearts of the Europeans . . . But on with the dinner! The main dish consisted of quantities of rice with spiced pork, sauce, and gravy. The beverages were especially delightful—a soothing drink prepared from the milk of the coconut, and a mild palm wine.

"This dinner was worth the trip," thought the adventurers with satisfaction. "We won't want food for six months more."

All at once a huge platter of roast fish and ginger was served. The Westerners began to feel alarmed. After all, the capacity of the human stomach is limited. But could a guest refuse? Taking heart, for they were brave men, they attacked the fish and by sheer courage disposed of it.

"The danger is past," they thought faintly.

But wait . . . The enemy was advancing with fresh power. Platters of fish and rice steamed in. Recklessly the Europeans fell upon the dish—and collapsed. But so did the king of the islands. And they all snored away the effects of the food.

The king was a strange specimen to Magellan. "A savage!" thought the commander. "Look at him! Tawny in color, his body painted and nearly naked; gold rings in his ears, gold studs in his teeth. He is short and fat, a lover of ease and quiet. Though he is a just man, he is also arrogant; nobody may speak to him except through a tube. His Royalty must not stoop; therefore when he has occasion to enter a room with a low doorway, he has to go by way of the roof. Such queer customs, too! For instance, to show his affection for you, he shoots out his clenched fist at you. And when he is old, he will be thrust aside unceremoniously and his children placed in command. What savages!"

And the native probably thought: "What strange people these Spaniards are! So parched looking, and as skinny as skeletons! Why did they risk their lives to come here? Isn't their home comfortable? How impressed they were with that metal, gold! They seemed to worship it. The worst of them is their uninteresting faces. There is no "make-up" on them, no life—just the skin of an animal with no art on it to make it human. And their bodies they cover all up with rags, as if they would shun the air and sunshine. Such queer customs, too. To show affection each squeezes the other's palm."

The image of the Spice Islands, now called the Moluccas, and his friend Francisco made Magellan restless. It was time to leave the pleasant haunts of the Philippines.

One day, about three years after Magellan left Spain, the people of Seville saw a singular float wearily making its way up the Guadalquiver. So battered was it that even the ghostly emblem it bore, *Victoria*, failed to make it recognizable. Straining in every joint, the ship anchored at last as the curious crowd stared from the dock. A few faces on deck seemed familiar.

With a cry of surprise, the watchers exclaimed, "It must be Magellan's *Victoria!* Where is the rest of the fleet? Where is Magellan?"

Juan del Cano stepped forward, pale and cadaverous as a spectre. "Our leader is dead," he said sadly, "buried in the Philippines. Of the two hundred eighty men who started full of hope from San Lucar, only eighteen of us are returning; of five ships, only one."

The crowd rushed on board to embrace the eighteen heroes, and to mourn with them the loss of Magellan.

"But," said del Cano, brightening, "we have found the Spiceries, which were Magellan's goal . . . When we left the Philippines, with anguish at our great loss, we sailed to Borneo, which is the largest island in the world. After staying awhile in the wonderful palace of the sultan, over the Celebes Sea we rode straight to the Spiceries, to the Isles of Ternate and Tidore.

"We asked for Francisco Serrano to sadden him with news of the death of his best friend. But it was unnecessary. It seemed as though the two friends were bound in death as in life. The shadow of death had no sooner fallen upon Magellan in the Philippines than it hastened to take his friend, too, on the island of Ternate."

There was little more to tell. Homeward the *Victoria* had sailed, by way of Vasco da Gama's water, around the Cape of Good Hope, up the West coast of Africa, straight to Spain. Clear around the globe of the earth the eighteen heroes had gone.

With this journey, all further guesses about the shape of the earth were made unnecessary. Magellan, and his comrades, swept aside the myths of an Atlas upholding the world on his shoulders, of a flat ocean from whose edge you fell headlong, and similar fearsome tales. That the world is round, this first circumnavigation of the globe showed.

The world's debt to Magellan, the one who gave us this proof, will be remembered as long as ships sail through the Strait of Magellan, and men glance skyward. For, in the heavens of the southern hemisphere, two star clusters have been named the Magellanic Clouds.

FROM

Daniel Boone

JOHN MASON BROWN

The story of the growth of America is closely bound up with the exploits of Daniel Boone. This picturesque, lovable and courageous pioneer believed that he was especially ordained to open up the West for his country. Again and again, he pushed out to new frontiers—North Carolina, Kentucky, West Virginia, Missouri—not only for himself but for other settlers whom he guided to new lands and new homes. After he had blazed the famous Wilderness Road into Kentucky and founded Boonesborough, he was ready to adventure further west. But not before he had some dramatic encounters with the Indians—whom he understood better than any other frontiersman of his time. He not only fooled the Shawnees into adopting him, but persuaded them to delay their attack on Boonesborough, and then he escaped in time to prepare the settlers and foil the Indian attack.

An Eventful Sunday

SUMMER is a friendly and relaxing time. Its greens are soft as cushions; its colors gay and party-like. Its lazy heat is comforting. When its days are sun-drenched everything seems at peace, and peace seems to be everywhere.

On the 17th of July, 1776, even Boonesborough had a peaceful look. That it was Sunday only added to the calm. The past few months had been tranquil enough. Those Indian massacres, which had sent so many frightened settlers back across the mountains, had taken place in the cold, leafless weeks of December. They now seemed a long way off, almost as far away as the red-coated armies on the coast.

As was proper on the Sabbath, there had been a reading of the Bible in the morning. As was no less proper for an older man on a Sunday afternoon, Daniel, sleepy from his midday meal, had gone to his cabin to take a nap. After he had removed his moccasins and before he dozed off, it perhaps crossed his mind that the stockade which by connecting the cabins would turn Boonesborough into a fort, had not been completed. The stockade ought to be finished. He knew that. Yet on such a lolling summer's day surely it could wait.

The sun, which had added to Daniel's drowsiness, kept the young people out-of-doors. They were playing by the river. Among them was Daniel's daughter Jemima, whose shouts and laughter her father may have dimly heard before he went to sleep.

Jemima had two friends with her, the Calloway sisters—Betsey, who was sixteen and Fanny, who, like Jemima, was fourteen. The three girls decided to go out in the settlement's only canoe. When they had drifted downstream about a quarter of a mile, they saw beyond a clump of bushes on the far bank some flowers they wanted to pick. While trying to land, they lost control of their boat.

They did not suspect that in the bushes, towards which the Kentucky's current carried them, five Indians were hiding. These Indians had been watching the canoe, hoping this very thing would happen. At the right moment they plunged into the water and dragged the screaming and struggling girls ashore. They then silenced them by threatening to kill them and hurried them through a ravine up and over a hill.

Some say the girls were not missed until milking time, others that their screams were heard in Boonesborough and that Dan-

They dragged the screaming and struggling girls ashore.

iel, on hearing them, jumped up, grabbed his rifle, and raced to the river, more alarmed than his neighbors had ever seen him. He was so upset that he did not realize for hours (and then only when someone pointed it out) that he had not stopped to put on his moccasins.

Pursuing parties were organized at once, one on horseback headed by Colonel Calloway, one on foot led by Daniel. As Daniel advised, Calloway's group did not attempt to follow the Indians. Instead, they galloped north, in order to reach the ford of the Licking River first and stop the red men if they got that far with their captives. To Daniel and his group fell the task of picking up the trail, shadowing the Indians, and, most difficult of all, overpowering them before they had a chance to kill the three girls.

Daniel found that the trail was not so hard to follow as he

Daniel and his group were to pick up the trail.

had feared. This was due to the courage and ingenuity of the three girls. They did not have Boone and Calloway blood in them for nothing. In spite of being closely watched by the Indians, they managed to give hints of their course by breaking twigs and tearing off and dropping tiny bits of their garments. Each time Daniel and his men came upon one of these markings, their hopes increased. Even so, they were well aware of the difficulties which lay ahead of them and of the dangers faced by the girls.

Daniel realized the braves would become less and less careful the farther they went and the safer they felt themselves to be. The end of the thirty-five-mile chase came at noon and was terrible in its suspense. When the white men crept close to the Indian party, they were delighted to see that the three girls were unharmed. But Daniel and his men knew that one false move by them would cost the girls their lives.

Luckily, the Indians were busy cooking and, therefore, were caught off guard. The frontiersmen took careful aim and fired just as their presence was discovered. Two of the warriors were killed; the other three ran into the canebrake and escaped.

In spite of knives and a tomahawk thrown at the girls by the departing braves, and John Floyd's mistaking Betsey for a squaw and almost braining her with his rifle butt, the young women were saved. The party that returned them to Boonesborough came back in triumph. They were soon rejoined by Colonel Calloway and his men who, having encountered no Indians, had rightly decided that Daniel must have accomplished his mission.

They had not been home long when exciting news reached the settlement. In distant Philadelphia the Representatives of the United States in General Congress met, had pledged their lives, their fortunes, and their sacred honor to support an all-important document. It was to change man's thinking about himself, his rights, and his government. It proved to be what has been called the "birth certificate of a nation." America had made her final break with the British Crown. She had broken a new path, too, and proclaimed her freedom by issuing the Declaration of Independence.

In time the men and women in the wilderness would know the blessings brought them by this document. For the next few years, however, every cabin on the frontier, including Daniel's, would mainly know the terrors and trials of war and how hard and constant a struggle the fight for liberty always must be.

Captured by the Shawnees

A year and a half after Jemima's capture, Daniel was to have his own experiences as a prisoner of the Indians. In the bitter cold of a freezing January he and twenty-nine men had left Boonesborough for the Lower Blue Licks.

They had important work to do. The settlements were in desperate need of salt. In the past it had been sent to them by the seaboard colonies, but the Revolution made the sending of such supplies inconvenient, if not impossible. Fortunately, there was plenty of salt in Kentucky's salt springs or "licks." To prepare it for human use, these waters had to be boiled down in large iron kettles. The pioneers had lacked such kettles until Virginia sent some by pack horse across the mountains. It was with this newly arrived equipment that Daniel and his men went to work.

They had been at the Lower Blue Licks for a month during which, as they worked undisturbed, they had made quantities of salt. They thought their task almost done, and were looking forward to being relieved by another group of salt-makers, when disaster abruptly overtook them.

Towards sundown on the 7th of February Daniel was struggling in a snowstorm to return to camp. He had been out hunting and the horse he led was carrying fresh buffalo meat for himself and his men. Although the horse shied nervously on approaching a fallen tree, Daniel blamed the blinding snow for this. Within a few seconds he knew better. Four Shawnee

Four Shawnees jumped from behind the tree.

braves jumped from behind the tree and, though Daniel tried to run away, soon captured him.

The four braves forced Daniel to go with them to their nearby camp. On reaching it he realized at once how serious his situation was. A hundred and twenty warriors were gathered there under Chief Blackfish. With them, dressed and painted like Indians, were James and George Girty, those white traitors to the American cause. Their brother, the even more infamous Simon Girty, would figure darkly in Daniel's life in the coming years.

All the men at the Indian camp had heard of Daniel, all knew the importance of their prisoner. They gave him a loud welcome, shook hands with him, and pretended to greet him as a friend. Among those most pleased to see him were some of the very braves from whom he had escaped eight years before after they had warned him to beware of the stings of the "wasps and yellow jackets." These braves were so delighted to have him in their power again that they could not help laughing. Daniel, knowing the ways of Indians, fooled them all into thinking he was as happy to be with them as they were to have him.

They soon told him their plans. They announced they were going to attack Boonesborough and wished him to guide them there. When they added that they expected Daniel to persuade his group of salt-makers to give themselves up before the expedition started, they presented Daniel with one of the most difficult decisions he ever had to reach. To make a choice affecting his own life was easy enough; to make one which affected so many other lives was a terrible responsibility.

As he listened to the Indians, the beat of Daniel's heart may have quickened but the expression of his face remained unchanged. He thought of Rebecca and the children. He thought of the men with him and their families. He remembered that the stockade at Boonesborough was finished only on one side. He realized that, without his twenty-nine companions and those who might be coming to relieve them, the defenders of Boonesborough would be hopelessly outnumbered by their attackers.

How he could save Boonesborough was Daniel's only concern.

To save it, he knew he must delay the threatened attack, trust to luck, and sacrifice the few for the many. To gain time, he went so far as to promise the Indians that he and his party of salt-makers would give themselves up and go with them peacefully to their Ohio villages. The Indians in return promised not to hurt their captives.

Daniel pointed out that without attacking Boonesborough they would already have collected a large number of prisoners. He argued that, if the Shawnees went north and stayed there until the snow was gone, their expedition would be far simpler to carry out. It would be better equipped too, because they could buy more arms with the twenty pounds which Governor Hamilton would pay for each American captive delivered alive in Detroit. Daniel, who could play the Indian game as well as any Indian, added as a final inducement that if the Shawnees waited for the spring he would himself guide them to Boonesborough and persuade the settlement to surrender.

The Indians were won over by Daniel's arguments; so were Daniel's men. Though some of the settlers protested sullenly, they admitted the wisdom, both for themselves and their families, of laying down their rifles and going north with the Shawnees.

The red men showed at once how unreliable their promises were. They had guaranteed not to hurt their captives but, now that the white men were helpless, many of the braves were eager to kill them. A council, at which Daniel was allowed to speak, was held to determine their fate.

It lasted for two hours and was presided over by Blackfish, a kindly chief and a man of character who wanted to live up to the agreement. The vote was close—frighteningly close—but it was accepted as binding. In spite of Blackfish's eloquence, only sixty-one warriors were in favor of sparing the prisoners, while fifty-nine voted to murder them all except Daniel.

After this council the journey to Ohio began. On the way, Daniel was the first to be forced to run the gauntlet. Running the gauntlet was the odd ritual of torture with which Indians welcomed their prisoners. To red men it was at once a test and a game. It was their way of learning which were the weaklings and which the strong.

They would stand in two rows on either side of a line, and, armed with sticks, stones, antlers, or tomahawks, beat the man who ran between them. Only the hardiest survived, and often these suffered permanent injuries. Since the Indians considered this a sport, they were as willing to cheer their victims as to destroy them. Daniel won their admiration by zigzagging down the course at great speed, using his head as a mallet and knocking over several braves, to the delight of the others, and coming out of the ordeal with only a few bruises.

Chief Blackfish's "Son"

The trip north was uncomfortable. The winter uncommonly cold. Little or no game was found. Often the shivering party had nothing except slippery elm bark to chew on. Every night the prisoners were tied up and watched by guards. Many of the white men grumbled, but not Daniel. His fellow salt-makers were amazed to see how cheerful he was, how much he joked and laughed, and how happy he seemed to be. The more experienced of them understood the trick he was playing, and played it too. There were others who refused to follow Daniel's example and even began to doubt his loyalty.

After passing through several villages, the Shawnees led their captives to their largest town, Little Chillicothe. The Indians there were overjoyed at such a sizeable catch of Americans. They were surprisingly friendly, too; so friendly that Daniel and at least sixteen of his group, who pretended to be contented, were solemnly adopted into the tribe.

Adoption was an old Indian custom. More than being an act of forgiveness, it was, especially if the prisoners were young men or boys, a sensible method of getting recruits. By means of it families that had lost their sons in battle gained new sons. These were chosen from the captives who were best behaved and most courageous. Once it was clear that a prisoner would not try to escape, a warrior would take him into his wigwam, treating him with as much affection as if he were really a member of the family.

Glad as they were to have their lives spared, neither Daniel nor his men can have enjoyed the ceremony of being adopted. It took a long time and had its embarrassing features. What was worse, it hurt.

According to one of his early biographers, who had talked often with Daniel, the hair of the man being adopted was plucked out until only a tuft some three or four inches in diameter was left on the crown of his head. The scalp lock was then cut, tied with ribbons, and decorated with feathers. Next the candidate would be undressed and led, usually by squaws, to a river or stream where he would be washed and rubbed "to take all his white blood out." Thereafter, when he had scrambled into his clothes, he would be escorted to the council-house. The chief would make a welcoming speech, the new brave's face and head would be fashionably painted, and what the Indians considered a feast would be served.

When he was plucked and painted in this fashion, Daniel was a Shawnee. At least, he was outwardly. He was fortunate in having as his new "father" no less a person than Blackfish himself, whose attention he had attracted from the first. The chief became genuinely fond of Daniel and so did his squaw. They called him Sheltowee, meaning Big Turtle, and looked upon him with pride as their son.

To Daniel, as to his men, it seemed the winter months would never end. The wigwams were cold, smoky, and drafty. They were dirty, too, and filled with fleas and bedbugs. The food, consisting of beans, pumpkins, dried corn, hominy, and game, was neither pleasant to look at nor easy to swallow, since often all of these would be dumped into one kettle and boiled until they became a greasy mess.

In spite of such hardships and the inner worry he knew, Daniel gave the appearance of being happy. When he was allowed to hunt, he brought what he had killed home to his red "father." If he found himself in a shooting contest with some Shawnees, he remembered the lesson he had learned long ago in the Yadkin. He shot well enough to show his skill but never well enough to make his rivals jealous.

If Daniel laughed, talked, and whistled a lot, he also listened. Little by little, from hints dropped here and there, he pieced together the plans being made for the attack on Boonesborough in the coming spring. He also kept his sharp eyes open, noting every detail of the countryside through which he passed. Mostly he waited, wondering if the chance would ever come for him to escape, and hoping it would come before it was too late.

The Indians continued to be proud of having so many white prisoners. What they counted a triumph Daniel was later to say was an error. He thought the Shawnees never made a greater mistake than when, by taking white men into the heart of their country, they enabled their captives to learn the exact locations of their villages and the paths leading to them. In the avenging years ahead, when American forces were to sweep through this Indian country under such leaders as Anthony Wayne and George Rogers Clark, burning these villages and destroying crops, Daniel was to be proved correct.

That was in the future. For the moment the Indians had it their way, and their way was not easy for Daniel. Often he had to bite his lower lip hard not to lose his self-control. He suffered acutely whenever he saw some of his own men—his Boonesborough neighbors and friends—beaten without mercy or compelled to run the gauntlet because of having shown their hatred of their captors.

A few of the victims of these tortures looked at Daniel with accusing eyes, not realizing what he was doing and beginning to believe he was a traitor. Daniel read their thoughts and understood their feelings. Nonetheless, he continued to play his game, reminding himself with all the strength he had that what mattered most to him and to these men was Boonesborough, which must be warned and strengthened in time.

Early in March, 1778, Blackfish decided to go to Detroit. He wanted to see Henry Hamilton, the British lieutenant-governor there, and to sell him those surly Americans no Indians wished to adopt.

Blackfish took his new "son" along with his party, and Daniel saw face to face the man who, rightly or wrongly, was hated and feared up and down the frontier as the "hair-buyer." Hamilton, realizing how valuable Daniel could be to the English cause, treated him with respect. He showed him many courtesies, not guessing that Daniel was fooling him just as he had fooled the Shawnees.

The governor was surprised and delighted to have Daniel produce from the leather bag he wore around his neck the captain's commission he had been issued when he served with the British colonial forces in Lord Dumore's War. Daniel carried this commission because he knew that Indians, if ever they caught him, would be impressed by a document which established him as an officer in the army of their British allies.

Hamilton was no less impressed. He was the more convinced of Captain Boone's loyalty to the Crown when Daniel said he would undertake to persuade the citizens of Boonesborough to surrender and follow him back to Detroit. This offer pleased Hamilton to such an extent that he attempted to obtain Daniel's liberty by offering to pay Blackfish a hundred pounds for him. Blackfish, however, refused to let him go, insisting he was too fond of his new "son" to lose him.

Even when Blackfish and his party prepared to leave the fort at Detroit, Hamilton's kindnesses to Daniel continued. As a farewell present he gave Daniel a pony, saddle, bridle, blanket, and some silver trinkets. The truth is Hamilton was so taken in that on telling Daniel good-by he talked to him about his duty to *their* Most Gracious Majesty, King George III.

When he got back to Little Chillicothe, Daniel saw at once that the long-discussed plans for attacking Boonesborough were becoming definite. The village had changed. It had lost its peaceful winter look and was an armed camp. The air was heavy with talk of war, and signs of the war's coming were everywhere. The beat of the tom-toms had quickened. They now pounded like the hearts of angry men. Runners were being sent out to race from town to town with the war pipe. Each day strange Mingos, Delawares, and Shawnees were appearing, impatient and prepared for action.

This different feeling and these different conditions did not make life easier for Daniel and the other adopted Americans. Adding to their troubles were things which had happened both during and after Blackfish's visit to Detroit. While the chief was there, one of the shrewdest of the pioneers, a man named Johnson who since his capture had pretended to be a half-wit, escaped. He was the first to reach Kentucky with news of the coming invasion and details as to the whereabouts of the Shawnee villages.

In May this same Johnson led a small raid against one of these Ohio towns. As proofs of his success, he came home with some stolen horses and a sickening number of Indian scalps. Early in June some other men from Boonesborough made a similar surprise attack on another village, collecting many horses and killing several Shawnees.

The Indians were angered and alarmed by these expeditions. Since they left they could no longer trust their white "sons," they began to guard them more closely. As the days crept by, Daniel, though he continued to smile, flamed with impatience. It began to look as if his chance would never come. Then, unexpectedly on the 16th of June, it did come, and in a way that must have made Daniel laugh.

This time it was the Indians who needed salt. Some braves had gone to make it at the salt springs of the Scioto. Their leader was Blackfish, who had brought Daniel with him. According to one story, the Shawnees were hard at work and keeping, as usual, a watchful eye on Daniel. The day would have passed like all those other days of captivity, had not such a tremendous flock of wild turkeys suddenly filled the sky that, for a moment, the Indians forgot about Daniel.

Such a moment was all Daniel needed and all he had been praying for. He dashed for the woods and disappeared, and kept on dashing for the next four days. During those four days Daniel, who was now forty-four, covered a hundred and sixty miles and had only one meal, some meat from a buffalo he killed at the Blue Licks. Although exhausted and half-starved when he approached the little group of cabins for which he had been heading, he did not care. He had reached Boonesborough. In time, he hoped.

FROM

Paul Revere and the Minute Men

DOROTHY CANFIELD FISHER

Revolution was brewing in the American colonies and the British were doing their best to suppress it. The rebels had hidden an important store of arms and ammunition at Concord in preparation for the conflict. When the British learned about this, they dispatched a column of troops to capture it. But the Colonists were alert to the situation. They sent Paul Revere, a fearless leader among the Revolutionists, to warn the people of Lexington and Concord. Here is Dorothy Canfield Fisher's story of Revere's famous ride, and the beginning of the war that made America a nation.

The Two Lanterns

IN the dark, in front of the house of Robert Newman, sexton of Christ Church, Paul Revere slowed down. He could see through the lighted windows that the front room of the Newman house was filled with British officers. They were doing what Boston people mostly saw them doing—playing cards, drinking and having a loud, jolly time together. How could a man known to the English get at the sexton without being seen? As he hesitated, a man standing in a shadowy corner of the street began to walk casually along. When he reached Raul Revere, he said in a low tone, "Go ahead. I'll follow you." It was the sexton. Paul stepped forward.

The two men were alone in the street. Over his shoulder Paul asked, "How did you get out? Did they see you?"

The sexton answered, "Out of a window. Over a shed-roof. No, they didn't."

Nothing more was said until they turned, in front of the old church. Another man was waiting in the shadow there. He was to stand guard, while the sexton climbed up the long steps of the tower.

The three men stood close to the door of the church and talked in whispers. "How long shall I leave the lanterns in the window, Mr. Revere?"

"That's hard to say. Not long. I've told the Charlestown people to be on the lookout. So remember, not a glimmer till the lanterns are in the window. British sentries on the ship are watching and our chances are better if the British don't guess what we're up to."

The man who was to stand guard broke in anxiously, "But Mr. Revere, a light won't hurt as long as it's inside. Climbing in the dark he'll risk breaking his neck."

"No he won't," said Paul. "I know every inch of the tower. The steps are all right so long as you keep well over to the left side with a hand against the wall to guide you. There's an opening where the bells hang. The patrol on the Somerset might catch a flash through the cracks . . . or our watchers at Charlestown might think it showed a single lantern, and start off before you got the two hung out. We can't take any chances." He turned to the sexton. "Now, remember, two lanterns. I told the Charlestown Committee it would be two if the Regulars start by boat."

"I hope they see it, Mr. Revere, it's a long way to Charlestown."

"They'll see it," answered Paul. "I was a bell ringer here when I was a boy. Many's the time I've looked over at Charlestown from the top of this tower. And back at it from Charlestown. I know just the place over there where you can get a clear view. The Committee will be there, watching. They'll catch the first gleam."

The other asked, "But you are on your way to Charlestown now. Why are signals needed?"

"I'm on my way. But I may never get there. If my boat is sighted from the *Somerset,* it'll be sunk by shot. If I don't get over to them, the Charlestown Committee is to send another rider out to try to get through with the alarm."

The sexton murmured respectfully, "It's a great risk you are taking."

"I'm not the only one. You're doing as much. If they ever find out who hung those signals, you'll land in Boston Jail."

"I'm proud to take that risk, Mr. Revere."

"So am I," said Revere heartily. He went on. "Now remember, it must be two lanterns you show. Be sure to hang them well apart so the Charlestown folks can be sure there are two of them."

The sexton unlocked the church door, paused a moment, and said in a loud voice, "God help you this night, Mr. Revere."

"Amen!" said the other man.

The sexton pulled the door shut and locked it. The man on guard took his position in the shadow of the church door, looking up and down the empty street.

Paul Revere walked steadily on to whatever was before him—shooting, hanging, or glory.

Near the place where his boat was hidden, two men sauntering in the mild April evening on different sides of the street turned when they saw him. The three men walked separately as though they had no connection with each other. It was a quiet part of the city. Nobody noticed them as, one by one, they turned into a dark alley.

They did not come out. Now they were in a small boat, the two men at the oars. In the stern sat Paul Revere, very straight, very still. Just below the handles, the oars were wrapped in flannel, at the place where they rub against the oarlocks as they are pulled to and fro, so the usual clinking noise was muffled. They made not a sound. But of course, as they were dipped in and out of the water, the wet blades flashed in the light from the rising moon. No help for that.

Not a word was said. They knew what to do—to keep as far away as they could from the ship with its sixty-four guns. Paul Revere kept his head turned towards the great warship and those guns.

How could the watch on the frigate help seeing the boat? The moon was not yet risen but he himself could see, easily enough, the lines of boats beyond the ship, going back and forth ferrying the Regulars across to Cambridge. No others were to be allowed out that night. If anybody on the deck of the tall ship should happen to glance around, he couldn't help seeing the telltale silver flash of those wet oars. How could that flash be missed by a watch set there to make sure no boat was out?

The silent men at the oars knew they were risking their lives. They pulled steadily towards the Charlestown shore. The silent man, sitting straight and easy at the stern, did not take his eyes from the anchored ship looming up tall, black, threatening. From its guns, at any instant, death might dart out at him.

Where could the British patrols be? Perhaps all gathered on the other side to watch the boats carrying the troops to Cambridge? Or one of them might have caught sight, already, of the forbidden attempt to cross. Perhaps one of the guns was being leveled at them this instant. He sat motionless, breathing deeply, wondering if they had now gone far enough so that he could swim to the Charlestown side—if he were not killed in the first fire from the ship. His fixed gaze on the huge black hulk of the *Somerset* shifted with a jerk. Something else had come into view. He caught sight of an object near them. He turned his head cautiously. It was a tree! Why, there was land, close at hand. They were getting near to the Charlestown side. They hadn't been seen. Was it possible that they hadn't been seen?

Still without a word, the men at the oars pulled in closer and

In the stern sat Paul Revere, very straight, very still.

closer to the stony beach. Paul Revere gathered the long skirts of his riding coat around him. The bottom of the boat grazed the stones. The oarsmen lifted the oars and looked at him. The moment had come. They had made it.

Their pause was but an instant. In one powerful leap, their passenger was out of the boat. They rowed on without him. They rounded the point. They were out of sight. They were still alive, as they had hardly hoped they would be when they had pushed off from the Boston shore.

Paul Revere was still alive too, his skin crawling with taut suspense. He drew a long breath, took off his hat, passed his hand over the back of his neck to smooth down those hairs that had seemed to stand up coldly as he braced himself against death. He put his hat back on, and walked steadily up the sloping shore. He knew where to go. And shortly he had found his way through the dark to the Charlestown house where he was expected.

They told him that his signals had been seen. They had a horse waiting for him. But all roads, they said, were watched by British officers on horseback.

"There are back roads," he said. "Short cuts through the fields. I know them, the British don't."

They brought out the horse, saddled and bridled. He took one look at the fine animal—he never forgot what a good horse it was—and thought to himself that no heavy British army mount could compare with it.

"*If I see them before they see me . . .*" he thought.

One of the Charlestown men said he had already tried to send a messenger out to Lexington to give the warning. But he shook his head sadly. "I doubt that my man will ever get through the British net. He's probably been picked up by some of those officers by this time. Has William Dawes started?"

"He was to try to get out through the English sentries on the Neck. I don't know if he made it."

"They've strung a net around Boston like a spider's web. Dawes will never slip through."

Paul Revere thought, standing by that fine fleet horse, the reins in his hand, "I'll get through. *If I see them first. . . .*"

He was in the saddle. The little knot of men looked up at him. The moon had fully risen now. They saw him plainly. Would they ever see him again? Everything now depended on Revere. Would he get through? Could he get through? Would he perhaps at the very first turn of the road be captured or forced to turn back?

They held up their hands in a gesture of goodbye. Now there was nothing more to say. The man on the horse nodded silently and rode away at a sober, careful, rapid trot. In the saddle from which he might be shot down at any moment, he sat as straight as he had in the boat during the perilous trip across the water. They stood looking after him till there was nothing to see but darkness. Would he get through? Would they ever see him again?

On Moonlit Roads

The man on the horse fixed his mind on one thought: "*I must see them first.*"

He must not ride so fast that he would run into an ambush. He must not ride so slowly that those red-coated troops now being landed could reach the first village before he did. For it would be enough, although not all he wanted, if he could reach even the first few farmhouses on the road to Lexington before the Regulars did. Just let him rouse two or three families, and tell them the British were on the way. The alarm would be passed along, to those beyond. The Minute Men would spring to their arms. The boys too young to carry a gun would be off on horseback to wake up people who lived on lanes and back roads and to get other big boys to go farther. The old men would start the drums beating so they could be heard for miles, would pull furiously on the ropes of the church bells to throw out their wild summons to fight. Yes, it would be enough if he could get through the empty wasteland back of Charlestown to the first cluster of houses, at a crossroads. Let him be shot down there—he would have done what he was out to do.

But what he wanted was to get through to Lexington. Two of the most important men on the American side—Samuel Adams and John Hancock—were in Lexington. The British hoped to take them by surprise. If they did, they'd be sent back to London to be hanged for treason—as Paul would be if he were caught. He felt that come what might, he *must* get through to the first settlement. If he possibly could, he must reach Lexington to make sure the two leaders of the Americans were safe. And it would be well if he could go on from there to Concord, although the alarm, if he could start it, might well have spread to that town without him.

That was what he intended to do. He knew he could do it—*if he could only see the British patrols before they saw him.*

As he rode out over the empty moorland back of Charlestown, there was not a sound except the hoofbeats of his horse, trotting cautiously when he came to a place where trees or bushes cast a shadow, let out to a full run on open stretches clear in the moonlight. The patrols would never show themselves in the open. They would hide in the shadows.

His keen black eyes ranged everywhere at once, searching the distance, focused intently on every dusky thicket beside the road. At any instant, just as in the boat, a shot might leap out at him. And now not only from one place on which he could keep his eyes. From anywhere. From either side of the road, behind him, from in front of him. But how much better this was, with something active he could do, than that dreadful passage on the water, sitting helpless, the hair on the back of his neck rising in suspense.

He checked his speed to peer sharply around a turn of the road, he loosened the reins, touched his mount's flanks with the spurs, and leaned forward over the mane as the horse broke into a run.

Nobody knows what thoughts went through his mind in that desperate race. Did he remember again that if he were caught he would be hanged? Did he remember his father's saying that all a brave man needs is a fighting chance, just one?

We don't know. But we do know, as though we were inside his mind, that one thought a man might have had never once occurred to him—the simple idea that all he had to do to be safe was just to turn his horse into the thick woods, anywhere. He could stay there, hidden, till everything was all over—whatever that night might bring. He was alone. Nobody was there to see what he did. Nobody would ever know. He could say the British patrols chased him into the woods and he lost his way.

He rode straight ahead, his quick eyes shifting from side to side of the road, his quick mind flashing over what he knew of British ways.

Any man of sense who had fought Indians, if he were set to guard a road on a moonlit night, would cover up anything on his clothes that might catch the light. But Revere thought of Braddock, of the British soldiers he had seen at Albany, of those he had watched drilling on the Common at Boston. He was sure that no British officer would ever spoil the looks of his uniform by covering up a well-polished buckle, a white strap or a cockade. So, as he rode on, trotting cautiously, or galloping wildly, he watched for anything that might show white or catch the light. *He must see them first.*

He did.

Under those trees, what was that white patch? Nothing natural was as white as that. And that gleam, as from something brightly polished? His quick hands drew his horse to a stop.

He saw them now. Two officers on horseback, almost invisible in the shadow cast by a tree. The white came from their ribbon cockades. The reflected gleam was from the pistol holsters kept so brilliantly shiny by the common soldiers who did the work for them.

Now the officers had seen him too, in spite of his dark coat, dark hair and pulled-down black hat. They had a plan to stop him. One of them launched his horse plunging straight at him.

The other turned and dashed off up the road to head him off if the first one did not make the capture.

But Paul Revere had seen them first!

He swung his horse about, and struck in the spurs. In the instant of time since his eye had caught that first gleam of white, his ready mind had made a plan to fit that exact place. He would go straight cross-country at top speed, to another road.

As clearly as though it were before him on a map, he saw exactly what fields to cross, what stone walls to leap—and there was a pond, with clay banks that were slippery. He would know how to dodge that, with his little native-born horse. The Britisher on his great military charger would not.

He was off. The officer was taken aback at the idea of leaving the road, but spurred his handsome mount to follow. Again Paul Revere's back hairs crawled on his neck, as his taut body expected a shot from behind. But his mind knew no fear.

He kept his horse galloping at full speed, he watched the rough field over which they were racing, but he turned his head just enough so that he could see from the side of his eye where the British officer was. He was no nearer than in that instant on the road when he had sprung out to block the way. He was farther. Yes, he was dropping behind!

Paul leaned low over his horse's neck, put his weight well forward, kept his eyes fixed on the ground ahead rushing up towards them, dropping behind. Huckleberry bushes, great rocks, a clump of trees. There was the pond—its banks treacherously covered with grass. He swung his horse far to one side and felt, to his joy, a clatter of stony ground under those flying hooves. Behind him the British horse had gone straight ahead over what looked like grass land, had slipped when its feet struck the clay, was sliding down the bank, plunging and floundering wildly. His rider, thrown to one side of the saddle, struggled to get his balance.

Paul Revere shook out the bridle and gave his horse his head. He had almost come through to the Mystic River. Once there, he would find a wooden bridge into the first village on the road to Lexington. If he could get as far as that.

Through the trees, he saw a road! It was a little country road. Did the British know about it? Would it be patrolled? Before leaving the woods, he drew rein to look up and down. The road was empty. He took his horse out on it in a run, raced down to the bridge and galloped across, the loose planks rattling under those flying feet.

He was in Medford. He had made it. He was alive.

The village lay dark and sleeping in the night just as it would have been—defenseless—a few hours later, if he had not come through.

None of us need ever hope to be happier than Paul Revere was as he galloped his horse down that dark village street and along the lane till he came to the home of the captain of the Medford Minute Men. He leaned from his saddle to hammer on the door with the handle of his whip. A window flew up. Through the dark came Paul Revere's shout, "*The Regulars are out!* On their way to Concord."

That was enough. Everyone knew what was meant by that cry. Knew what to do. Was ready to do it. Before Paul was even back on the road, one half-dressed boy was racing for the church to ring the tocsin bell, an old man with silvery hair had stepped from the next house, his drumsticks flying on his drum, another boy was in a barn saddling a horse. Lights came on in houses. Windows were flying up.

"The Regulars are out," shouted the dark rider to one side or the other, as he raced by. "Start a boy up to Cobble Hill to give the alarm there."

"The Regulars are out. On their way to Concord. Get somebody over the Menot Flats, to those houses."

"The Regulars are out."

A wave of hatred flowed over those country hearts at that name.

"The Regulars are out." The village was flaming in excitement, the Minute Men were running from their houses, muskets in their hands, to form a line on the Common, ready to head for Lexington and Concord.

On the moonlit road beyond the village, the man on horseback rode hard. Sometimes before he reached a house, the swift beat of his horse's hooves, loud in the silent night, had wakened the people in a sleeping home. If a light showed in a window, if a head was thrust out, he did not draw rein, but shouted as he passed, "*The Regulars are out*. Give the alarm." If there was no sign of life, he rode up to the door and hammered on it fiercely till someone from inside called back. Then, "The Regulars are out. Get the alarm going," and he rode on, sure of what would follow.

House after house sprang from sleep to action. Mile after mile the rider covered at headlong speed. Then as he came to the top of a slope, there was the town of Lexington.

It was after midnight. The two American leaders were asleep in the minister's house where they were lodged. A sergeant's squad had been set to watch the house. When Revere came thundering in, they sprang up to stop him. Not a soul there yet knew what Paul Revere had come through to tell them.

"The Regulars are out," shouted Revere.

He was heard inside the house. His voice was known. John Hancock called out, "Come in, Revere." The door opened, he went in, and exploded his great bomb of news. Behind him one of the guard had run across to the church. As he told his story, the bell began to clang out its alarm. He raised his voice to be heard over its loud pealing.

"Over a thousand British troops are on the way. I saw them when I left Boston at ten o'clock tonight. Crossing the river in boats. They may arrive any moment now. The alarm has been given, all round about. The Minute Men are arming and gathering."

There was a wild hurry in the house as the two men, so vital to the American side, made ready to leave.

Half an hour later, William Dawes rode in. He had bribed his way past a sentry on the "Neck," shaken off one patrol and ridden the roundabout road through Roxbury. The two express riders were well satisfied with their night's work. They had a bite to eat, took a drink, and considered what to do next.

As his wife had reminded him, Paul had taken orders from the Committee of Safety to Concord only two days before. Most of their military stores were already hidden. And as for the alarm, that had already spread far and wide. Near and far they could hear bells tolling and muskets fired as warning signals. Just the same, they wanted to finish what they had started.

Paul and Dawes turned their horses towards Concord, and a young Dr. Prescott rode along with them. He lived in the district, knew everyone and all the lanes and byroads.

This time, halfway to Concord, there were not two, but four British officers suddenly blocking the way. The Americans were forced into a field where six more British were waiting. In the darkness and confusion Dawes slid off his horse and managed to hide in the bushes. Prescott jumped a stone wall and rode off. But Paul was squarely cornered with a pistol cold against his forehead.

"Who are you? Where do you come from?"

Paul thought quickly. Someone might recognize him. Boldness was his only hope. "My name's Revere," he said. "I left Boston about ten o'clock."

They could hardly believe him. It was only just past midnight. How could anyone have made such quick time? But at his name they broke out into angry words and threats.

Then a bell, quite near, started ringing. The British looked at one another, worried. They quieted down and one of them, remembering orders, tried to explain why they were here. "We're only out after deserters," he said.

Paul saw his chance. "I know better. I know what you're after. But you won't get it. The alarm has been given everywhere. And it's spreading."

The British put their heads together and talked in tones too low for Paul Revere to hear. Then they took the reins out of his hands and led his horse in their midst back along the road to Lexington. The major waved his pistol and said, "As for you, Paul Revere, don't try to escape or I'll blow your brains out. You go back with us. We'll send you to England to be tried and hanged for treason."

Paul answered briefly. "Do as you like about that. But what chance have you to get to Boston? There are only ten of you. Your troops are hours away. There are at least five hundred Minute Men heading here at this minute. In an hour there will be thousands more."

It was slow work leading Revere's horse. The road was dark and lonely. The Englishmen got uneasy and alarmed. With good reason. What chance did they have against a whole countryside swarming with armed men who hated them?

All at once a gun was fired. In the darkness, it rang out very loud. The officers drew their horses sharply to a halt.

"What was that?" the British major snapped out.

"Only another alarm gun. They're being fired like that everywhere from here to Connecticut. You've a mighty slim chance of getting back to Boston with whole skins." Revere spoke out boldly though he knew he was still in mortal danger.

The British officers had another short whispered talk. "Dismount," they told him. As Revere had hoped, they began to see that they had a better chance to escape without being burdened with a prisoner.

They mounted one of their sergeants on Paul's horse and, spurring their mounts to a run, vanished down the road.

FROM

Young Nathan

MARION MARSH BROWN

Nathan Hale was brought up in a simple country family, where there was little wealth but much character. Just out of Yale, he was beginning to teach school when he enlisted in the Connecticut militia. At the time of his arrest, the young Captain—disguised as a deserting schoolteacher—had volunteered for the dangerous mission of getting information about the British forces on Long Island. He did this knowing that he could be executed without a trial. He was, on the very next day. His was such a short life. Yet America gained such a glorious symbol for love of freedom when Nathan Hale freely gave up his life at the age of twenty-one years and three months.

Destiny Fulfilled

THE captors were silent at the oars, and Nathan's thoughts raced desperately on plans for escape. But beneath his fear ran an undercurrent of bitterness. To be betrayed by your own kin was hard. How much had the Eustacia affair had to do with it? He saw again the black anger of fallen pride on Sam's face the night Eustacia had told him of her engagement. But his Tory sympathies had been strong too. At any rate, regardless of the reason, Sam had betrayed him. He could jump from the boat and swim for shore, but if the rowers did not overtake him, certainly Sam would be waiting when he reached land. Probably it was best to wait, trusting to the blind future.

He hadn't long to wait. The boat rounded a bend, and a British man-of-war, hidden behind a wooded point, loomed into sight. Steadily the oarsmen pulled toward it.

Nathan found himself delivered to a Captain Quarme. Outwardly at ease he repeated the story he had told his captors. He was relieved to see that Captain Quarme believed him.

"We'll take you up to General Howe tonight," Quarme said. "That's orders—all rebel deserters to headquarters. Howe'll fix you up."

Nathan's relief was gone; a chill ran down his spine. "He'll fix you up!" If no means of escape offered itself before then—Courage! Courage!

The long day wore on. Would they find the papers if they searched him at headquarters? What was poor Asher thinking as the hours went by and he did not return? In some way the papers concealed in his shoes must get through to Washington.

His heart was heavy as the *Halifax* docked at Turtle Bay at sunset, and its friendly young captain sent him on his way under armed guard. All day long he had believed that some means of escape would present itself. He was on the side of right, and right would prevail. But as he was marched to the mansion at Mount Pleasant where General Howe had his headquarters, his confidence sagged. Twilight settled about him. This was the hour he had expected to be approaching the familiar white mansion on Murray Hill. Instead, he was nearing the headquarters of the enemy's high command. His heart ached with despair.

He scarcely saw the wide lawns, with their prim borders, or the few patches of color left in the formal gardens. He had expected to be shown immediately to General Howe, and was surprised when he was turned over to the officer of the day, a handsome, well-set-up fellow of about forty whose name was Montressor. But of course! This was merely a routine matter; deserters were brought in every day. He was no different from any other deserter. Perhaps there was still a chance. If they didn't discover the papers, he would find a way out.

A Sergeant North took him by the arm.

"Proceed, Sergeant," Montressor ordered, and stood quietly at one side.

Sergeant North began a routine search. He unbuckled Nathan's belt. "Take off your boots," he commanded.

Nathan's fingers were cold, but he knew he must display no nervousness. This was the crucial moment. There was still a chance. If only they didn't find the inner soles! They fit well; he had made sure of that at the outset. He pulled off one boot and dropped it to the floor. The noise it made sounded in the room like a shot.

The sergeant reached for the boot, and Nathan bent to remove the other one. Don't watch the sergeant! Don't act nervous! Go right on with the boot as if nothing were happening! He didn't raise his eyes from what he was doing, yet he could see the sergeant turn the boot over and look at the bottom as if to determine how many miles it had tramped and then run his fingernail along the seam to see if the stitching had been ripped.

Nathan tugged at the other boot. He dropped it on the floor and glanced at Montressor. Montressor's eyes were following the sergeant's movements intently as the man ran his hand down inside the boot he held. There was no sound in the room, unless it was the beating of Nathan's heart. It sounded as loud in his ears as the beating of drums.

Into the quiet, the captain spoke three words. "Your knife, Sergeant."

They fell like a death knell on Nathan's ears. He could not even pray. In fascination his eyes moved to the sergeant. He had opened his knife and was running it down into the boot. Now he was prying with the point. By the sudden set of his lips, Nathan knew what he had found.

Captain Montressor stepped to the sergeant's side, and Nathan's head dropped for an instant in despair. Then he took a long breath, set his lips, raised his head, and squared his shoulders. Captain Montressor and the sergeant pried the insole out and removed the neatly folded sheets of thin paper with their carefully written words and their carefully drawn plans.

Captain Montressor looked at Nathan. "I didn't think you looked like an ordinary rebel deserter," he said.

Suddenly Nathan realized that the British officer's eyes were sorrowful.

"The other boot," Montressor said to the sergeant and tossed the one from which the insole had been removed to Nathan. "Get it on."

Nathan obeyed with numb fingers. One boot on, then the other. He wasn't thinking; he could only feel. His whole heart cried out to Alice. He stood between two guards that had come at Montressor's call. His body dragged, carrying a heavy load of failure and despair. Yet he made himself walk like a soldier as he followed the captain, who carried the sheets of paper spread out in his hand like a fan.

The door opened on a room of startling beauty, dominated by a white fireplace bordered with lovely delft-blue tiles, like a delicate gem exquisitely set. But Nathan's eyes, usually so quick to see beauty, saw only the man who sat behind a large mahogany desk. He might have been General Washington. He had the same military bearing, the same white-powdered wig.

Captain Montressor handed Howe the papers. There was now only one way it could end.

General Howe examined the sheets and looked up. "Drawings of our groundworks and fortifications. And notes in Latin. This can mean, of course, but one thing."

"Yes, sir," Nathan replied. It was the first word he had spoken, and his voice sounded far away to him and as if it came from another person.

"Do you have anything to say for yourself?" General Howe's words were clipped.

"Nothing except what you can see. I was inside your lines to obtain information."

"You are not in uniform."

"No, sir."

"What is your rank?"

"Captain."

"Your name?"

"Hale. Nathan Hale."

The general turned back to the papers before him. There was no sound in the room but the light crackling of the thin sheets as he turned them. The minutes ticked away. Nathan tried to swallow but found it difficult. The general continued to study the notes.

"Captain Hale," he said finally, "I've never seen so excellent a set of drawings or so complete a set of notes." He looked intently at the young man standing straight and tall before him, and continued: "We could use such a man as you, if you would be interested in joining the British ranks. We would make it well worth your while, both in salary and in position."

Suddenly Nathan became taller. "Nothing," he said, "could make me turn traitor to my country!"

"You leave me but one course, Captain Hale."

"Yes, sir."

"It is my unpleasant duty to sentence you to be hanged as a spy tomorrow morning at sunrise. God be with you. That will be all. Captain Montressor." Howe's fingers shook as he gathered up the thin, neatly covered sheets of paper that lay on his desk.

"Take Captain Hale to the provost marshal and acquaint him with General Howe's orders," Montressor snapped at the guard.

Nathan scarcely saw the provost marshal to whom he was delivered. Suddenly a loud, rough voice snarled at him:

"Another dirty rebel, are ye—and a captain! You low-livered son-of-a—"

"I beg your pardon—" Nathan began. Never, in his twenty-one years had he been so addressed. Startled from his numbness, he saw a short, fat, coarse-featured red-faced man with an animal brutality in his eyes and on his curling lips. In his ugly fat hand the man held a blacksnake, which he twitched menacingly against his boot.

He must be around sixty years of age, Nathan thought, and he must have spent those years viciously to have a face so deeply engraved with lines of brutality.

He had gone so far in his thoughts when a sudden, sharp pain cut across his limbs. The man had lashed out with the twitching blacksnake.

"I beg your pardon!" mimicked the provost marshal. "Captain mama's boy! You'll whine and cry for your mama before we're through with you–"

The color rushed to Nathan's face.

Provost Marshal Cunningham laughed and snapped out an order to the guard. "Throw the cursed pup in the greenhouse and put on a double guard."

What a strange place to spend the last night of his life, Nathan mused, looking about him at the odd, exotic plants that were withering away for want of care since the master of the house had fled before the British. He sat down on a wooden bench, his legs weak. Disconnected pictures flashed through his mind: Abigail, the night the Deacon had brought her home, so pretty and so kind; Alice, in her bright red hood, the day he had gone to Old Jeff's store to meet her; the family sitting in their pew at church, his father all stiffness from his back to his mustaches, the little boys trying so hard to wiggle inconspicuously, little Joanna sighing because her legs were weary from dangling, Elizabeth, with her smooth braids, sitting almost as still and straight as the Deacon; Alice, sitting beside his sick bed only a few short weeks before; Abigail again, grayer and older, looking up from the churn with eyes full of tears when he had told her how much she meant to him and saying, "I'll never forget what you've said, Nathan."

A lump rose in his throat and stuck there. Abigail had always insisted that he was going to do something great in the world. He had hoped that he could do something that would be of some good to mankind. And now this–to die as a spy! How sadly disappointed Abigail would be in him! And Alice, and Enoch, and pa, and Alden, and Tallmadge, and Hillhouse, and Dwight, and Hull! Hull had tried to save him from this journey.

The worst of it was being so terribly alone. He ached to have Alice with him, her hand to cling to, the steady light in her eyes to help him through the long hours till the dawn. The misery of his failure was acute: the stigma attached to the death of a spy, cruel. What would this last blow do to Alice? He knew a moment's black despair; then another picture flashed into his mind and buoyed him up: Alice before the fireplace, that last night of his furlough, saying, "Nathan, the old coat of arms has always meant a great deal to you, hasn't it?" And his own reply, "I've always thought it stood for a very special brand of courage." It was now that he must call up that special courage from somewhere out of the deep heritage of the Hale past.

He did not know how long he had sat without moving on the hard seat in the center of the greenhouse, but it must have been hours. Suddenly he came to himself. He must hurry. The dawn might not be far off, and there were things he must do. He moved stiffly toward the door and spoke to the guard standing inside. Lost in his black thoughts, he had not been aware of the soldier's presence.

"I wonder if I might have pen and paper," he asked, "and a candle to see by. I'd like to write some letters."

"I'll see what I can do." The guard's voice was kind. He summoned an outside guard. "See if you can get paper and pen and a candle for the prisoner," he said.

"The order has to go to Cunningham," the second guard replied doubtfully.

"I know, but try."

"And a Bible, if you would," Nathan added.

He paced the length of the greenhouse, waiting for the guard to return. He would write to Alice, and his father, and Abigail. He would like to write to Enoch too, and Elizabeth, if he had time. Elizabeth had named her new little son for him.

There was commotion outside the greenhouse, and the coarse, angry voice of Cunningham. The door opened and the provost marshal stormed in, swaying drunkenly, the candle in his hand lurching precariously.

"Where is he? Where is he?" he shouted. "The lousy, white-livered ass. Waking me up in the middle of the night to ask for a Bible! Oh, there you are! What do you think I am, a priest? I'll teach you to wake me up—" The blacksnake came down, but Nathan was too quick for it. He sprang to one side, grabbed the whip from Cunningham's unsteady hand, and handed it to the outside guard.

Cunningham lurched out the door in pursuit of his black-snake.

"I'm sorry, sir," the guard said, closing the door and turning the key. "He's drunk. And besides, he's a black devil."

"You did your best," Nathan told him. His breath was coming fast. He went back to the rustic bench, dropped to his knees, and prayed.

He was still on his knees when the first dim light began to mold vague forms out of the darkness. The voice of Cunningham fell heavily on the early stillness, his words still thick. Nathan rose and found that his heart was pounding hard and fast.

It was a relief to be led out into the open air. The stars were still visible. He had always loved them. This would be the last time he would see them.

Cunningham was noisily giving orders. Nathan paid no attention to what he said, but he did give heed when a quiet voice broke into Cunningham's bluster.

"Provost Marshal, may I not make your prisoner at ease in my tent until your preparations are completed?" It was Captain Montressor.

Cunningham was too busy to be bothered. "Yes, yes," he sputtered, paying slight attention.

"My tent is right here," Captain Montressor said at Nathan's side. "I think you would be more comfortable waiting there, Captain Hale."

"Thank you," Nathan said, his voice husky with appreciation.

It was good to receive a word of kindness when he needed human comfort so badly.

"Is there anything I can do for you?" Montressor asked, when they were inside the tent.

"I should like very much to have pen and paper—and a Bible," Nathan replied quickly. Perhaps there was still time to write a word to Alice.

"But the chaplain?" Montressor asked in surprise, reaching for writing materials. "Didn't he—"

"I have not seen a chaplain."

Montressor's lips set in a tight line. He handed Nathan paper, pen, and ink, then threw back the lid of his army trunk to find his Bible. "Sit there at the table," he said over his shoulder.

Nathan took up the pen and wrote quickly. His hand was steady. It seemed to him that his mind had never been clearer. Captain Montressor found the Bible and laid it on the table before him. There was no sound in the tent except the even, steady scratching of the pen. Montressor glanced at the light that was growing steadily brighter in the east.

"Is there any passage in the Bible I could find for you?" he asked.

"Yes, if you would, please—the Sermon on the Mount." Nathan did not look up, nor pause.

Montressor turned the pages to the fifth chapter of Matthew and laid the open book on the table. The noise of Nathan's pen stopped abruptly.

"Do you think you could see that these get through the lines for me?" he asked. "One is to my father, and one to my sweetheart."

"Certainly, certainly," Montressor replied, agitation in his voice.

Nathan reached for the Bible, and his eyes ran hungrily over the familiar words: "Blessed are the poor in spirit: for theirs is the kingdom of heaven. Blessed are they that mourn: for they shall be comforted. . . . Blessed are they which are persecuted for righteousness' sake. . . . I am not come to destroy, but to fulfil."

The stillness in the tent was broken by Cunningham's bellowing approach. He stooped to enter the tent, then straightened and stood glaring at the scene before him.

"You—you—" Anger choked him. He snatched the Bible from Nathan's hand and sent it hurtling to a far corner. "Readin' the Bible, air ye, ye lousy, white-livered coward."

Cunningham reached for the letters that lay on the table. He picked them up, ran his eyes over the pages, and tore them to bits. The fine pieces of white paper fell like snow on the cold ground.

Nathan's throat ached. Now they would never know how he thought of them at the last, how he loved them, why he had done this thing.

He walked out of the tent and marched up the hill. His lips moved. "God, make Alice feel the warmth of my love always. I promised it to her." They entered an apple orchard at the top of the hill. For a moment Nathan felt a strange comfort. The sweet, tangy smell of the ripening fruit brought home very near. Then he saw the rope dangling from a straight limb of a red-laden tree, and beside it a ladder.

"Up on the ladder!" Cunningham barked hoarsely.

Nathan obeyed.

"Face front!"

He turned. There was a motley group of curious townspeople below him and a number of redcoats. He did not really see them. There would be no friendly face to whom he could turn, no one who would care. Then his eyes rested on the figure of an officer standing at attention, his face strained, and his eyes full of compassion. It was Montressor. As Nathan's eyes came to rest on the British captain, Montressor raised his hand in a quick salute.

Nathan closed his eyes and prayed as the rope was placed about his neck.

Cunningham's bullying voice, sharp with sarcasm, cut through

His voice was clear and firm. "I only regret. . . ."

to his consciousness. "Now, Captain Hale, let's have your dying speech."

That was the bitter moment. What was there to say at the end of a life with which he had hoped to do so much, a life in which no "great things" had been accomplished, a life that was ending ignominiously?

Could he have known that his death was to arouse and inspire the American troops, uniting them as nothing else could have done, the weight of failure would have lifted. Could he have known that he was rendering such a service to his country as he had longed to render, the hour would have been less dark. Could he have known that he was not giving his life in vain— But he did not know.

Suddenly, however, he seemed to see the coat of arms over the fireplace at Coventry. Courage! He straightened his shoulders, lifted his head, and looked out over the crowd below. His voice was clear and firm.

"I only regret that I have but one life to lose for my country."

Cunningham himself kicked out the ladder, and the pink of the dawn—a new dawn for the cause of American independence —went black before Nathan Hale's eyes.

FROM

George Washington: Leader of the People

CLARA INGRAM JUDSON

The life of Washington seems like a model of heroic devotion and service to his country. Yet it is pleasant, too, to read about his boyhood in this book and discover some of his more human—and charming—failings. Young George was extremely sensitive and hot-tempered, and he disliked his teacher. But he idolized his older brother Lawrence, who was like a father to him—since his own father had died when he was eleven. A chance to learn surveying meant a lot to young George, because it gave him his first long trip and his first taste of the frontier. And of course he turned out to be a good surveyor.

A Young Surveyor

ALL the next day George was restless and uneasy. He had never asked a favor of the Reverend Marye. How should he word his request to learn surveying?

While he curried Whitefoot, George muttered to himself, saying over sentences and tactful approaches. None seemed good. Marye was a stern man; aloof from his pupils. George went to bed Sunday still puzzled as to what he should say.

Monday morning, George was waiting at the dock when the ferryman came. When they crossed the river, he hurried up the hill to school. Marye was at his desk, but the other pupils had not yet arrived. George walked to the desk and spoke quickly, but respectfully.

"Good morning, sir. Will you please teach me to be a surveyor?"

Marye stared at him astonished. George shifted his weight from his left to his right foot and locked his hands behind him. He never quite knew what to do with hands when Marye got that pained expression on his stern face.

"I have found my father's surveying tools," George explained, "and I would like to learn to use them."

Marye frowned at the urgency in George's tone.

"You have a strange notion about your rate of progress," he complained. "A surveyor needs trigonometry and logarithms which you have not yet studied. When I consider that you are ready, we may, perhaps, speak of this again. Now get to the lesson of today."

George turned and walked to his bench. His hands trembled with rage, and his blood was hot. Trigonometry? Logarithms? If he needed those subjects, why didn't Marye teach them?

"I am top boy in arithmetic," George thought rebelliously. "Yet he talks to me as though I were young Sam." He took a quill and pulled out his knife to whittle a point. But his eyes were blurred with rage. The quill was soon a heap of scraps.

James, his seatmate, watched him with amusement. "Wish I'd got here earlier," he thought. "The master's got old George in a rage this time. Wonder what's up?"

George picked up a second quill, sharpened it and began to write. But his hand raced angrily over the paper. The day was half gone before he could put his mind on his work.

Later, at home, George went to the storeroom and handled the surveyor's chain. It was long and heavy; the links rattled mysteriously in the dim light.

"Father would have taught me," George assured himself. "He

"You have a strange notion about your rate of progress," he complained.

would like me to be a surveyor. Marye spoke as though there was much to learn. I must talk with Lawrence."

The first chance to go to Mount Vernon came some weeks after George's fourteenth birthday. Then Mrs. Washington sent him with a message to Lawrence. It was a Saturday and he arrived in time for dinner. As usual there were guests. But after the meal, Lawrence drew George into his study; he saw that the youth had some special matter on his mind.

"I want to ask you about school—and surveying, Lawrence," George began when they were alone.

"Surveying?" Lawrence said. "Isn't that a new idea?"

"I found Father's chain when Mother and I cleaned the storeroom," George went on. "I asked the master to teach me but he put me off. School is very tiresome, Lawrence. Two of the boys have left for England. James quit this week to help on his father's plantation. New boys are so *young*. I am the tallest and oldest in the room. I want to learn what I need for a *man's* work."

Lawrence stroked his long chin thoughtfully.

"Father meant you to go to England, too. But your mother is not willing for you to be away so long. You would need three or four years—I had to admit that."

George was silent. Perhaps Lawrence had some plan for him.

"I have been wondering about a profession for you. Ferry farm will be yours; but the soil is light. It will not produce a good living by itself. Would you like to go to sea?"

"To sea!" George's jaw dropped in astonishment. "Oh, Lawrence, that would be wonderful!" His eyes glowed, and visions of wide sails and a deck where he was master floated before him. "I would like that vastly better than surveying. How do I begin?"

"Oh, you might get an appointment in the King's navy. Our family has influence, and Colonel Fairfax would help you. Or you might get on a merchant ship out of Yorktown."

"But if Mother will not let me go to England, will she let me join the navy?" George asked in sudden dismay.

"Well, that is a point," Lawrence admitted. "At least we can ask her. I shall ride back with you tomorrow."

The next day, when Lawrence tactfully made his suggestion Mrs. Washington settled the matter at once.

"George is not to go to sea," she said firmly. "Remember, he is my son, not yours, Lawrence Washington."

For a time, George was bitterly disappointed. But with the coming of spring and summer, he began to forget. He continued at school, occasionally visiting Mount Vernon.

In September, Lawrence and Colonel Fairfax stopped at Ferry farm for a brief call.

"We are on our way to see about some land beyond Fredericksburg. I took the opportunity to see that you are all well," Lawrence told Mrs. Washington.

"No, we cannot stay, thank you," Colonel Fairfax replied to her invitation to dinner. "We have to pick up George Byrne and his helpers in town." They chatted briefly and left.

George hung over the fence, watching them down the lane. "*I* could have helped them," he grumbled. As the riders turned into the main road he recalled the name "George Byrne."

"He is a surveyor. Maybe *he* could teach me!" Suddenly George felt energetic and amiable. Young Sam was cleaning the water trough in the horse lot. "Want help, Sam?"

Sam stared—and handed over a scrub brush. The boys got the trough clean. Then they watched while the stableman connected up a wooden pipe and filled the trough with fresh spring water.

The next day, George made inquiries at the town wharf.

"George Byrne?" one of the idlers answered. "Sure I know him. Best surveyor around here. He's out on a job now."

George waited several days. Then he went to Byrne's house and pounded on the knocker. A friendly looking man in his middle thirties opened the door.

"I am looking for Mr. George Byrne," George said.

"You've found him." Byrne opened the door wide and motioned for George to enter. The room was a kind of office; surveying tools were scattered over the floor and a long table was littered with maps, papers, ink-spots, and quills.

"I am George Washington from Ferry farm, across the river. Perhaps you knew my father, Augustine Washington," George said.

"That I did," Byrne agreed. "I've helped him on many a survey—but that was some time ago."

"Yes, sir," George replied. "And now I want to be a surveyor myself. Would you teach me?"

"What do you want to be a surveyor for?" Byrne asked curiously. "You have a farm to manage."

"My mother will manage the land for some years yet," George explained, flushing. "Since I found my father's surveying chain, I have the urge to learn the profession. I can figure and keep accounts," he added with a glance at the littered table. "And I could go with you and carry the rod and chain."

"Um-m-m." Byrne was thoughtful. George had seen a gleam in his eye when figures were mentioned, so he enlarged that point.

"I could make a map like this, sir, if you would let me."

"Surveying is not all gentlemen's work, sitting at a table," Byrne said quickly, "though that is important—and I hate it. You'd have hours of tramping in the mud, climbing mountains, wading creeks—you'd hardly care for all that." He eyed George curiously.

"I like the outdoors, sir," George said. "All you say makes me want to learn the more."

"Well, then," Byrne rose, his mind made up, "come tomorrow. I'll leave here at eight. Wear your topboots, son, you'll need 'em."

"Shall I bring my chain, sir?" George asked hopefully.

"Not tomorrow. You'll lug mine."

They were gone four days. Byrne found his helper useful. He told George to come on Tuesday of the next week. New settlers were arriving west of town and wanted boundary lines surveyed before they built cabins. Fortunately this was spring vacation when George often went visiting, so his mother did not object.

During that summer George took several trips with Byrne. Occasionally he served as rodman for other Fredericksburg surveyors. He learned to measure the boundaries of a piece of land, to stake corners or note a certain tree as a marker. He learned to set the measurements on a map and to show rivers and creeks. His drawing was neat and the lettering clear; the owner was sure to be satisfied. He also got a book of logarithms and studied it.

On a visit to Mount Vernon, George surveyed Lawrence's turnip field and some hilly land nearby. Lawrence was astonished and very pleased at the neat maps.

One day Byrne handed George two pounds in pay—real money, not tobacco, which was more often used as money in the colony.

"Mine?" he exclaimed, amazed.

Byrne grinned. "You're doing a man's job—no reason why you shouldn't be paid for it."

The future seemed dazzling. George liked his work, and he liked having his own money. He started an account book, saved his earnings, and felt manly and affluent. He doubted that he would go back to Marye's school the next year.

In the late autumn of 1747 when George was nearing sixteen, Lord Thomas Fairfax came to Belvoir for a long visit. He was the owner, George remembered, of the great tract of land which men called the Fairfax Proprietary—six million or more acres in the Northern Neck. Peter Jefferson (father of four-year-old Thomas) and Joseph Fry had risked great danger trying to survey this land between the Potomac and the Rappahannock rivers. But the survey was never completed.

Lord Fairfax had come from England to see about this land. He was a middle-aged man with many oddities of dress and manner. George enjoyed his tales of England; if his father had lived he would be seeing those interesting places himself.

But his lordship was not the only attraction at Belvoir. Nancy's young sister Sarah had suddenly blossomed into a pretty young lady and a friendship with Nancy's older brother, George William Fairfax, was developing. George Washington had had little contact with young people except at Belvoir and he enjoyed them. As it turned out, those friendships brought him his first important business opportunity.

On a late winter day, the Lawrence Washingtons and George rode over to Belvoir to call. They found Lord Fairfax pacing the floor excitedly. He held an open letter in his hand and shook its pages as he talked.

"Squatters moving onto my land!" he exclaimed angrily. "They claim the land belongs to anyone who is there to use it!" His lordship strode the length of the room nervously.

"Lord Fairfax has a letter by the post from Philadelphia," Sarah explained to George. "It says that many settlers are moving

"Squatters moving onto my land!"

into his Proprietary. One gathers that he doesn't like it." Sarah smiled at George, amused at her relative's anger.

"You cannot do anything until you have a full survey," Colonel Fairfax said patiently. "I have told you that, sir."

"Then get a survey now," his lordship snapped. "You have written to—what is that man's name?"

"James Genn, surveyor for Prince William County," the colonel said. "The best man in the Northern Neck."

"All right. If he is that good he will not wait around for warm weather. Get him off now. I have to know my rights." Lord Fairfax subsided into a big chair as Sarah and her father gave their attention to their visitors.

George followed Sarah to the spinet. As they talked, her fingers made a soft melody of chords.

Presently George noticed Colonel Fairfax, addressing Lawrence.

"While Genn is there, he could survey that land you and I bought. We might make a nice profit if we had plots ready to sell."

"That is good sense," Lawrence agreed.

"My son wants to go with Genn," Fairfax continued, "though he would be no help. Why not have your brother go too? I hear he is doing well with his surveying. How about it, George?"

"Sir!" George was taken aback to have a question called across the room. Colonel Fairfax grinned and explained.

George's eyes gleamed. "I would like it very much, sir," he answered fervently.

"But William," Lawrence protested, "George is barely sixteen! Genn's trip is important. He may not care to have a boy along."

"Boy!" Fairfax chuckled. "You talk like an older brother! Look at George—he's grown-up! Likely the tallest in the party. Rides better than most. I wager he knows more about land than any helper Genn will have along."

George flushed and Lawrence said, "Well then . . ."

So the surveying party was planned. George put extra boots

and clothing in his saddle bags. Then he put in a parchment-covered blank book. That was to be his diary of the journey.

George Washington and George William Fairfax left Belvoir on the second Friday in March. They rode forty miles through pouring rain to Neville's Ordinary, an inn where they stayed the first night. The next day they rode on and met Genn and his supply train. Genn had helpers for carrying two tents, supplies of salt meat and cornmeal, and his tools.

They crossed the Blue Ridge mountains at Ashby's Gap and the first sight of the Shenandoah Valley thrilled George. They traveled on through the little village of Winchester to Thomas Cresap's place, a center for fur traders near the place where the South Branch pours into the Potomac.

George wanted to study the stockade and storehouse carefully but he was interrupted by the arrival of a party of thirty Indians. They talked loudly to Cresap and seemed to be complaining.

"Is anything wrong?" George asked Cresap.

"They've been on the warpath," Cresap replied, "and they're annoyed because they caught no white settlers. They got only one white scalp."

George had a sudden queasy feeling in the pit of his stomach. Genn's party, including himself, were white men!

Cresap noticed his face and roared with laughter. "We don't count. I'm a trader, and you're my friend. Indians never scalp a man who is useful to them—only settlers who take the land."

The answer was a relief but George continued to eye the visitors with fascination mixed with horror. They were quite unlike any Indians he had seen so he wrote of them in his diary:

". . . we had a War Daunce there manner of Dauncing is . . . They clear a Large Circle and make a Great Fire in y. middle then seats themselves around it y. Speaker makes a grand speech telling them in what Manner they are to Daunce after he had finished y. best Dauncer jumps up as one awaked out of a sleep and runs and jumps about y. Ring in a most comical Manner he is followed by y. Rest . . ." George admired the gourds they rattled and their drum, made of deerskin stretched over a container of water.

He wrote all this and more by firelight, with diary upon his knee, and with original ideas about spelling. Indeed, words were not too well spelled in school until after Samuel Johnson published his dictionary five years later.

From Cresap's, Genn took his party northwest as far as Wills Creek on the North Branch. George's work was to take field notes of boundaries, and his knowledge of trees was of great service. Often an old deed would give as a boundary "large hickory and a red oak" or "two redbuds and a black walnut." George could recognize trees at a distance and soon he was acting as second man on the surveying team.

They met few people until early in April when they came across a few Germans from Pennsylvania, who followed Genn's party for some hours. George tried to talk with some and was astonished that he could not understand their replies.

"They're as stupid as Indians," he complained to Genn.

The surveyor laughed. "They're not stupid. They speak German. They cannot understand you, either." This was George's first experience with a foreign language.

On "Fryday" the eighth of April he wrote: ". . . we Camped this Night in ye Woods near a Wild Meadow where was a Large Stack of Hay after we Pitched our Tent and made a very Large Fire we pull'd out our Knapsack . . . every (one) was his own Cook our Spits was Forked Sticks our Plates was a large Chip as for Dishes we had none". This was a night after they had shot wild turkeys.

George was sorry when the five weeks' journey ended. Beds at Mount Vernon were comfortable; food was the best. But there was a thrill about wilderness travel that he had never known on a plantation. He wondered how and when he could take such a journey again.

FROM

Narcissa Whitman: Pioneer of Oregon

JEANETTE EATON

As a little girl Narcissa loved to listen to stories about the Indians. She heard how savage and cruel they could be, but also how they needed friends to teach them. And when people needed help, Narcissa just had to give it. She got her chance when she married Dr. Marcus Whitman and they set out on the long hard trip over the Oregon Trail. It was the first time a white woman had ever crossed the Rockies. They built their mission, and the lovely golden-haired Narcissa was teacher, friend, nurse, doctor, and gardener to the Indians. She knew that they lived in constant danger from the Indians, yet she kept working for them right up to the hour when they killed her and her husband. Too late they realized that they had killed their best friends. Today the Whitmans are honored as the founders of Oregon, and courageous Narcissa as the ideal American pioneer woman.

Going West

ONE morning Whitman called his associates together. Baggage had to be still further reduced because the heavy farm wagon could not be taken over the mountains and everything in it had to be shifted to pack animals.

"I'm setting the example," said the leader, "by selling my black suit and overcoat. Yes, and all my fine white shirts."

"Your shirts, Marcus!" His wife looked at him dumbfounded. "Why, the ladies of the parish made those for you just before we left home!"

"I know, but I shan't need them in the wilderness, nor my good suit either." Determinedly he flung the package of clothes into one corner of the tent.

"But that leaves you almost nothing except what you have on!" Half laughing, half angry, Narcissa turned to Mrs. Spalding for sympathy. "If you sell your clothes, Marcus, I'll sell mine. I refuse to dress if you can't. Furthermore—" she folded her arms and tried to look grim, "I'll write to your sister Julia and tell her what you did with the gift shirts."

That argument finally broke Whitman's resolution. When the caravan started out on the 21st of June, the doctor's clothes were safely packed on one of the mules. He had, however, carried one point against all opposition. Nothing could persuade him to abandon the light wagon. At last the company officials were so convinced that they gave him an extra man to help at the bad spots and even decided to drive one of their own wagons to the rendezvous.

"On to the Rocky Mountains!" That was the zestful cry as the long pack train started from Fort William. But at first the way was painfully difficult. Up and down through ragged country went the steep trails. It was hard to tell who had the worst struggle, Whitman and his helpers with the wagon or the Indian boys with their cattle. Both these groups were late every night in reaching camp.

Narcissa was usually pacing up and down near the campfire watching for them. She would run up to the clattering wagon and ask breathlessly, "Marcus, did you see any Indians?" Grinning down at her, he would answer, "Nary a one!" He tried to reassure her by saying that the Indians would be afraid to attack a member of the caravan. But she would always say, "Not if they find you alone! You could do nothing against them." She envied Mrs. Spalding whose husband never left her side.

When they had made the last ford before reaching the mountains the going was better. The grade was very marked but it was gradual, and lofty ridges between which they slowly crawled replaced the choppy, brush-covered hills. One morning the guides pointed out Independence Rock. Even Easterners knew this landmark because of the many stories published about it. Two explorers who had climbed it long ago on the 4th of July had given the rock its name. The lofty, flat oblong of stone looked like a giant's chest set down upon the plain. Most of the party climbed to the top for the magnificent view. Toward the east loomed the shapes of the Laramie Mountains and to the west appeared the lower ridges of the Rocky Mountains blurred in mist.

That climb was an interesting interlude. But a far greater moment came for Narcissa next day. She was dressed and out of the tent at dawn. The sky was brilliantly clear and as she looked around her breathing stopped with a gasp. Towering on both sides of the wide plain were white-crested peaks. It was her first view of the eternal snows. From then on she watched the snowy mountains hour by hour. They were always different, always the same. The sight of them gave her a peculiar feeling of triumph.

The plain they were mounting was the famous South Pass through the Rocky Mountains. Now the nights were so chill that Marcus was glad he still had his overcoat to serve as an extra cover for Mrs. Spalding. Up and up and up they went over the endless, gradual grade. When clouds lifted, the azure sky and the dazzling white of the snowy peaks made Narcissa feel as if she were soaring into space. Now she didn't mind how slowly they pushed their way upward. The spectacle was too magnificent for impatience. On the 4th of July the climax of the trip was reached. Fitzpatrick halted the caravan and rode back to the mission party.

Up and up they went.

"Friends," he said with a ring in his tone, "we've reached the Great Divide. From this point melting snows run east and west. The watershed of the continent! All the way north to Canada and west to the Pacific lies the Oregon country. Whoever settles it first—British or Americans—gets it. Take a good look now. From here we begin to descend."

The Great Divide! Even a dull imagination must leap up at the term. But the eyes refused to believe. Secretly Narcissa confessed that she had always imagined the crossing meant a climb over some final peak from which one could get a view of east and west. But this slow ascent through the South Pass—could it really have brought them to the roof of the continent? Were it not for the snow fields on the mountains, she would never have guessed they were nearly a mile and a half above sea level.

Far more dramatic was what happened next day. The caravan had just reached the Sweetwater River in the southwestern part of our present state of Wyoming. Suddenly William Gray, who was riding beside Narcissa, gave a startled cry, "Lord save us! Indians!"

Over a rise of ground appeared the shapes of riders speeding toward them. On the instant the air was rent with yells. Gray seized the bridle of Narcissa's plunging horse and swiftly headed in behind the wagon. Mrs. Spalding's face looked out dead white. The sound of hoofs tramping up from the rear blended with the frightened shouts of the two cattle drivers. Spalding came running to the wagon, his eyes bulging with terror. Up ahead guns were firing. In a mad tear the marauders came on, swaying crazily in their saddles, waving arms, shooting rifles. Where was Marcus? Narcissa looked for him wildly. To her horror she saw him reining in his horse to face the onslaught. Slowly the caravan was coming to a halt.

All at once she understood. A white flag waved from one of the rifle barrels. Her ears caught the sound of a mighty laugh rolling down from the leaders of the column. These were friends! Along the line flashed word that a party from the rendezvous was greeting the caravan. Voices roared, "It's Joe Meek and his band!"

Still shaky, Narcissa rode out to join her husband. A tall fellow galloped up with a mad swoop and a swift turn of his steed which brought him beside Marcus. "Dr. Whitman, welcome back to the West!" he cried. "Guess you remember me—Captain Bridger's scout?"

Whitman remembered. Laughing, he said to his wife, "This is Joseph Meek, the most famous trapper in all the western lands."

She looked into a thin, hard face which crinkled with a smile. How young he was! Dark eyes fixed her with a curious wistfulness. But now there were other hands to shake. A number of the Nez Perce tribe had come to see the white teachers. All were presented. When the missionaries tried out the phrases they had learned from Richard and John, the Indians were delighted. They replied in sonorous words of welcome.

Something of that same respect tinged Joe Meek's casual manner. When the caravan began to move again, Narcissa found the scout riding on beside her. He asked if she knew all the good work her husband had done the year before at the rendezvous. When he had taken out an arrow-head from Captain Jim Bridger's back and then other arrow-heads from suffering Indians, everybody knew Whitman was a great doctor. The whole crowd was glad to have him back. Deeply pleased, Narcissa asked Meek if he had had a good year of trapping.

"Fine, ma'am," he replied. "And me and my partners had many good fights, too, with the Indians this spring. Blackfeet, Bannocks, Crows—none of them savage tribes war able to get the best of us. We sent a-plenty to their happy hunting grounds!"

To a missionary bent on saving Indian souls this was a remarkable approach. But somehow Narcissa couldn't be shocked. For an hour she was entertained by Joe Meek's stories of bear hunts and the narrow escapes which were everyday adventures in a roving trapper's life. Finally a signal was given for the departure of the visitors. With a lift of his hat Meek took leave of Mrs. Whitman. Whooping at the top of their lungs, the cavalcade dashed away in a cloud of dust and in no time at all were out of sight.

At the evening halt Narcissa found her husband and Spalding in grave consultation. A letter had been brought to Whitman by one of the Nez Perce chiefs. It was from Samuel Parker. He was not meeting Dr. Whitman at the rendezvous nor anywhere else. He was taking ship at Vancouver to go home around Cape Horn. This meant that the newcomers were not going to profit by Parker's long stay in the West. He left them neither instructions nor advice about the location of the mission—a deep disappointment to everybody. Now it was more important than ever to get all possible information at the rendezvous.

This meeting was held on Green River near its junction with the Sandy River not far from the present-day border between Wyoming and Idaho. The caravan reached it on July 6th. Long before its arrival there was another wild greeting by scouts and Indians who rode out to escort the pack train to camp. Drums beat, savage howls burst like rockets. Indian horsemen, hideous with war paint, tore madly up and down Fitzpatrick's long line.

Then came the first sight of the great meet. On the flats along the river was set up a forest of tents. A hundred horses stamped in the corrals. Smoke from campfires rose through the clear mountain air. Here with their year's catch of furs came men who worked for the American Fur Company, independent trappers, Canadian voyageurs, and Indians from many tribes. This was the one sociable event in the lives of lonely mountaineers and their reckless high spirits gave the place the air of a circus. With shouts, halloos, and shrill whistles, they rushed upon their friends of the caravan.

But the welcome given the two women was not of the same boisterous order. As they rode slowly toward the camp, a group of squaws ran forward. They were dressed in their finest costumes and were gay in ribbons and beads. With gestures of respectful joy, they lifted Eliza and Narcissa from their saddles, kissed them on both cheeks, took their hands, and with soft murmurs expressed profound joy that the white teachers had come at last.

Gesturing to the newcomers to seat themselves on blankets spread out upon the ground, the Indians made a circle around them. Narcissa whispered to her companion, "We're just like queens holding court!" First a chief came bowing and pushing forward his gorgeously dressed wife to shake hands. Others followed. Richard and John stood by to serve as interpreters.

Suddenly John bounded forward crying out a word familiar to the missionaries. It meant "Father!" The tall Nez Perce brave shook hands with his son and then held him at arm's length to see if he were really the same. Now it was Richard's turn. Hats were doffed, hands were shaken. The grave greetings revealed such overwhelming affection that Narcissa was not surprised to see Richard's black eyes moist with tears.

Marcus strode up to Narcissa, his dark blue eyes sparkling with excitement. "It's true that they want us to come, isn't it?" he cried. "It's worth all the effort. It will be fine to teach these good people."

Next day Narcissa showed her husband a scene which sharpened this impression. Beneath the shade of a big live oak tree Mrs. Spalding sat in the center of a group of Indian women with a Bible spread out on her lap. As she talked to them, they looked eagerly from the printed page to her moving lips. From the rapt expression of those dark faces it was plain the lesson had some wondrous magic even though it was not understood.

Every morning Mrs. Spalding held her class and every morning it grew larger. The Indian women talked to Narcissa and proudly showed her their infants. But it was the scouts and traders who claimed most of her attention. All that first day in camp they paraded past her tent, strutting, touching their beaver hats, and casting curious glances at her. When they finally got courage to talk to her, they said she reminded them of their sisters, "back in the States." She understood. To these uncouth wanderers the

Every morning Mrs. Spalding held her class.

presence of a white woman suggested the homes they had left behind.

None of the mission party had any sleep the first nights because of the noisy carousing. Card-playing, smoking, drinking, swearing, fighting—such were the joys of the rendezvous. To people who had given up everything to try to teach the Indians, these evils seemed peculiarly horrible. Selling liquor to the redskins was, indeed, against government regulations. But Whitman warned his associates against taking any other stand than that of setting a good example.

"To attack the conduct of these fellows would be worse than useless," he said with a stern look at Spalding. "Getting to the Columbia River is impossible without the friendly help of mountaineers!"

After that warning, Narcissa was pleased to hear from Joe Meek that she had the sense of humor to take the rendezvous in the right spirit. He came to see her every day and talked of his adventures. With rough eloquence he told her how much he mourned his brave and beautiful Indian wife, known as the "Mountain Lamb." She had been killed that year by an enemy arrow. Meek said he would never have supposed he could miss anyone so much.

Narcissa saw all too little of Marcus these days. He was kept busy treating patients. But whenever he could join the group of mountaineers around his wife's tent, he plied them with questions about the western country. The scouts agreed that the Nez Perce Indians near the Columbia River were the best of all the tribes. Not only were they a friendly people, but they were more intelligent and less lazy than most of the others. This opinion was approved by an important newcomer to the rendezvous.

He was the fur trader from Boston, Nathaniel Wyeth. From Fort Hall he had come down with two Hudson's Bay men and a small pack train. Fitzpatrick brought him to the mission camp and presented him to the group. Wyeth was a genial gentleman, ready to help with information and advice. He told them Samuel Parker was leaving by ship because his health hardly permitted his taking the overland trip a second time. Wyeth had much to say also about the Methodist Mission south of the Columbia River.

Wyeth strongly advised placing the Presbyterian mission in the Nez Perce country. He also urged the doctor to change his plan of going north with the Indians and trappers. "The two Hudson's Bay traders who came with me are going back to the Columbia district," he said. "Their route is more direct and you can go with them. They are excellent men, both. I'll bring them around to meet you tomorrow."

Whitman was delighted by this good fortune. He and the others liked their prospective guides on sight. They were men of commanding air and courtly manners, and they had been trained in the Hudson's Bay Company to maintain strict discipline. They wouldn't allow their mule drivers and trappers to stay at the rendezvous amid the wild carousing, but set their camp some miles away. When the traders had agreed to guide the Whitman party northward, they advised Marcus to move everybody over to the company's camp. The change was made with alacrity. After that the nights were quiet.

Even that separation, however, disturbed the Indians. The squaws wanted to know the plans of the white people. "You will live with us?" asked the Cayuse women. "No, you will come to our tribe!" declared the Nez Perces. Around Eliza and Narcissa a small storm arose. All they could say was, "We do not know yet. We will send you word."

Another scene of the same sort took place on the day of final departure. When the traders were ready to go the missionaries rode over to the rendezvous to say good-by to their friends. The Cayuse and the Nez Perce Indians begged harder than ever to be the ones chosen by the white teachers. Such eagerness was heartening and all the members of the party thought the fortnight had been most profitable. Mrs. Spalding was better. The animals were rested. Most important of all was the sense of being launched upon the life of the West. They felt so much more familiar with conditions that the future was no longer the terrible unknown.

Two days of travel, however, made the known present seem bad enough. The weather was scorching hot. Trails over the high mountains and into rough gulches were perilous. The nervous strain of staying in the saddle while her horse picked its way along a precipice or slowly jerked down an almost perpendicular slope of rocks left Narcissa exhausted by night. Added to this was her anxiety about Marcus. Every few minutes he would have to help the men lift the wagon over rocks or hold it back on steep grades. A large party of Indians went with them as far as Fort Hall and these tireless travelers refused to stop for a noon rest. All day the trail had to be endured on a diet of tea and dried buffalo meat.

Each evening when the halt was called, Marcus and Narcissa scanned one another anxiously to judge the effect of the day's hardship. Joking about the trials, she said, "I tried to find some of mother's bread and butter along the way, but caught no sight of it." Yet she was never too weary to be excited by the strange formation of the huge rocks, all the stranger for being so brilliantly tinted in red and deep rose and green. Some shapes looked to her like castles and some like the thrones of pagan gods. Others were fortifications made by the angels of Lucifer. At night coolness descended from the heights to refresh the body. Then the stars, like separate worlds of light in the clear air, drew the fainting spirit up to contemplation of mysterious harmonies.

It was the wagon that kept all harmony from the day. It was an unceasing nuisance. One day it jammed between rocks in a creek and twice on a steep mountainside it upset. That evening Narcissa made her husband roll in a blanket while she dried his wet clothes before the fire.

"You're a stubborn man, Marcus," said she in a tone of detachment. "You'll wear yourself out with this wagon. You're getting thin. On such terrible paths as we have to follow it's a wonder your wagon isn't turning somersaults all the time."

But neither words nor accidents broke Whitman's resolution.

A few days later Narcissa was following Gray's horse in the long single file. As she came over the top of a rocky ridge, she found the whole party halted. For an instant her heart was pounding. Then Spalding called out, "The axle-tree of the wagon is broken!" She had a treacherous spasm of joy. Now Marcus would have to leave the wretched thing where it was! But no. The men set about turning it into a two-wheeled cart and presently it was bumping and rattling on its way again.

The cattle grew footsore. Mrs. Spalding became such a weary ghost of a woman that everyone feared she might collapse entirely. Even Gray was ill for a day or two. Nevertheless, fired by insatiable interest in this fascinating land, the five travelers rode ten miles out of the way to see the famous soda springs in the present region of eastern Idaho. With scientific curiosity Marcus tested the water with acid and with soda. It fizzed and bubbled furiously, but proved good to drink. The weirdness of that muttering underground stream was in keeping with the awesome beauty of the crimson rocks piled in masses or detached like pinnacles.

Riding back to camp that afternoon, Narcissa said to the others, "Wouldn't you give a fortune to see a stretch of woods? Or just something green! I've never even imagined such a barren land."

Yet, as Gray pointed out, the guides somehow found a little grazing spot for camping sites every night. The courteous Scotchmen commanding the party sent their guests large antelope steaks whenever the hunters brought in game. They did everything, indeed, except temper the heat. Now it hardly lifted at night. The skin felt scorched and the mouth dry. Narcissa said the daily text should be, "The Heavens over my head are brass, and the earth iron under my feet."

Nearly three hundred miles they had advanced from the rendezvous, walking and riding and driving cattle. On August 3rd, the sixteenth day of this stretch a promise of rest offered. Across the hot basalt rocks, the lava ridges, and the dry levels a habitation made by man loomed like a castle of delight. It was Nathaniel Wyeth's Fort Hall.

The captain in charge of it turned amazed eyes upon the two women. He questioned, he exclaimed, he gesticulated in the effort to believe they had made the fearful trip. His admiration for their courage took the form of trying to make them comfortable and of showing them, after they had rested, the tiny vegetable garden of which he was so proud. "We'll have turnips for dinner!" he declared.

To the travelers that homely vegetable, served with fried bread and topped off with stewed service berries, made a wondrous feast. At dinner it was announced that the party would start on the next noon. The Indians were now going straight over the northern branch of the Rockies to their homeland. Two of them, however, offered to travel with the mission party and help with the animals. One of the two went by the extraordinary name of Chief Rotten-Belly.

Next morning Narcissa wrote up her journal in the delightful coolness of the fort. But at two o'clock the relentless forward march began. Almost at once the Easterners caught their first sight of the famous Snake River which curls across western Idaho and, turning north almost on the boundary between that modern state and Oregon, goes on up to empty at last into the Columbia River. Even at that point where its banks are low, Narcissa recognized this river as one of the dramatic personalities of the West. Sometimes between swampy banks of rushes, sometimes between enormous cliffs of sheer rock, the Snake twists its tortuous way.

Marveling at the width and wicked swiftness of the river, Narcissa said to the Scotch leader, "Do you know what the Snake reminds me of? One of those wild, willful horses the Indians catch on the plains. This stream looks so untamed!"

She was sorry when the route left the river's course. For the next two weeks the travel tale was a record of dust, heat, swamps, mosquitoes, and the sandy desert, covered with harsh sage and flanked by bare, brown mountains. No individual today, used to traveling by train or automobile, can possibly imagine what that daily plodding was like. In twelve hours the modern motorist comfortably covers the distance in that region which then required a fortnight of terrible effort. Yet in the changing light of morning and of evening there is great beauty in the desert. Narcissa loved to see the fierce outlines of rocks and mountains soften and grow purple in the slanting shafts of light or creeping shadow.

"There are times," Marcus said to her one day, as he helped her from the saddle, "when I'd like to catch an eagle for each of us and fly up to the Columbia. Especially when we have to ford rivers!"

Many rivers had to be crossed in this section. Two of them were wide and dangerous. Twice some of the pack animals came near drowning. Once, perched on the tallest horses, the women made a crossing of nearly half a mile. Water came up to the bellies of their animals and just one stumble meant drowning in the swift stream. Now there was another threat.

One late afternoon Narcissa was walking her horse beside Richard. She was almost asleep in her saddle, lulled by the heat, the monotonous pace, the rhythmic creak of the wagon which Marcus was driving just ahead of the cattle. Almost a mile in the distance was the faster-moving pack train. Suddenly the distant thud of swiftly galloping hoofs made her sit up, broad awake.

It was one of the Scotch traders who acted as chief scout. He began to shout even before reaching Marcus. "Make haste! Make double time—all of you! I've stopped the train up there. We've got to close in and stick together. A band of Indians is sighted."

Skillfully wheeling his horse, cracking his whip, shouting, the trader helped drive the cattle swiftly forward. Narcissa acted as outrider to keep the stragglers in line. The three Nez Perce boys padded forward with their beasts at a run. Marcus urged his steeds to a trot. Within ten minutes, enveloped in a cloud of dust, they had all caught up with the motionless pack train. In a wide circle around the entire outfit, trappers, scouts, and Indians squatted on the ground with rifles ready.

Taking a look at his wife and seeing that she was not at all afraid, Marcus began to chat with the Hudson's Bay men. This was the region where the Shoshone and Blackfoot Indians prowled. They wanted horses above all, but were not averse to scalps. Eagerly Narcissa searched the horizon, but nothing moved from behind sagebrush or crouching rock or giant cactus. Nor was there an alarm that night, although sentries took turn on guard. Nevertheless, for days and days she knew no peace when the boys or Marcus fell behind.

Everyone was overjoyed to reach the Snake River once again at the salmon fisheries. At the halt there everyone partook of delicious fresh broiled fish. It was fascinating to them all to watch the beautiful salmon leaping up the rapids. But the stay was spoiled for Narcissa by a bit of bad news Marcus brought her. Because the horses were getting exhausted, the luggage had to be lightened still more and now there was no room in the wagon for her precious little trunk. She was told she had to give it up.

Marcus caught her bending over it and murmuring, "Poor little trunk, I am sorry to leave thee. I thank thee for thy faithful services and that I have been cheered by thy presence so long."

"Narcissa!" he cried. "Stop! I have a reprieve for you. At least you don't have to abandon your box entirely. Our leader will put some things in it and have it taken up to the Columbia River. There he'll give it back to you, I'm sure."

That was far better than losing it. Another pleasant relief was a cool breeze which for hours made travel almost comfortable. Best of all was arriving on August 19th at Snake Fort. There for two and a half days the party rested and was well fed by the Hudson's Bay Company officials whose post it was. The women washed their clothes and all spent a Sunday of prayer and peace and thanksgiving. Once more the well-springs of courage gushed to the surface. Ready now for the last sprint!

FROM

Abe Lincoln Grows Up

CARL SANDBURG

This remarkably fine biography of Lincoln will give you a new insight into the boyhood forces that shaped this great and complicated man. He loved practical jokes and muscle contests, as well as learning. The picture of him sprawled out with a book, reading by the light of the fireplace, is a true one; but it's equally true that he was a tough and wiry outdoors fellow—a good shot, an extraordinary wood chopper and wrestler. Lincoln's mother died when he was very young, but in Sally Bush he was lucky enough to get a wonderful stepmother. She was sympathetic to his moods and to his special humor. And it was she—against the wishes of his own father—who encouraged his hankering for books and insisted that an education would not be wasted on young Abe.

Gentryville's Strong Boy

WHEN he was eleven years old, Abe Lincoln's young body began to change. The juices and glands began to make a long, tall boy out of him. As the months and years went by, he noticed his lean wrists getting longer, his legs too, and he was now looking over the heads of other boys. Men said, "Land o' Goshen, that boy air a-growin'!"

As he took on more length, they said he was shooting up into the air like green corn in the summer of a good corn-year. So he grew. When he reached seventeen years of age, and they measured him, he was six feet, nearly four inches, high, from the bottoms of his moccasins to the top of his skull.

These were years he was handling the ax. Except in spring plowing-time and the fall fodder-pulling, he was handling the ax nearly all the time. The insides of his hands took on callus thick as leather. He cleared openings in the timber, cut logs and puncheons, split firewood, built pig-pens.

He learned how to measure with his eye the half-circle swing of the ax so as to nick out the deepest possible chip from off a tree-trunk. The trick of swaying his body easily on the hips so as to throw the heaviest possible weight into the blow of the ax —he learned that.

One winter morning he wiped the frost from the ax-handle, sniffed sparkles of air into his lungs, and beat a steady cleaving of blows into a big tree—till it fell—and he sat on the main log and ate his noon dinner of corn bread and fried salt pork—and joked with the gray squirrels that frisked and peeped at him from high forks of near-by walnut trees.

He learned how to make his ax flash and bite into a sugar-maple or a sycamore. The outside and the inside look of black walnut and black oak, hickory and jack oak, elm and white oak, sassafras, dogwood, grapevines, sumac—he came on their secrets. He could guess close to the time of the year, to the week of the month, by the way the leaves and branches of trees looked. He sniffed the seasons.

Often he worked alone in the timbers all day long with only the sound of his own ax, or his own voice speaking to himself, or the crackling and swaying of branches in the wind, and the cries and whirs of animals, of brown and silver-gray squirrels, of partridges, hawks, crows, turkeys, sparrows, and the occasional wildcats.

The tricks and whimsies of the sky, how to read clear skies and cloudy weather, the creeping vines of ivy and wild grape, the recurrence of dogwood blossoms in spring, the ways of snow, rain,

These were years he was handling the ax.

drizzle, sleet, the visitors of sky and weather coming and going hour by hour—he tried to read their secrets, he tried to be friendly with their mystery.

So he grew, to become hard, tough, wiry. The muscle on his bones and the cords, tendons, cross-weaves of fiber, and nerve centers, these became instruments to obey his wishes. He found with other men he could lift his own end of a log—and more too. One of the neighbors said he was strong as three men. Another said, "He can sink an ax deeper into wood than any man I ever saw." And another, "If you heard him fellin' trees in a clearin', you would say there was three men at work by the way the trees fell."

He was more than a tough, long, rawboned boy. He amazed men with his man's lifting power. He put his shoulders under a new-built corncrib one day and walked away with it to where the farmer wanted it. Four men, ready with poles to put under it and carry it, didn't need their poles. He played the same trick with a chicken house; at the new, growing town of Gentryville near by, they said the chicken house weighed six hundred pounds, and only a big boy with a hard backbone could get under it and walk away with it.

A blacksmith shop, a grocery, and a store had started up on the crossroads of the Gentry farm. And one night after Abe had been helping thresh wheat on Dave Turnham's place, he went with Dennis Hanks, John Johnston, and some other boys to Gentryville where the farmhands sat around with John Baldwin, the blacksmith, and Jones, the storekeeper, passed the whisky jug, told stories and talked politics and religion and gossip. Going home late that night, they saw something in a mud puddle alongside the road. They stepped over to see whether it was a man or a hog. It was a man—drunk—snoring—sleeping off his drunk—on a frosty night outdoors in a cold wind.

They shook him by the shoulders, doubled his knees to his stomach, but he went on sleeping, snoring. The cold wind was getting colder. The other boys said they were going home, and they went away leaving Abe alone with the snoring sleeper in the mud puddle. Abe stepped into the mud, reached arms around the man, slung him over his shoulders, carried him to Dennis Hanks's cabin, built a fire, rubbed him warm and left him sleeping off the whisky.

And the man afterward said Abe saved his life. He told John Hanks, "It was mighty clever of Abe to tote me to a warm fire that night."

So he grew, living in that Pigeon Creek cabin for a home, sleeping in the loft, climbing up at night to a bed just under the roof, where sometimes the snow and the rain drove through the cracks, eating sometimes at a table where the family had only one thing to eat—potatoes. Once at the table, when there were only potatoes, his father spoke a blessing to the Lord for potatoes; and the boy murmured, "Those are mighty poor blessings." And Abe made jokes once when company came and Sally Bush Lincoln brought out raw potatoes, gave the visitors a knife apiece, and they all peeled raw potatoes, and talked about the crops, politics, religion, gossip.

Days when they had only potatoes to eat didn't come often. Other days in the year they had "yaller-legged chicken" with gravy, and corn dodgers with shortening, and berries and honey. They tasted of bear meat, deer, coon, quail, grouse, prairie turkey, catfish, bass, perch.

Abe knew the sleep that comes after long hours of work outdoors, the feeling of simple food changing into blood and muscle as he worked in those young years clearing timberland for pasture and corn crops, cutting loose the brush, piling it and burning it, splitting rails, pulling the crosscut saw and the whipsaw, driving the shovel-plow, harrowing, planting, hoeing, pulling fodder, milking cows, churning butter, helping neighbors at house-raisings, log-rollings, corn-huskings.

He found he was fast, strong, and keen when he went against other boys in sports. On farms where he worked, he held his own at scuffling, knocking off hats, wrestling. The time came when around Gentryville and Spencer County he was known as the best "rassler" of all, the champion. In jumping, foot-racing, throwing the maul, pitching the crowbar, he carried away the decisions against the lads of his own age always, and usually won against those older than himself.

He earned his board, clothes, and lodgings, sometimes working for a neighbor farmer. He watched his father, while helping make cabinets, coffins, cupboards, window frames, doors. Hammers, saws, pegs, cleats, he understood first-hand, also the scythe and the cradle for cutting hay and grain, the corn-cutter's knife, the leather piece to protect the hand while shucking corn, and the horse, the dog, the cow, the ox, the hog. He could skin and cure the hides of coon and deer. He lifted the slippery two-hundred-pound hog carcass, head down, holding the hind hocks up for others of the gang to hook, and swung the animal clear of the ground. He learned where to stick a hog in the under side of the neck so as to bleed it to death, how to split it in two, and carve out the chops, the parts for sausage grinding, for hams, for "cracklings."

Farmers called him to butcher for them at thirty-one cents a day, this when he was sixteen and seventeen years old. He could "knock a beef in the head," swing a maul and hit a cow between the eyes, skin the hide, halve and quarter it, carve out the tallow, the steaks, kidneys, liver.

And the hiding-places of fresh spring water under the earth crust had to be in his thoughts; he helped at well-digging; the wells Tom Lincoln dug went dry one year after another; neighbors said Tom was always digging a well and had his land "honeycombed"; and the boy, Abe, ran the errands and held the tools for the well-digging.

When he was eighteen years old, he could take an ax at the end of the handle and hold it out in a straight horizontal line, easy and steady—he had strong shoulder muscles and steady wrists early in life. He walked thirty-four miles in one day, just on an errand, to please himself, to hear a lawyer make a speech. He could tell his body to do almost impossible things, and the body obeyed.

Growing from boy to man, he was alone a good deal of the

time. Days came often when he was by himself all the time except at breakfast and supper hours in the cabin home. In some years more of his time was spent in loneliness than in the company of other people. It happened, too, that this loneliness he knew was not like that of people in cities who can look from a window on streets where faces pass and repass. It was the wilderness loneliness he became acquainted with, solved, filtered through body, eye, and brain, held communion with in his ears, in the temples of his forehead, in the works of his beating heart.

He lived with trees, with the bush wet with shining raindrops, with the burning bush of autumn, with the lone wild duck riding a north wind and crying down on a line north to south, the faces of open sky and weather, the ax which is an individual one-man instrument, these he had for companions, books, friends, talkers, chums of his endless changing soliloquies.

His moccasin feet in the winter-time knew the white spaces of snowdrifts piled in whimsical shapes against timber slopes or blown in levels across the fields of last year's cut corn stalks; in the summer-time his bare feet toughened in the gravel of green streams while he laughed back to the chatter of bluejays in the red-haw trees or while he kept his eyes ready in the slough quack-grass for the cow-snake, the rattler, the copperhead.

He rested between spells of work in the spring-time when the upward push of the coming out of the new grass can be heard, and in autumn weeks when the rustle of a single falling leaf lets go a whisper that a listening ear can catch.

He found his life thrown in ways where there was a certain chance for a certain growth. And so he grew. Silence found him; he met silence. In the making of him as he was, the element of silence was immense.

A Good Stepmother

He took shape in a tall, long-armed cornhusker. When rain came in at the chinks of the cabin loft where he slept, soaking through the book Josiah Crawford loaned him, he pulled fodder two days to pay for the book, made a clean sweep, till there wasn't a blade left on a cornstalk in the field of Josiah Crawford.

His father was saying the big boy looked as if he had been roughhewn with an ax and needed smoothing with a jack-plane. "He was the ganglin'est, awkwardest feller that ever stepped over a ten-rail snake fence; he had t' duck to git through a door; he 'peared to be all j'ints."

His stepmother told him she didn't mind his bringing dirt into the house on his feet; she could scour the floor; but she asked him to keep his head washed or he'd be rubbing the dirt on her nice whitewashed rafters. He put barefoot boys to wading in a mud-puddle near the horse-trough, picked them up one

He walked their muddy feet across the ceiling.

by one, carried them to the house upside down, and walked their muddy feet across the ceiling. The mother came in, laughed an hour at the foot-tracks, told Abe he ought to be spanked —and he cleaned the ceiling so it looked new.

The mother said, "Abe never spoke a cross word to me in his life since we lived together." And she said Abe was truthful; when Tilda Johnson leaped onto Abe's back to give him a scare on a lonely timber path, she brought the big axman to the ground by pulling her hands against his shoulders and pressing her knee into his backbone. The ax-blade cut her ankle, and strips from Abe's shirt and Tilda's dress had to be used to stop the blood. By then she was sobbing over what to tell her mother. On Abe's advice she told her mother the whole truth.

As time went by, the stepmother of Abe became one of the rich, silent forces in his life. Besides keeping the floors, pots, pans, kettles, and milk-crocks spick and span, weaving, sewing, mending, and managing with sagacity and gumption, she had a massive, bony, human strength backed with an elemental faith that the foundations of the world were mortised by God with unspeakable goodness of heart toward the human family. Hard as life was, she was thankful to be alive.

Once she told Abe how her brother Isaac, back in Hardin County, had hot words with a cowardly young man who shot Isaac without warning. The doctors asked Isaac if they could tie him down while they cut his flesh and took out the bullet. He told them he didn't need to be tied down; he put two lead musket-balls in between his teeth and ground his teeth on them while the doctors cut a slash nine inches long and one inch deep till they found the bullet and brought it out. Isaac never let out a moan or a whimper; he set his teeth into the musket-balls, ground them into flat sheets, and spat them from his mouth when he thanked the doctors.

Sally Bush, the stepmother, was all of a good mother to Abe. If he broke out laughing when others saw nothing to laugh at, she let it pass as a sign of his thoughts working their own way. So far as she was concerned he had a right to do unaccountable things; since he never lied to her, why not? So she justified him. When Abe's sister, Sarah, married Aaron Grigsby and a year after died with her new-born child, it was Sally Bush who spoke comfort to the eighteen-year-old boy of Nancy Hanks burying his sister and the wraith of a child.

A neighbor woman sized him up by saying, "He could work when he wanted to, but he was no hand to pitch in like killing snakes." John Romine made the remarks: "Abe Lincoln worked for me, but was always reading and thinking. I used to get mad at him for it. I say he was awful lazy. He would laugh and talk —crack his jokes and tell stories all the time; didn't love work half as much as his pay. He said to me one day that his father taught him to work, but he never taught him to love it."

A misunderstanding came up one time between Abe Lincoln and William Grigsby. It ended with Grigsby so mad he challenged Abe to a fight. Abe looked down at Grigsby, smiled, and said the fight ought to be with John Johnston, Abe's stepbrother. The day was set for the fight; each man was there with his seconds; the mauling began, with the two fighters stripped to the waist, beating and bruising each other with bare knuckles.

A crowd stood around, forming a ring, cheering, yelling, hissing, till after a while they saw Johnston getting the worst of it. Then the ring of people forming the crowd was broken as Abe Lincoln shouldered his way through, stepped out, took hold of Grigsby and threw that fighter out of the center of the fight-ring.

Then Abe Lincoln called out, "I'm the big buck of this lick." And looking around so his eyes swept the circle of the crowd he let loose the challenge, "If any of you want to try it, come on and whet your horns." A riot of wild fist-fighting came then between the two gangs and for months around the Jones grocery store there was talk about which gang whipped the other.

After a fox-chase with horses, Uncle Jimmy Larkin was telling how his horse won the race, was the best horse in the world, and never drew a long breath; Abe didn't listen; Uncle Jimmy told it again, and Abe said, "Why don't you tell us how many short breaths he drew?" It raised a laugh on Jimmy, who jumped around threatening to fight, till Abe said quietly, "Now, Larkin, if you don't shut up I'll throw you in that water."

Asked by Farmer James Taylor, if he could kill a hog, he answered, "If you will risk the hog I'll risk myself."

He had the pride of youth that resents the slur, the snub, besides the riotous blood that has always led youth in reckless exploits. When he was cutting up didos one day at the Crawford farm-house, Mrs. Crawford asked, "What's going to become of you, Abe?" And with mockery of swagger, he answered, "Me? I'm going to be president of the United States."

Driving a horse at the mill, he was sending the whiplash over the nag and calling, "Git up, you old hussy; git up, you old hussy." The horse let fly a hind foot that knocked down the big boy just as he yelled, "Git up." He lay bleeding, was taken home, washed, put to bed, and lay all night unconscious. As his eye winkers opened the next day and he came to, his tongue struggled and blurted, "You old hussy," thus finishing what he started to say before the knockdown.

The horse let fly.

FROM

Man of Molokai: The Life of Father Damien

ANN ROOS

When Father Damien of Belgium was sent to Honolulu, he heard about the pitiful plight of the lepers banished to the island of Molokai. He volunteered to go there. With vigorous energy and devotion, he set to work to bring some order and hope into these lives of utter despair. It took enormous courage to overcome the handicaps of the island, and the resistance of the lepers themselves. And Father Damien realized that if he were not careful he might contract the awful disease; but that never for a moment restricted his contacts. One day he poured boiling water on his foot and felt no sensation; he knew what that meant. The next Sunday, he electrified his congregation when he casually began his sermon with, "We lepers . . ." Now he felt that he could accomplish even more because the last barrier had been removed—he was in every sense one of them.

Damien, the Leper

THE disreputable old straw hat flapped gently in the wind as Father Damien surveyed his domain. He had climbed halfway up the incline and stood gazing below at the rocky shelf which was Kalawao.

From the distance a cluster of little cottages and a longer building marked the leper settlement. The lone cabin under the great pandanus tree, near the cemetery, was Damien's house, erected by his own hands during his first year of residence. He observed it with approval. It was sturdy and comfortable, and lately he had added an extra room for his infrequent guests. This fine cottage was quite an advance from his first hard bed on the ground under the pandanus tree, he thought.

But nevertheless he regarded the great tree with a certain sentiment. It had been his first haven during those first terrible weeks when life at the leper colony had seemed an agony of hopelessness and desolation. His house had been built in its shade, and with the matter-of-fact acceptance of the idea of death common to the inhabitants of this island he had selected it as the spot where his grave should one day be dug. Indeed, so attached to this thought had he become that he was greatly disturbed one day to discover one of the leper grave-diggers starting to dig a new grave under the big tree for a man recently dead.

"Stop, man—why do you dig here? Do you not know it is forbidden?" His shabby cassock had fluttered angrily as he hurried over to the lean brown man who was using a small pick to dislodge the rocky turf.

The man had straightened his back and looked bewildered. The cemetery was so crowded, he had thought a fresh location, with so many new dead—and this spot had seemed to him excellent—. But Damien, with a sternness rare in his dealings with the lepers, peremptorily bade him to refill the hole and find another spot.

His agitation surprised even himself. He had not realized how attached to the idea of being buried under the pandanus tree he had become until he saw the possibility threatened. Perhaps this sense of possession was unbecoming in a priest. He stood for a moment, irresolute. Would the Lord forgive him this small vanity?

But this morning, standing off on the hillside, he was permit-

"Stop, man—why do you dig there?"

ting himself to indulge in his favorite dream. The recent visit of the Princess Liluiokalani had culminated in a bewildering and heartening occurrence. The Princess Regent had heard that the Monseigneur Koeckmann, newly arrived Co-adjutor to the enfeebled Bishop Maigret, was soon to visit Molokai, and had entrusted him with a small box and a letter. Both were to be delivered to Father Damien.

The box had contained the beautiful insignia of the Order of Kalakaua, indicating the highest possible honor to be bestowed by the Royal House. The astonished priest had endured the elaborate ceremonial with chagrin and reluctance, for such public recognition was deeply painful to him. The jeweled insignia he removed as soon as possible and hid it carefully away lest he be asked to wear it again.

But the letter of the princess he read and reread, each time with a lift of the heart. For did it not mean that some of his thwarted dreams for his dear lepers might at last come to fruition?

"REVEREND SIR: [*it read*]:

"I desire to express to you my admiration of the heroic and distinguished service you are rendering to the most unhappy of my subjects; and to pay, in some measure, a public tribute to the devotion, patience, and unbounded charity with which you give yourself to the corporal and spiritual relief of these unfortunate people, who are necessarily deprived of the affectionate care of their relations and friends.

"I know well that your labours and sacrifices have no other motive than the desire to do good to those in distress; and that you look for no reward but from the Great God, our Sovereign Lord, who directs and inspires you. Nevertheless, to content my own earnest desire, I beg of you, Reverend Father, to accept the decoration of Knight Commander of the Royal Order of Kalakaua as a testimony of my sincere admiration for the efforts you are making to relieve the distress and lessen the sufferings of these afflicted people, as I myself had occasion to see on my recent visit to the settlement. I am,

Your friend,

LILIUOKALANI, REGENT."

Damien's eyes glowed happily behind the thick lenses as he gazed at the scene before him and laid out in imagination the leproserie of his dream. The leper's cottages would do for the present. But a large communal gathering place was needed. This would add to the social life of the lepers and provide meeting places for the Burial Associations and other clubs which he had encouraged into existence. The Chapel of St. Philomene was far too inadequate. He would repair the roof and add to the nave. Perhaps he would put in a small side-chapel to Our Lady.

But most of all he needed to build proper orphanages. This had been his dear and cherished project ever since his early days when he had been distressed at the great number of orphaned children who lived a wild and undisciplined existence, utterly without control or direction. Most of these did not have the disease, although their parents had died from the result of it. True, he had made considerable progress. For some years now the orphans had been gathered into two large crude buildings, one for the boys and one for the girls, and their lives had assumed a kind of order under the hand of Father Damien and a few of the adult lepers who were capable of helping him. The priest instructed the boys in carpentry and taught them to read and to write and to govern their small affairs by common discussion and voting. The girls were taught to sew and to prepare their simple food.

But the quarters were crowded and the leper teachers often desultory and half-hearted and so ill-prepared themselves that the quick minds of the children leaped far ahead of their instructors. Nuns he would have, decided Damien. A small group of able religious would soon bring peaceful order to the untidy orphanages. They would teach the smallest children and the girls and guide them into ways of dignity and usefulness, however briefly. Monks he would have as teachers for the boys, and as physicians in the hospital. The order and discipline of a religious community would prevail. Everyone would be busy and serene and selfless, living in God.

Molokai, he planned in happy abandonment, would have a

Father Damien ministered to the lepers.

leper settlement like the lazar houses of the Middle Ages, with their best features retained and modern medical practice added.

Father Damien sighed sharply with impatience as he remembered the slowness of official movements. It was hard to be so full of eagerness to get things accomplished and yet continually to be thwarted by delays and indifference. He tried to shake off a vague depression as he descended the slope to the plateau of the settlement. He suddenly felt old and tired. Life in this part of the world aged a man quickly, he thought. And of late he had been irked by a return of an old foot trouble, and often felt strangely unwell.

Lola lifted the tea-kettle away from the hottest part of the fire and padded over in her bare feet to the doorway. The last streaks of sunset had long since faded, and the sudden tropical night lay dark and quiet around the cottage.

She peered out anxiously. The good Father was later than usual. She would have to chide him again tonight for being so absorbed in his labors that he forgot to come back to eat his evening meal until it was cold and unappetizing.

With the privilege of long servitude, she often scolded Damien for neglecting his meals and the rest that he so badly needed. Hadn't he been looking particularly weary lately? Several of the parishioners had commented upon it and had bade Lola to remonstrate with him. But it had been quite useless. Over and over he had stayed so late in the hospital or in the cottage of a sick leper that, when he did finally arrive home, he was too weary to eat. He would sip a cup of hot tea and then fling himself in exhaustion on his hard pallet. Later, long after the old housekeeper had gone home to her own cottage, he would revive and perhaps eat a little. She knew this because in the morning she would find, partly consumed, the carefully prepared supper which she had laid out for him. His light would often burn late as he worked over his reports and letters.

Remonstrances did no good. He would laugh at the worried expression on the kind old face of his faithful housekeeper.

"I will rest later," he would say, amused at her evident concern. "There is so much to do now, Lola. Yes, later," and he seemed for a moment to be talking to himself, "later I will rest."

But he had never before been quite so late as tonight. He had spent the day at the neighboring settlement of Kalapaupa, and when that happened, he seemed to lose all track of time. The old woman padded back to the table and set the dish of freshly baked yellow taro pudding in the oven to keep warm. What a pity it would be hard and dry, probably, before Father Damien set his teeth into it. Was there no reasoning with the man?

Some time later the slow drag of footsteps outside told her that the priest was nearing the house, and as he stepped into the doorway, her housewifely resentment fled. His face looked drawn and dark. She could think of nothing to say but "Father—you are tired."

He sank into the stiff little wooden armchair and for a moment it seemed as though he could not speak.

"Very tired, Lola," he said at last. "It is a long walk from Kalapaupa."

"But your horse, Father—"

"My horse went lame this afternoon and I had to leave him at Kalapaupa. Poor old fellow—too many times have I urged him over the pass. He caught a stone in his shoe and I did not discover it soon enough. He will recover, but it seemed only fair to let him have a night's rest before asking him to use the sore foot again."

"So your feet, Father, will be sore instead," the old woman said with asperity.

The priest laughed. "And so they are, Lola. Sore and very dusty. Perhaps—" and he looked quizzically at her disapproving, wrinkled face, "perhaps I may use some of your good hot water to bathe them before I eat."

Lola was instantly solicitous. She carried a basin and towels into the bedroom and set the kettle of steaming water on the floor beside them.

Father Damien sat on the edge of his cot and pulled off his dusty boots. His feet were not serving him well of late. They often seemed hot and feverish and at night he had noted a peculiar itching sensation. Perhaps he should not do so much walking. He had frequently thought of contriving some sort of horse-drawn carriage for his trips from settlement to settlement, and perhaps now was the time to get to work on the idea. His own good horse would be excellent, once trained to the carriage-rein, and he had half a notion that a friendly non-leper planter over the mountain could be persuaded to part with one of several rarely-used carriages which stood in his shed.

He poured a little cold water in the basin and then lifted up the still bubbling kettle. The steam arose from the spout and clouded his spectacles. Blinded for a moment, his aim was not sure, and the water poured in a boiling stream over his bare feet.

A widening pool of water darkened the uneven wooden floor. The steam lifted and his eyes riveted to his scalded foot which looked swollen and red. The signs of the burn on his skin were unmistakable. Yet he had felt nothing.

For a long time he sat arrested, the kettle still in his hand.

Pasteur

SIR ARTHUR T. QUILLER-COUCH

THROUGHOUT the late autumn of 1870, while the Prussian troops were crushing upon the frontier of France, there dwelt in the little town of Arbois in the Jura, and in a cottage not far from the bridge which crosses the stream of the Cuisance, a middle-aged man, short of stature, plain of feature, noticeable only, when you met and passed him, for a pair of curiously deep gray-green eyes and the drag of a paralyzed left leg. This was Louis Pasteur, administrator of the École Normale in distant Paris, beloved there until yesterday by colleagues and pupils for his single-hearted devotion to science.

At Paris to-day there were no pupils left to teach. In spite of the privilege which freed *normaliens* from military service in exchange for a ten years' engagement at the university, the lads had enlisted eagerly. Pasteur's own son, a youth of eighteen, had started for the front. He himself had sought to be enrolled in the National Guard, until reminded that such service was not for a half-paralyzed man. The École Normale, deserted of young life and forlorn, had been turned into an ambulance hospital in readiness for the now inevitable siege. For some time the administrator haunted the empty laboratories and tried to continue his scientific researches. "Do not stay in Paris," his friends advised. "You have no right to stay; you would only be a useless mouth during the siege." So on September 5th Pasteur had packed up and started for Arbois, his native place.

There in the cottage by the bridge he tried to return to his books, his plans for future work. "*Laboremus*" ("Let us work"), he would repeat as in brighter days, looking up to cheer his wife and daughter, whose thoughts were at the front. But just then the town-crier's trumpet would sound up the street and with a heart wrung with anxiety for France the little man would rush out, mix with the townsmen on the bridge, listen breathlessly to the news—which grew worse and worse—and return to his room with tears in his eyes, despair in his heart.

To understand the indignant wrath that burned in a good Frenchman's heart during those days of humiliation, it must be remembered that Bismarck had brought this war about by means of a forged telegram. The whole business was a crime; and men, taught to believe that such a crime must be abhorrent in the sight of God, saw that it was successful, and wrote, as Pasteur wrote, "Should we not cry, Happy are the dead!"

He, well on in years and half paralyzed; he, dismissed from Paris as a "useless mouth"—what could *he* do towards lifting the *patrie* from the dust and restore her to her proud place among the nations? Nothing, as it seemed, or less than nothing.

But wait! If he had learnt anything in his laboratory, it was to think clearly; and it is wonderful what one clear perception in the brain of an honest man will sometimes do in this world. Pasteur had two such perceptions, both equally clear. He saw that the only true leadership among the nations—the only leadership worth regaining for France—was a leadership in well-doing, for which a nation, as a man, must have a trained intelligence. It does not suffice to mean well; one must learn the skill to carry that meaning into practice. He saw further—all question of right and wrong apart—that Germany had for years been setting a value on learning, education, intelligence, while France had been neglecting these things. "The real cause of our misfortunes lies *there*," he wrote to one of his pupils.

"It is not with impunity that a great nation is allowed to lose its intellectual standard. We are paying the penalty of fifty years' forgetfulness of science, of its immense influence on the destiny of a great people, and of all that might have assisted the diffusion of light . . . I cannot go on; all this hurts me."

The town-crier's trumpet would sound up the street.

Again:—

"Whilst Germany was multiplying her universities, setting up healthy rivalries between them, honouring her masters and doctors, creating vast laboratories and stocking them with every instrument and appliance, France was giving but a careless attention to higher education. . . . *The cultivation of science in its highest expression is perhaps even more necessary to the moral condition than to the national prosperity of a nation.*"

This clear perception he never lost, though now and again passion might cloud it for a moment as he thought of his country's humiliation.

"The best kind of revenge," says an old philosopher, "is not to be like them;" and Pasteur's revenge was to be of this nobler kind. "I know not what destinies Fate has in store for me," he wrote; "but I do feel most deeply that if I had to choose between the present situation of France and that of Prussia, I should decide for the former." Let us see what this modest man of science did towards lifting France out of her disasters; but first let us see how his life had been preparing him for the attempt.

The Pasteurs had four children—three daughters, and little Louis, born at Dôle on the 27th of December 1822. Louis Pasteur grew and thrived, and was sent in due course to the elementary school of Arbois. Neither here nor at the Arbois College, to which he proceeded, did the boy show any special cleverness, unless it were at drawing, a gift inherited from his father. His father pondered much on the future of his one boy, so tractable and studious, but possessing, so far as could be seen, but this one modest talent.

M. Romanet, headmaster of the Arbois College, did something to reassure the father. He had perceived that young Louis's mind, while it worked slowly, was unusually conscientious: he never supposed "this" or "guessed" that, but before affirming, waited until he was absolutely sure. M. Romanet talked with the parents and hinted at the École Normale. They hesitated, demurred; finally, at the close of October 1838, in a shower of rain and sleet, young Louis Pasteur and a school friend, Jules

Vercel, were hoisted with their luggage on board the country coach and driven off for Paris, hiding themselves from the weather under a tarpaulin beside the coachman.

They were received in Paris by a good fellow-countryman, M. Barbet, who kept a small school in the Latin Quarter. But although Louis did his best to work, his homesickness was acute, and soon became intolerable. It so preyed on his mind that at length good M. Barbet wrote a letter to his parents. One day in November Louis had word that a friend wished to speak with him in a café at the end of the street. He went, and found, at a small table behind the shop, a man sitting with his face in his hands. It was his father. "I have come to fetch you," he said.

So back Louis went. He was ashamed of having let his feelings master his will. He turned again to his pastel drawings and worked feverishly, restlessly; but all the while his conscience was accusing him. He had run away from his duty, and honour bade him return. Since he could not trust himself for a second assault on Paris, he sought and obtained his father's leave to go to the college at Besançon, where he could pass his *baccalauréat* and prepare himself, still with an eye on the École Normale. Besançon is scarcely fifty miles from Arbois, and his father visited it three or four times a year to sell hides from the tanyard.

In 1840 he took his degree of Bachelor of Letters, and in August 1842 that of Bachelor of Science, passing both examinations creditably, but without special distinction. He was eager by this time to make another attempt on Paris, whither Charles Chappuis, a beloved and intimate college friend, had preceded him. His father refused his consent for some time, fearing a repetition of the 1838 fiasco, but at length gave way. And in October Louis made his second start.

As before, he boarded with good M. Barbet. He was no longer a homesick boy, but a grown lad, able to take care of himself, eager to learn, regular in attendance at the Lycée St. Louis and the lectures at the famous Sorbonne. At the end of the school year was admitted fourth on the list to the École Normale. It was in keeping with his character that he at once wrote to M.

Barbet, who had boarded him gratis in return for his teaching some of the younger pupils, offering to give some further lessons on his half-holidays as a small token of his gratitude for past kindnesses.

It is related that in his hurry to enter the École Normale he presented himself some days before the other students, and was allowed to sleep in the empty dormitory. His parents soon began to worry about his health; and not without excuse, for he spent so much time among the retorts and test-tubes that his comrades nicknamed him "the laboratory pillar." On half-holidays he taught M. Barbet's classes. All his recreation consisted in an occasional walk with Chappuis, when the two would dispute over the comparative claims of philosophy and science—for Chappuis was taking his course in philosophy.

One day—they were walking in the gardens of the Luxembourg —Pasteur began to talk excitedly of tartaric acid and an allied but highly curious substance called "paratartaric" or "racemic" acid. What bothered Pasteur, and did not bother Chappuis at all, was this—that while in combination with soda, or again with ammonia, these two acids produced crystals which in other respects could not be distinguished from one another, a beam of light passing through these crystals was quite differently refracted; just as a ray falls differently through a prism and through a flat sheet of glass. Here were two crystals alike in shape and apparently in every other respect; yet the tartaric slanted the light, and the racemic passed it straight through. Of course this is an extremely rough-and-ready way of stating a problem over which Pasteur had been brooding for months, and with which he wearied his friend during their walk, explaining that (nobody knew why) certain crystals reflected light to the right hand, others to the left, while others again remained inactive. "Why should this be?" the young man eagerly demanded.

This crystallography had taken hold of Pasteur; and, having passed through the ordinary examination course at the École Normale with more than fair credit, he plunged into the study with a newcomer at the laboratory, one Auguste Laurent, a young professor full of bold ideas. These two worked together until their experiments were interrupted by Laurent's promotion as assistant to M. Dumas, the great chemist, at the Sorbonne. Pasteur worked on alone. The differences in crystals occupied his spare thoughts even during the Revolution of 1848, when young men in Paris threw up barricades in the holy cause of the republic and chased Louis Philippe from his throne. Like most generous youths of his time, he had visions of a France devoted to the ideas of liberty and fraternity—a state of free men and brethren. But the struggle over and apparently successful, he returned to his crystals.

If an object reflected in a mirror—say a table or a square flight of steps—has its two sides alike or "symmetrical," you can lay the image of the thing over the thing itself, and they fit. But if the staircase be spiral, you cannot lay its image exactly over it; the one turns to the right, the other to the left; and a right hand seen in a mirror is a left hand.

Now Pasteur, examining the crystals of tartaric acid, discovered—what had escaped all previous observers—that they had little facets on one side, and always on the same side, to the right. "Now," reasoned he, "if the paratartaric or racemic crystals have these facets on *both* sides, we shall know exactly why, with them, the ray is neutralized and falls straight." To his disappointment, these crystals, too, were faceted only upon one side, but not on the same side. It occurred to him to pick them out one by one and sort them, putting on one side those which turned to the right, and on the other those which turned to the left. Having done this, he mixed an equal number of each kind together, and threw the ray upon the mixture.

The equal and opposite facets exactly neutralized one another, and the light fell straight. "I have it!" he cried, and rushing from the room embraced a casual curator who happened to be coming down the corridor.

In Paris the report of a scientific discovery spreads quickly. The report of this one reached the great chemist Biot, aged seventy-four, who had spent the best years of his life in studying crystals, and was inclined to be sceptical. Pasteur heard of his disbelief, and wrote very modestly asking him for an interview. An appointment was made.

Every detail of that interview remained for ever fixed in Pasteur's memory. Biot began by fetching some paratartaric acid. "I have most carefully studied it," he said to Pasteur: "it is absolutely neutral in the presence of polarized light." Some distrust was visible in his gestures and audible in his voice. "I shall bring you everything that is necessary," continued the old man, fetching doses of soda and ammonia. He wanted the salt prepared before his eyes.

After pouring the liquid into a crystallizer, Biot took it into a corner of his room, to be quite sure that no one would touch it. "I shall let you know when you are to come back," he said to Pasteur when taking leave of him. Forty-eight hours later some crystals, very small at first, began to form; when there was a sufficient number of them Pasteur was recalled. Still in Biot's presence, Pasteur withdrew them, one by one, and divided them into two groups—left and right.

"So you affirm," said Biot, "that your right-hand crystals will deviate to the right, the plane of polarization, and your left-hand ones will deviate to the left."

"Yes," said Pasteur.

"Well, let me do the rest."

Biot himself prepared the solutions, and then sent again for Pasteur. Biot first placed in the apparatus the solution which should deviate to the left. Having satisfied himself that the deviation actually took place, he took Pasteur's arm and said in these words often deservedly quoted: "My dear boy, I have loved science so much during my life that this touches my very heart."

Thanks in great measure to Biot's enthusiasm, the young man's reputation spread among the scientific bigwigs, who were delighted to find him as modest personally as he was ambitious for the cause of learning. In the autumn of 1848 he was offered

He took Pasteur's arm.

a professorship of physics at Dijon, a post which he exchanged in the following January for a professorship of chemistry at Strasburg. A new rector, M. Laurent, had recently been appointed to the Academy of Strasburg—a man of excellent heart and charming manners, blessed with a wife and three daughters, all—and it is saying a great deal—as good as he deserved. Together they made of the academy a home where professors and pupils alike found a cordial welcome, and witnessed a family affection which was none the less merry and cheerful for being trained upon the highest principles and ideals. Pasteur, made welcome with the rest, fell in love with the youngest daughter, Marie. The discovery of his passion dismayed him, for the family was of a higher social position than his own, and he had no wealth to compensate for this inferiority. But with that simple directness which was a part of his nature he wrote to M. Laurent, professing his suit:—

"My family is in easy circumstances, but with no fortune—I do not value what we possess at more than 50,000 francs; and as for me, I have long ago decided to hand over to my sisters the whole of what should be my share. I have therefore absolutely no fortune. My only means are good health, some courage, and my position in the university."

The answer was delayed. Meanwhile Pasteur was sadly afraid that Mademoiselle Marie would have nothing to say to him. "There is nothing in me to attract a young girl's fancy. But my recollections tell me that those who have known me very well have loved me very much." The proposal was accepted, and he was married on May 29th, 1849. "I, who did so love my crystals!" he wrote whimsically. But from the first Mme. Pasteur made up her mind that the laboratory must come before everything, and her husband become a great man of science.

The next few years were occupied with hard work and domestic happiness. He studied his crystals with infinite patience, and at length, on June 1st, 1853, he was able from his laboratory at Strasburg to send the following telegram:—

Monsieur Biot, College de France. Paris. I transform tartaric acid into racemic acid; please inform M.M. Dumas and Senarmont. "The discovery," he wrote, "will have incalculable consequences." As a by-product, one may mention, he obtained from it the red ribbon of the Legion of Honour.

In September 1854 he was made professor and dean of the new Faculty of Science at Lille, the greatest industrial town of Northern France. It is the centre of a country of distilleries, and Pasteur, besides organizing his classes and attracting pupils by the hundreds to his lectures, flung himself into the study of fermented liquors, especially the ferments of alcohol. This study led him to hope that one day he might even solve the question of "spontaneous generation." Can life start into being of itself, without deriving that existence from other life? "You will never find your way out," Biot warned him. "I shall try," said Pasteur.

Pasteur set himself to work. He had just been elected administrator of his beloved École Normale. He said his farewells at Lille, returned to Paris, set up his scientific installation in two attics close under the roof, and so started on a campaign of research which lasted four years. It is, of course, impossible here to follow the paths by which he reached the answer to that all-important question. He sought it in his garret laboratory—he sought it on the summits of the High Alps; for gradually he became convinced that the air we breathe, even the most rarefied, contains dust, which in its turn contains germs of animal life, and that therefore no discoverable thing on this planet comes, or can come, into life of itself. If from nothing else, it receives life from the germs of the all-surrounding air.

At length, on April 7th, 1864, Pasteur entered the lecture-room of the Sorbonne and explained to a crowded audience—for "all Paris" had gathered to hear him—his discovery. With the aid of a phial or two he showed that "there is now no circumstance known in which it can be affirmed that microscopic beings come into the world without germs, without parents similar to themselves. Those who affirm it have been duped by illusions."

Thus, before an audience as critical as any in the world, this unassuming servant of science stood up and in a few quiet words, without eloquence or a trace of self-glorification, slew the false doctrine of "spontaneous generation," and slew it for ever.

He was attacked on all sides—attacked as being, among other things, an enemy of religion. "There is here," he answered, "no question of religion, philosophy, atheism, materialism, or spiritualism. I might even add that these do not matter to me as a scientific man. It is a question of fact. When I took it up I was as ready to be convinced by experiments that spontaneous generation exists as I now am persuaded that those who believe in it are blindfolded."

Leaving his critics to dispute amongst themselves, he hastened back to his study of wine and fermented liquors. From this, just as he was starting on fresh discoveries, he was summoned to investigate a disease among silkworms which threatened to ruin the silk-growing industry in the south of France, and indeed over all Southern Europe. In the early days of Louis Philippe's reign this industry had been worth one million francs a year to France. Of a sudden all this prosperity fell away. Disease swept the mulberry tree—the "tree of gold," as it was called—of all its yield, and the plague spread everywhere, even to China. By 1864 healthy eggs could be found nowhere but in Japan. His old friend Dumas, now a senator, begged Pasteur to visit Alais, the silk-growing centre of Southern France, and attempt to stamp out the disease, which manifested itself in the form of tiny dark spots like a sprinkling of pepper grains. Pasteur obeyed, and set up a laboratory at Alais, where the cultivators grumbled, wanting to know why a "mere chemist" had been sent to them instead of an experienced silk-farmer. Pasteur answered, "Have patience."

Those days at Alais were made sorrowful by the death of his father and of his youngest child, his two-year-old daughter Camille. He himself began to suffer from symptoms of failing health; but he worked on, examining thousands of silkworms under the microscope, and gradually getting to the root of the complicated "corpuscle disease." During this time he was much cheered by the success of his old experiments in the preservation of wine by heating it, now that the government was putting his theories into practice on a large scale. He found time to improve the vinegar industry at Orleans by teaching the merchants there to follow scientific principles; and attacked the ministry in a pamphlet for cutting down the new laboratories at the École Normale—this at a time when millions upon millions of francs were being spent on the new Opera House!

"If the conquests useful to humanity touch your heart—if you are jealous of the share your country may boast in these—then, I implore you, take some interest in those sacred dwellings sneeringly described as *laboratories*. . . . Some nations have felt the wholesome breath of truth. Rich and large laboratories have been growing in Germany. St. Petersburg has spent three and a half million francs on a Physiological Institute, England, America, Austria, Bavaria, have made generous sacrifices. Italy has made a start. And France? France has not yet begun."

He was approaching his conquest of the silkworm disease; he was sure of success. He had separated the pure seed from the infected, and was growing healthy worms in distant "colonies" to restore the industry, when, on October 19th, 1868, paralysis struck him down, deadening the whole of his left side. In the dark struggle before speech failed him he explained his own symptoms to the doctor, smiling, but with the brave smile of one who had no illusions. For a week he lay between life and death; and then, to the amazement of his pupil M. Gernez, who had scarcely left the bedside, started of a sudden to dictate a note on the silkworm disease quite clearly and concisely, in words which actually appeared in report to the Academy of Science.

There were days of doubt after this. But his recovery was steady on the whole. On January 18th, 1869, exactly three months after his paralytic stroke, he insisted upon being carried back to Alais. The Lyons Silk Commission wrote to Alais, asking if it were possible to procure some guaranteed healthy seed. Pasteur's answer was to send four boxes of silkworms' eggs, with this message: "I have the honour to submit to you (1) one parcel of eggs which should succeed; (2) one parcel which should perish of the corpuscle disease; (3) one parcel which should perish of the flachery disease; (4) one parcel which should perish of the corpuscle and the flachery diseases combined."

All happened as he predicted. Success was achieved. He spent the remainder of his convalescence at Villa Vicentina in North Italy, a silk-growing centre, spreading the good work, and in July 1870 returned by easy stages to Paris, making a detour to visit Vienna, and stopping a couple of days at Strasburg, his old home, soon to be lost to France. By the time he reached Paris the war had broken out.

Such, then, was the man—already, and in spite of his modest bearing, not undistinguished—who in the small cottage at Arbois swore to devote the remainder of his life to the uplifting of France. In his anguish he remembered the honorary diploma he had received two years ago from the German university of Bonn. From Arbois he returned the parchment to that university with a letter saying, "The sight of it is now odious to me, and I feel offended at seeing my name, with the qualification of 'illustrious,' placed under a name which is henceforth an object of execration to my country—that of your king, William."

The protest or challenge may seem weak enough and undignified to us, whose patriotism has never known what it means to endure a helpless shame. Amid the brutalities of war the finest intellects that have lived for peace may find themselves helpless indeed. Even thus helpless was Pasteur when, having been for long without news of his son, who had been fighting before Héricourt, he with his wife and daughter started off on January 24th, 1871, in a broken-down chaise, along roads choked with snow, to search for the lad. After journeying for some hours in bitter weather the travellers found a wayside inn near Montrond, and spent the night there. Next day they jolted through a pine forest, in a silence unbroken save by the masses of snow that dropped from the branches. On the 27th reached Pontarlier. The town was full of straggling soldiers, some huddled around bivouac fires in the streets, others dying in the church on the very steps of the altar, others foraging for straw along the roads between the bodies of horses half snowed under. For long they could hear no news. "All I can tell you," reported one soldier whom they interrogated, "is that out of 1,200 men of that battalion there are but 300 left."

As they were questioning another a passer-by stopped and said, "Sergeant Pasteur? Yes, I know him. I slept by him last night at Chaffois. He is ill. You might perhaps meet him somewhere on the road thither." Back the Pasteurs started in their chaise, now almost a wreck. They had just passed through the Pontarlier gate when a rough cart met them. A soldier, wrapped

"Sergeant Pasteur? Yes, I know him."

in his greencoat and holding by the edge of the cart, gave a cry of surprise. He clambered down, and mother and father embraced their son.

Such scenes were by no means rare in that winter of 1870–71, so terrible for France. Pasteur carried his invalided son off to Geneva and nursed him back to strength, so that the lad was able to get back to France and rejoin his regiment. The parents moved back to Lyons, where they lodged with Mme. Pasteur's brother, Dean of the Faculty of Science there. For Arbois had by this time been cruelly invaded, and was a Prussian depôt; while Paris had passed from siege and bombardment to surrender and civil war. Amid these trials Italy remembered the man who had done so much for her peaceful industry, and offered him a professorship of agricultural chemistry at Pisa, with a high salary. Pasteur declined. "I should feel," he wrote in his letter of refusal, "that I deserved a deserter's punishment if I left my country in her distress to seek material gain better than she can offer me."

He accepted an invitation from an old friend and pupil, M. Duclaux, and became his guest at Royat, where the two set up a spare room as a silkworm nursery. This was in April 1871, and before summer was well advanced Pasteur had found a brewery hard by, and was deep in the process of brewing pure beer. He found the maltsters of this Chamalières brewery working by rule of thumb, ignorant of the science of their trade, and producing yeast pure and infected without knowing one from the other. Pasteur, as he taught them better methods, became as deeply interested in pure beer as he had been aforetime in pure wine. He resolved to visit England, the country of vast breweries, where surely, thought he, the principles of the manufacture would be understood. In London, where he came to learn, he was quickly able to teach. The breweries, starting from his advice, underwent a great reform, particularly in the matter of cleanliness. As Pasteur soon demonstrated, beer that contains no living germs will not decay, or "go bad" as we say.

A study of beer does not strike one at first sight as a highly promising start towards restoring self-respect to a great nation. But let us mark what followed. The study of ferments in beer led to the study of virus; that is to say, Pasteur asked himself the illuminating question, "*If germs are the secret of disease in wine and beer, may not germs also be the secret of much human disease?*"

He regretted bitterly that he was not a medical man. He foresaw, and accurately enough, that his further researches would arouse bitter criticism within the ranks of a close profession; and it was mainly in the hope of arming himself against this opposition among men who spoke of him as a "mere chemist," a "poacher on the preserves of the physicians," that he consented in 1873 to be elected an Associate of the Academy of Medicine. In his own mind he armed himself with the thought that to vanquish one disease was a nobler feat, and farther reaching, than to vanquish a whole army of Prussians. It might be possible to save more lives than these enemies of France had ever destroyed.

Already throughout Europe earnest physicians were engaged in that study of contagion out of which was emerging a complete revolution in medicine and surgery; and already, though he had but faintly suspected it, some of the greatest had been working on lines suggested by Pasteur's researches. That there may be no doubt of this let us quote from a letter addressed to him on February 13th, 1874, by the great English surgeon Lister, the discoverer of the antiseptic method:—

"I do not know whether the methods of British surgery ever meet your eye. If so, you will have seen from time to time notices of the antiseptic system of treatment, which I have been labouring for the last nine years to bring to perfection.

"Allow me to take this opportunity to tender you my most cordial thanks for having, by your brilliant researches, demonstrated to me the truth of the germ theory of putrefaction, and thus furnished me with the principle upon which alone the antiseptic system can be carried out."

There were some indeed, who, when in 1874 the National Assembly voted a life annuity of 12,000 francs to Pasteur, supposed that the stricken man, always in danger of a second paralytic stroke, would now retire and end his days in tranquillity. But Pasteur had no such intention: "He considered that not to work was to lose the whole object of living." He went back to his laboratory. Our story cannot attempt to follow him through his researches into the causes of anthrax (that terrible disease of animals), bubonic plague, chicken cholera, yellow and other fevers; but it may take as a sample of the whole the discovery by which his name is still most widely known—the preventive treatment of hydrophobia.

The problem of this horrible disease had haunted his mind for years, and by degrees came to occupy all his thoughts. The experiments, as may be guessed, were attended with no little danger. One day, for instance, Pasteur having wished to collect some saliva direct from the jaws of a rabid dog, two assistants undertook to drag a mad bull-dog, foaming at the mouth, from its cage. They seized it by a lasso and stretched the ferocious creature on a table, where they held it down while Pasteur, by means of a glass tube held between his lips, drew a few drops of the deadly saliva.

He located the seat of the disease in the nervous system. By a series of inoculations on rabbits he first learnt to predict with astonishing accuracy the time before, in each animal inoculated, the virus would take effect, and then set himself to decrease the strength of the virus—to reduce it to a *preventive*, as vaccine is a preventive of smallpox. Pasteur cut out a bit of the medulla (the lower part of the brain, where it meets the spinal cord) from a rabbit which had just died of the virus. This fragment he suspended in a dry phial, closed by cotton-wool to prevent the entrance of any dust. As the medulla shrank and became dry the strength of the virus in it gradually decreased until at the end of fourteen days it was quite gone. This medulla Pasteur crushed, mixed with pure water, and injected beneath the skin of several dogs. Next day he inoculated them in the same way with medulla which had been drying for thirteen days, and so on, until the medulla was used of a rabbit that had died the same day. These dogs not only escaped hydrophobia; they took no disease from the bites of mad dogs.

Pasteur repeated these experiments again and again, until absolutely certain that he had the cure of hydrophobia under his hand.

But a man may be a hundred times sure of such a discovery by repeating experiments so hazardous upon animals. It yet requires a tremendous moral courage to put it to the proof upon a human being.

On Monday, July 6th, 1885, a little Alsatian boy, Joseph Meister, was brought by his mother to Pasteur's laboratory. The child, aged nine, had been bitten two days before, on his way to school, by a mad dog. The dog had rushed upon him and he had fallen in the roadway, thinking only of covering his face with his hands and screaming. A bricklayer rushed up, beat the brute off, and picked up the boy, who was covered with blood and saliva. The dog's master, a man called Vone, came up and took the dog home, when it bit him in the arm. Vone at once shot it. Little Meister's parents carried the child off to a doctor, who cauterized the wounds, and advised his being taken at once to Paris. Vone, anxious on his own account as well as for the child, came also.

Pasteur reassured the man. His coat sleeve had wiped off the dog's saliva, and his shirt sleeve was hardly pierced. He might safely return to Alsace, and he promptly did. The child had fourteen wounds. Could Pasteur venture to risk on him the preventive treatment which he had tried again and again, and with steady success now, upon dogs? He suffered anguish of mind: but he reflected on the hideous death that almost infallibly awaited little Joseph, and he hardened his heart. Still he would not operate until he had consulted the wisest friends known to him in Paris. He made an appointment with the mother to call again at five o'clock, and went off to lay the case before these friends. They advised him to begin the inoculation at once.

At five o'clock he did so. It was a very slight operation—a mere pin-prick in the side, with an injection of a few drops of a preparation fourteen days old. The child, who had been crying bitterly with the fear of it, soon dried his tears on finding that this was all the pain he had to undergo. Pasteur in the course of the day had provided a comfortable room for mother and child, and the boy was soon happy playing with tame rabbits, guinea pigs, white mice. Further inoculations followed, with virus which steadily increased in strength. On the 11th Pasteur wrote, "The child sleeps well, has a good appetite, and the inoculated matter is absorbed into the system from one day to another without leaving a trace. It is true that I have not come to the test inoculations."

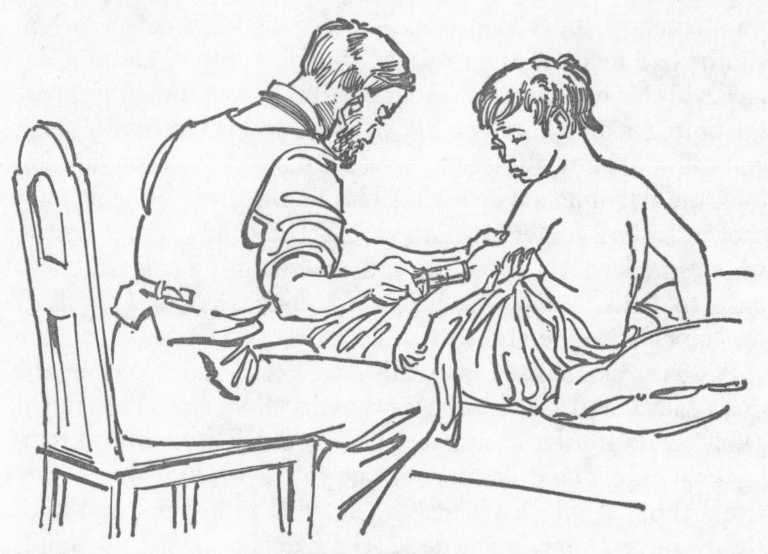

It was a very slight operation.

As this time approached Pasteur's anxiety robbed him of sleep. At night visions haunted him: he saw this innocent child "suffocating in the mad struggles of hydrophobia." In such hours it was useless to tell himself that this would almost certainly have been the end had no treatment been attempted. The inoculations took ten days. After the final one, and when little Meister had been put to bed (first claiming a kiss from "dear Monsieur Pasteur"), the great healer broke down. Sleep would not visit him that night; he felt sure the boy would die. But morning came, and little Meister, awakening without a trace of feverishness, began to call for his pets.

The cure was complete. Pasteur, having done all that his science could do, went off to take some needed rest at a quiet, almost deserted, country place in Burgundy, but within reach of the telegraph. Telegrams came, but all were reassuring. The boy returned to his home: still the news was good. By degrees all fear was at an end.

To me this vigil by the bedside of a waif of a boy—when we consider all it means, to what it has led, and to what it will continue to lead—appears the culminating point in the life of a truly heroic man; a man, though modest, greater than famous conquerors who have founded empires. In his remaining years honours poured in upon him, as patients flocked to him, from every part of Europe. They were alike the tribute of the nations to France—his beloved France. He died—overtaken at length by his old enemy, paralysis—peacefully in his bed, his one hand resting in his wife's, his other on the crucifix. I came once in the great Church of Notre Dame upon a side chapel piled high as a man's waist with wreaths of immortelles. They had been piled on the grave of Pasteur. How many of them, one wonders, came from men and women whose lives he had snatched from torment and prolonged?

He had accomplished his vow. He had turned the eyes of the world again upon France, for help. His own words rise up before me as this story concludes, words spoken by him to the Medical Congress of all Nations assembled at Copenhagen on August 10, 1884:—

"In the name of France I thank M. le President for his words of welcome. . . . Science is of no country. But though science has no country, the man of science must keep in mind all that works towards the glory of his country. In every great man of science will be found a great patriot. The thought of adding to the greatness of his country sustains him in his long efforts, and throws him into the difficult but glorious scientific enterprises which bring about real and durable conquests."

Florence Nightingale

SIR ARTHUR T. QUILLER-COUCH

THERE is a story that at a dinner given to the naval and military officers at the close of the Crimean War, each guest was asked to write on a slip of paper the name of the person whose services during the late campaign would be longest remembered by posterity; and that when the papers were examined all agreed on one name—"Florence Nightingale." And indeed, while the results of Crimean battles are today almost nothing, the great work which Miss Nightingale undertook and carried through in the hospital at Scutari outlasted the signing of peace, and has ever since, for more than fifty years, been carrying on its impulse, extending its influence, bringing comfort to thousands of homes. The testimony of that dinner-table, accurate though its forecast was, might be extended today from the campaign in the Crimea to that campaign which men and women have been carrying on ever since against alleviable human pain. If—looking around upon all the hospitals, infirmaries, dispensaries, nursing associations, boards and officers of health, district nurses, with which our country is blessed today—one were asked, "Who, under Almighty God, was the source of it all?" the answer would still be—"Florence Nightingale." And it has all come about because one woman prepared herself for a call not anticipated, and because, when the call came and found her, she had the courage to obey it instantly.

On March 27, 1854, Queen Victoria's message to Parliament announced that negotiations were broken off with Russia, and that she felt bound to give aid to the Sultan. Next day her

Majesty's formal declaration of war was read from the steps of the Royal Exchange amid wild enthusiasm. The people, urged on by the press, were spoiling for a fight; they had known no serious battle since Waterloo, and were confident, even hilarious, over the prospect.

But a nation which elects to be bellicose should first take care that it is military—which means, to be thoughtfully prepared for war, from its strategy down to the last details of commissariat and hospital. British people in 1854 vainly supposed that all could be done by bayonet-thrusting (on which, as it turned out, they could depend, so far as it went); but the troops were scarcely landed before dismal stories reached home of our unpreparedness in all these details. Mr. (afterwards Sir) William Howard Russell, the famous war correspondent for the *Times*, reached our first encampment, at Gallipoli on the Dardanelles, to note with shame the completeness of the French arrangements—"hospitals for the sick, bread and biscuit bakeries, wagon trains for carrying stores and baggage, every necessary and every comfort"—as compared with ours.

"In every respect the French can teach us a lesson in these matters. While our sick men have not a mattress to lie down upon, and are literally without blankets, the French are well provided for. We have no medical comforts—none were forwarded from Malta."

From Gallipoli to Scutari on the Bosporus, and from Scutari to Varna, these complaints, as we follow Russell's letters, grow steadily more serious:

"I regret very much to have to state that for several days last week there was neither rice nor sugar, no preserved potatoes, nor tea, nor any substitute for these articles, issued to the men; they had, therefore, to make their breakfast simply on ration brown bread and water. After breakfast they were paraded and exercised for an hour or two in the hot sun (on one occasion for more than four hours), and the result has been that sickness increased rapidly. The dinners of the men consisted of lean ration beef boiled in water and eaten with brown bread, without any seasoning to flavour it. The supplies ran out, and it was no fault of the commissariat that they did so. Who was to blame? I don't pretend to say."

They were disembarked upon the shores of the Crimea.

Thus fed, and herded in insanitary camps, the men were soon attacked by dysentery, then by cholera, and began to drop off like flies: this, be it observed, long before they had so much as caught sight of the enemy. On September the 14th and 15th they were disembarked from ships upon the shore of the Crimea, and, still before a blow has been struck, we read—

"It is clear that neither afloat nor on shore is the medical staff nearly sufficient. I myself saw men dying on the beach, on the line of march, and in bivouac, without any medical assistance; and this within hail of a fleet of 500 sail, and within sight of headquarters."

The battle of the Alma was fought on the 21st. After the victory—

"When I was looking at the wounded men going off today, I could not see an English ambulance. Our men were sent to the sea, three miles distant, on jolting *arabas* or tedious litters. The French—I am tired of this disgraceful antithesis—had well-appointed covered hospital vans, to hold ten or twelve men, drawn by fine mules, and their wounded were sent in much greater comfort than our poor fellows, so far as I saw."

Above all, the French had nurses—Sisters of Mercy, women trained at home in convents for the work—who in camp and hospital moved from stretcher to stretcher, from bed to bed, administering food and medicines, allaying the tortures of the wounded. Our men had no such help. Russell's descriptions culminated in this appeal in the *Times*:—

"Are there no devoted women amongst us, able and willing to go forth to minister to the sick and suffering soldiers of the East in the hospitals of Scutari? Are none of the daughters of England, at this extreme hour of need, ready for such a work of mercy? . . . France has sent forth her Sisters of Mercy unsparingly, and they are even now by the bedsides of the wounded and the dying, giving what woman's hand alone can give of comfort and relief. . . . Must we fall so far below the French in self-sacrifice and devotedness, in a work which Christ so signally blesses as done unto Himself? '*I was sick, and ye visited Me.*'"

Russell's appeal did not fall on deaf ears. In a few days hundreds of Englishwomen of all ranks were flooding the War Office with letters, beseeching leave to go out to Scutari as nurses. But to all such might be applied the words in which he had argued—of our deficiencies in baggage, pontoon trains, etc.—that these things can only be ready on the call of war through slow preparation in times of peace. "All the gold in the treasury cannot produce at command these great qualities in administrative and executive departments which are the fruits of experience alone. A soldier, an artilleryman, a commissariat officer cannot be created suddenly, no matter how profuse may be your expenditure in the attempt."

So it was with the nurses. These patriotic Englishwomen lacked one thing only—a capacity, even the smallest, to fulfil the services they were burning to undertake. They had received no training; they knew nothing of hospital duty, less than nothing of hospital organization. In 1854 there was, strange as it sounds, in England scarcely a nurse whom today we should entrust with the care of the meanest "cottage hospital." In 1854, one may fairly say a gently nurtured lady would sooner have offered herself to be a charwoman than to be a nurse. In a Protestant land the vocation of a Sister of Mercy, or of anything like it, did not fall within the dreams even of women devoted to religion.

These shoals of letters, all penned on impulses pathetically good, in the midst of the excitement and general futility of things, reached the War Office in due course, and were submitted to her Majesty's Secretary of State for War, who happened to be a remarkable man.

The Hon. Sidney Herbert (afterwards, for a brief while before his death, Lord Herbert of Lea), second son of the eleventh Earl of Pembroke, was born in 1810 and derived his Christian name from the famous Sir Philip Sidney, the hero of Zutphen and most perfect knight of Queen Elizabeth's reign. Men said that Philip Sidney, "the president of nobleness and chivalry," lived again in his nineteenth-century namesake; for beyond all doubt Sidney Herbert was one of the most fascinating men in Europe.

"He was strikingly handsome, with a commanding figure and courtly manners. He appeared to possess every social advantage —high birth, a great estate, a beautiful wife and children, one of the happiest homes in England, many accomplishments, a ready address, a silvery voice, irresistible manners, and a rare power for making friends. It was said that men would give up to Sidney Herbert what they would grant to no one else."

Such in 1854 was the Minister for War, who of a sudden found himself bombarded by hundreds of letters from Englishwomen begging to be sent out to the Crimea all burning to devote themselves, but all alike ignorant of the terrible duty they sought. Herbert's trained mind too surely perceived their incompetence as he read and rejected appeal after appeal. Where, in all this well-meaning hysteria, was any sign of capacity, of grasp, of power to lead and to organize? He could find none. Was there in England, then, no one woman endowed with strength of character for the task, and prepared by training with the skill for it? Yes, there was one—a gently nurtured lady and (as it happened) an honoured friend of his; one who for some years had studied nursing and knew more of its realities than did all those frenzied petitioners put together. His thoughts turned to her. Amid the hubbub of patriotism she had kept silence and made no sign, simply, as he could understand, because she knew, while others did not, the magnitude of the difficulty. He felt that, unless she volunteered, he could not ask her to take her life in her hands, to brave the cholera, the hardships, the exposure, the breaking toil, and, worse than these, the certainty of slanderous criticism from folk who, as public opinion then was, would cry aloud at the bare idea of a "lady" going out to nurse common soldiers.

But who was this lady?

A Mr. William Edward Shore of Tapton, Derbyshire, had in 1815 succeeded to the estate of his mother's uncle, old Peter Nightingale, a roistering squire of that county; and to the ownership of Lea Hall, high above the valley of the Derwent. As a condition of his inheritance he took, at the same time, the name of Nightingale. Three years later he married Frances, daughter of William Smith, Esq. of Parndon, Essex, for fifty years member of Parliament for Norwich, a constant and notable opponent of the slave trade. Mr. Nightingale was a cultured gentleman, whose mind had been broadened by travel, and for a few years he and his beautiful wife spent much of their time abroad, chiefly in Italy. Their first child, a daughter, was born at Naples and christened with the classical name of that city, Parthenope. About a year later, on May 12, 1820, a second daughter was born to them at the Villa Columbaia, near Florence. She too was named after her birthplace, and thus one of the best beloved of English heroines came by her melodious name—Florence Nightingale.

Mr. Nightingale being, in homely phrase, a stickler for education, lessons were not neglected. Parthenope and Florence did them together under a governess, their father supervising. Parthenope's accomplishments were the more artistic—she excelled her sister in music and drawing; Florence's the more severely intellectual. From her father she learned some Latin and Greek, with elementary science and mathematics. She read the standard authors, and showed great aptitude for foreign languages. There was plenty of out-of-door health with all this—scampers on ponies and rambles over park and dale; a certain relaxation, too, or routine in the summer months at Lea Hurst. But at Embley throughout the winter the routine of the schoolroom would be resumed, and went forward on very strict lines. Mr. Nightingale detested careless work. Mrs. Nightingale saw that her daughters became capable needlewomen, and that they learned to dance and carry themselves gracefully.

So in due course Florence Nightingale reached the age of seventeen, "came out" in the country society of Derbyshire and Hampshire, and "began to take her place as the squire's daughter," visiting the sick, organizing Bible classes, interesting herself in the village schools. "At Christmas-time her work basket was full of warm comforts for the poor. She was invaluable at bazaars," etc. In short, she was a very charming and fortunate young lady of the early Victorian period, and, like many another fortunate young lady, was taken to London for "the season," with its dances and other gaieties, and to Buckingham Palace to make her curtsy to the Queen.

Nevertheless there was something—her friends could not define it, and she herself was hardly conscious of it yet awhile—

which marked her out as different from those other young ladies. And if we define it now as a certain high seriousness, which so often appears, they know not how, in the youth of those destined to be great, the reader must not infer that Florence Nightingale was at this time, or ever in her life, a dull, solemn person. On the contrary, she had a shrewd wit and a very mirthful laugh; only there began to arise in her mind some obstinate questionings. Was this comfortable life of hers a really useful one? Or, if useful in its way, was it really effective? This district-visiting and distributing of goodies—did it go beyond "coddling," playing around the edge of a problem which was in truth both deep and terrible for those who had eyes to see? While so much relievable suffering went unrelieved in the world, was it right that women should be cramped, tied down to these petty, if pretty, ministrations? Was there no nobler work—work to be done thoroughly—work demanding stern, practical preparation?

She had pondered these questions, and her mind was still demanding the answer, when at this critical period in her life she met with a woman who could put her in the way of finding it. This was Elizabeth Fry, the Quakeress, whose courageous work in visiting the outcasts in our prisons had done so much to get those prisons reformed. The two women—the one old and stately and very wise, the other young and ardent—met as kindred spirits; yet it was understood from the first that Florence Nightingale had no desire to become Elizabeth Fry's pupil and assume the mantle when that aged prophetess laid it down. She had already decided on her own sphere of work. It was to be hospital nursing.

In this, as it happened, Mrs. Fry could help her. She was a friend of Pastor Fliedner, the founder of a nursing institution at Kaiserswerth, near Düsseldorf, on the Rhine, where Protestant "deaconesses" were trained to attend on the sick as "knowledgeably" as any Roman Catholic Sister of Mercy. From a crazy old summerhouse in which Fliedner had lodged one or two women—discharged prisoners—and taught them to lead useful lives, the institution had grown to an ample hospital, with branch hospitals scattered all over Germany, and from Jerusalem to Pittsburg in America.

It was in 1849 that Florence Nightingale entered the Deaconess Hospital at Kaiserswerth and donned its uniform—a plain blue cotton dress, white apron, and muslin cap. Her coming created a flutter among the deaconesses—all women of peasant birth—who found it hard to understand why an English lady of wealth and position should want to come and study among them. But the newcomer soon showed that she meant strict business. Years afterwards she wrote, "Three-fourths of the whole mischief in women's lives arises from their excepting themselves from the rules of training considered needful for men." And again, "I would say to all young ladies who are called to any vocation, Qualify yourselves for it as a man does for his work." This was strange doctrine in 1849, but Florence Nightingale acted upon it, having persuaded herself of its truth. She underwent two rigorous courses of training at Kaiserswerth, where the deaconesses came to adore her. After her return home Miss Nightingale published a little book on the institution, and prefaced it with some words on the principle her own career was soon to illustrate so splendidly, that women longing for a vocation should prepare themselves for it by business-like training. "Woman," she wrote, "stands askew. Her education for action has not kept pace with her education for acquirement. The woman of the eighteenth century was perhaps happier than her more cultivated sister of the nineteenth century. The latter wishes, but does not know how to do many things; the former, what she wished at least *that* she could do."

From Kaiserswerth she visited Paris, spent some time with the Roman Catholic Sisters of St. Paul, studied surgery, and compared French hospital systems and methods of organizing charity with those methods and systems she had already studied in London, Edinburgh, Dublin, and one or two foreign capitals. In the midst of this work her health broke down, and she returned to Embley. On her recovery she went up to London to take charge of the Harley Street Home for Sick Governesses, which had

"In the distance Magellan saw one of the most beautiful sights in the world—island mountains."

—Ferdinand Magellan

been brought low by mismanagement. In a few months she had brought order out of chaos; but again the strain proved too much for her bodily powers, and again she was forced to seek recovery in a restful life at Embley and Lea Hurst.

Here, then, was the woman to whom the War Minister's thoughts kept turning. He knew her intimately, and Embley Park lay within visiting distance of his own country home over the Wiltshire border; and, indeed, he and his wife had few dearer friends than Miss Nightingale, as she had none who took a warmer interest in her schemes than did the Herberts. He spoke to his colleagues in the Cabinet, and received their promise that if Miss Nightingale would undertake this work she should be given undisputed control, and be supported by the government. They promised, indeed, readily enough, but still he hesitated to write to her. For hers was the capable brain, as he knew, but it had already twice overtaxed her frail body. If she went to Scutari, she would take her life in her hands. Could he ask this sacrifice? He decided that a heart so noble as Florence Nightingale's would perhaps never forgive him if he denied this noble opportunity. On the 15th of October he sat down and wrote the fateful letter. After telling her of the lack of nurses at Scutari, and the number of offers he received daily from volunteers "who have no conception of what a hospital is," he went on:—

There is but one person in England that I know of who would be capable of organizing and superintending such a scheme. And I have been several times on the point of asking you if, supposing the attempt was made, you would undertake to direct it. . . . My question simply is, Would you listen to the request to go out and supervise the whole thing? You would, of course, have plenary authority over all the nurses, and I think I could secure you the fullest assistance and co-operation from the medical staff, and you would also have an unlimited power of drawing on the government for the success of your mission.

I do not say one word to press you, yet I must not conceal from you that upon your decision will depend the ultimate success or failure of the plan.

There is one point which I have hardly a right to touch upon, but I trust you will pardon me. If you were inclined to undertake the great work, would Mr. and Mrs. Nightingale consent? The work would be so national, and the request made to you proceeding from the government, your position would ensure the respect and consideration of every one. . . . This would secure you any attention or comfort on your way out there, together with a complete submission to your orders. I know these things are a matter of indifference to you, except so far as they may further the great object you may have in view; but they are of importance in themselves, and of every importance to those who have a right to take an interest in your personal position and comfort. I know you will come to a right and wise decision. God grant it may be one in accordance with my hopes. —Believe me, dear Miss Nightingale, ever yours,

SIDNEY HERBERT.

It so happened that, while Herbert was writing this letter, Florence Nightingale was seated in her garden pondering Russell's appeal: "*Are there no devoted women amongst us, willing and able to go forth and minister to the sick and suffering soldiers of the East?*" Hundreds were willing enough, she knew. But what of the ability she had been preaching—preaching for years? Was *she* able? Yes, if God would lend her strength.

She walked back to the house, and wrote to Sidney Herbert offering her services. Their letters crossed.

In just one week from that 15th of October, and while the public were still asking, "Who is Miss Nightingale?" she had her first batch of thirty-eight nurses marshalled and ready to start with her, and this, although the first advertisement in the newspapers had brought in applications which almost reduced her to despair with their hysterical foolishness. This first contingent was made up of fourteen Church of England Sisters, ten Roman Catholic Sisters of Mercy, three chosen by Lady Maria Forrester (who had been forming an independent plan for sending nurses to Scutari), and eleven selected from the miscellaneous volunteers who had answered the advertisement. A Mr. and Mrs. Bracebridge, two particular friends, accompanied the expedition;

a clergyman and a courier completed it. The "Angel Band" left London on the evening of October 21st. A few friends and kinsfolk had gathered at the railway station to see them off. She had wished for a quiet departure. Quietly dressed, she said her farewells with a calm smile of confidence meant to hearten those she left behind. Her own heart foreboded only too well the task that lay before her.

They reached Boulogne early next morning, to meet with a surprising reception. France was our ally in this war. Word of these good women and their mission had preceded them across the Channel, and they were met on the quay by a crowd of Boulogne fishwives who seized their trunks, and jostled and almost came to blows over the privilege of carrying their luggage on board the train. Tears ran down the faces of these honest women as they shouldered the boxes and staggered with them across the rails. Some gabbled messages to be conveyed to sons and husbands afar at the seat of war. Not one sou would any one accept, but hand-shakes again and again, and the train steamed out of the station amid cries of "*Vivent les sœurs!*"

After a short halt at Paris with the Sisters of St. Vincent de Paul, the party took train again for Marseilles, their port of embarkation, and here again the porters declined any fee for their services. The *Vectis*, a steamship of the Peninsular Line, awaited them, and through terrible weather she drove her way eastward to Malta, which was reached on October 31st. Here the nurses transhipped, and reached Scutari on November 4th, the day before the battle of Inkerman.

The barrack hospital at Scutari stood on a hill overlooking the waterway of the Bosporus, which by common consent is one of the loveliest scenes in the world. The building itself was palatial—an enormous quadrangle, each side of it close upon a quarter of a mile in length. Its galleries and corridors made up a total extent of four miles, and in the vast central court no less than twelve thousand men could be deployed. No hospital could appear more desirable—until one entered it and found a scene of filth and confusion not to be described. To right and left of the interminable corridors the wounded lay in closely packed rows, the majority of them with wounds undressed and fractured limbs still unset although days had elapsed since they left the battlefield. Many were starving; all lacked the barest decencies of life.

"There were no vessels for water or utensils of any kind; no soap, towels or cloths, no hospital clothes; the men lying in their uniforms, stiff with gore and covered with filth to a degree and of a kind no one could write about; their persons covered with vermin, which crawled about the floors and walls of the dreadful den of dirt, pestilence, and death."

After landing at the ferry below, the sufferers crawled or were dragged up the hill to reach the hospital and lie amid these horrors upon polluted beds, between sheets of canvas so coarse that many begged to be left in their blankets. At night, when the wards were lit only by the glimmer of candles stuck in empty beer-bottles, rats would venture out and bite the weakest of the sufferers, drawing blood; for the rats too were starving. One of Miss Nightingale's first actions, on entering the place, was to dislodge a Scutari rat from above a bed with the point of her practical British umbrella.

She arrived on November 4th. Next day was fought the hand-to-hand "soldiers' battle" of Inkerman—"the bloodiest struggle ever witnessed since war cursed the earth," wrote Russell—and before she could begin to cope with the miseries already about her, more were steadily accumulated, day after day and all day long, by the streams of wounded men pouring up from the ferry as the warships disembarked them, many bringing fever and cholera besides their wounds. They packed every inch of space in the vast hospital; many had to lie on the muddy ground outside, waiting until comrades died within and so made room. Medical stores had been sent out by the ton weight, never to reach Scutari. They lay rotting on the shore at Varna, or (an old trick of officialdom) had been packed in the holds of vessels *beneath* heavy guns and ammunition. These disasters culminated on November 14th, when the *Prince* transport, laden with stores, went ashore and was broken up in a furious hurricane.

They packed every inch of space in the vast hospital.

These were the days—days when all seemed hopeless—that really proved Florence Nightingale; days when she was known to stand for twenty hours at a time, dealing with fresh detachments of sick as they arrived, apportioning quarters, directing the nurses to their duties. She and her staff had taken up their quarters in a tower at a corner of the great quadrangle, and from her room, little by little, the presence of an organizing brain began to make itself felt along the miles of galleries. Fortunately government had given her full authority to back up her own power of command. The orderlies found that they could not scamp their work of inspecting the wards. Woe to one who brought a false report that all was right when Miss Nightingale, who had a knack of finding things out, cross-questioned him and discovered that all was wrong! The orderlies indeed soon became her devoted knights, and endured for her sake toils and vigils that far outwent their "official" duties. "Never," she said afterwards, "came from any one of them one word or one look which a gentleman would not have used. . . . The tears come into my eyes as I think how amidst loathsome scenes of disease and death there arose above it all the innate dignity, gentleness, and chivalry of the men, shining in the midst of what must be considered as the lowest sinks of human misery, and preventing instinctively the use of one expression which could distress a gentlewoman."

Even in those terrible early days she personally attended to scores of the worst operations. But for a time her work was done in the turret chamber, whence, as from the "conning-tower" of a modern battleship, the brain in command sent out its orders, bringing system out of confusion. A helpless kitchen was reduced to cleanliness, to order, finally to such efficiency that in one day it would turn out thirteen gallons of chicken broth and forty gallons of arrowroot for the sick, with plenty of well-cooked food for the convalescent. Distributors of government stores had to mend their ways and be punctual. A Levantine who had the washing contract, and broke it so repeatedly that two or three thousand sick lay without a change of linen, found himself superseded. In the course of the first three months Miss Nightingale, from her own resources and her friends', provided the ten thousand shirts. Next she set up a laundry in a house hard by the hospital, and—with the help of a fund started by the *Times*—had it fitted with ample copper tubs in which five hundred shirts, to name no other articles, were washed each week. Her nurses were never idle. What time could be spared from the bedsides of the sufferers was employed in tearing up bandages—miles of bandages—making lint, fashioning splints, sewing mattresses and pillows.

Possibly more distressful than the condition of the wounded and dying was that of the soldiers' wives, who had been allowed to accompany their husbands to Scutari, and who, left behind there, herded in the squalidest corners of the hospital. For these, too, Florence Nightingale cared. Some were widows, poor souls, and these were by degrees sent home. For the others she did her best, supplying them with food and clothes from her watch-chamber in the tower, organizing work for them—decently paid work—in her new laundry. They had been lodged, after official delays, in three or four dark rooms in the hospital basement; and in these cellars, from November to December, twenty-two children were born. Then fever broke out, through the bursting of a drain. Finally a Turkish house was procured and furnished out of private funds, and the poor women were lodged there. A school even was opened for the children. By Christmas Day of that bitter Crimean winter the barrack hospital had been swept of its filth; its inmates lay between clean sheets, and had invalids' food in plenty; and they drank—some of them out of medicine glasses—to the Queen of England, who had sent a Christmas message to her "beloved troops," and to their lady-in-chief.

Fifty additional nurses arrived with the New Year, and were drafted out on various services; for Scutari had a "general" as well as a "barrack" hospital, and there was the Kullali Hospital, across the Bosporus, and temporary ones at the front. The war had by this time settled down to a sullen siege of Sebastopol, and men were dying now, not of wounds, but from exposure in the icy trenches where sometimes they spent thirty-six hours at a

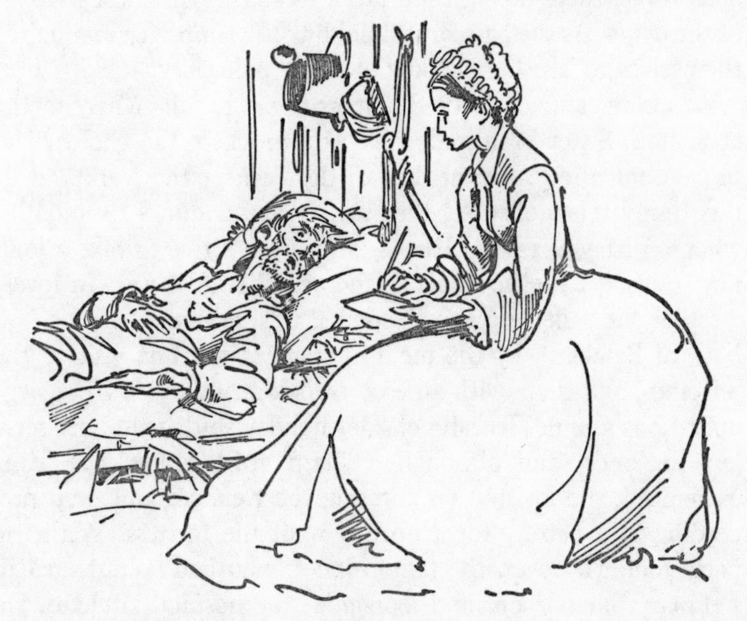

She would go her rounds taking the last message of the dying.

stretch, starved of rations, sleeping—when sleep overtook them —on the frozen mud. Cholera devastated them.

"The cholera was of the very worst type, and the attacked men lasted only four or five hours. Oh, those dreadful cramps! You might as well try to bend a piece of iron as to move those joints."

Against these cramps, as the sufferers were landed after tossing for a day or two on the Black Sea, nurses and orderlies worked heroically, wrapping the patients in blankets steeped in boiling water and sprinkled with chloroform. A very small proportion survived. Streams of stretchers bringing in the stricken men passed streams of stretchers carrying out the dead. For two months the death-rate stood at 60 per cent. Still fighting through the worst, Florence Nightingale, after the orderlies had retired to snatch some rest, would go her round, lamp in hand, along the endless galleries, moving from bed to bed, here pausing to soothe the delirium of a poor fellow who fancied himself still storming Sebastopol, there taking (and never forgetting) the last message of the dying. As she passed, still holding her lamp, sick men raised themselves to kiss her shadow on their pillows.

As spring came in devoted helpers began to fall—Miss Smythe at Scutari, Sister Winifred at Balaklava, where the cholera had broken out afresh. But at Scutari the back of the work had by this time been broken, as they say. It had endured six months, when on May 2, 1855, Miss Nightingale felt free to take a journey to inspect the hospitals at the actual seat of war. In lovely weather she sailed up the Bosporus, was welcomed at the harbour of Balaklava by the medical staff, paid a first visit to the hospitals, and then, with an escort, took a ride to view the siege operations around Sebastopol. Her holiday spirit made her reckless for once; and although a sharp artillery fire was being exchanged, she insisted on entering the trenches and even proceeding to a battery for a near view of the fortress. With the party rode M. Soyer, the famous chef, who had volunteered in February to come out and reorganize the hospital kitchens. He had done invaluable work, and today was in irrepressibly high

All shouted, "Bravo! Hurrah! Hurrah!"

spirits. "Before leaving the battery," he records, "I begged Miss Nightingale as a favour to give me her hand, which she did. I then requested her to ascend the stone rampart next the wooden gun carriage, and lastly to sit upon the centre mortar; to which requests she very gracefully and kindly acceded." Having beguiled Miss Nightingale into this position, the gallant Frenchman cried, "Gentlemen! behold this amiable lady sitting fearlessly upon that terrible instrument of war! Behold the heroic daughter of England—the soldiers' friend!" All present shouted, "Bravo! Hurrah! Hurrah! Long live the daughter of England!" The sentry of the Three Mortar Battery had been aghast at her incurring this peril. "My good young man," said Miss Nightingale, "more dead and wounded have passed through my hands than I hope you will ever see during the whole of your military career. Believe me, I have no fear of death." Yet the sentry was right, and her life too valuable to be lightly risked.

How valuable it was just then could be seen in the consternation that swept through the whole army a few days later, upon a report that Miss Nightingale had taken the Crimean fever. It was true. She had overtaxed her strength in visiting and reorganizing the Balaklava hospitals, and the fever had seized upon her weakness. For twelve days she lay dangerously ill, and on her recovery the doctors advised her returning at once to England. But she would not hear of this, and demanded to be taken back to Scutari, intending, as soon as her convalescence was assured, to return to Balaklava, and take up again the task of reforming the hospitals.

Her health, however, was barely re-established when, on September 8, the allies delivered their final assault upon Sebastopol, and in the following night the Russians evacuated the city, leaving it in flames. Peace was in sight, and amid the general rejoicings at home people were asking how best the nation could show its gratitude to the heroine of the war. Already Queen Victoria, anticipating the wish of her people, had put this question to Sidney Herbert. This was his answer:—

49 BELGRADE SQUARE, *July* 1855.

MADAM,—There is but one testimonial which would be accepted by Miss Nightingale. The one wish of her heart has long been to found a hospital in London, and to work it on her own system of unpaid nursing; and I have suggested to all who have asked for my advice in this matter to pay any sums that they may feel disposed to give, or that they may be able to collect, into Messrs. Coutts' Bank, where a subscription list for the purpose is about to be opened, to be called the "Nightingale Hospital Fund"—the sum subscribed to be presented to her on her return home, which will enable her to carry out her object regarding the reform of the nursing system in England.

The scheme was inaugurated at a public meeting on November 29th. At the meeting Sidney Herbert told a story that had reached him from a simple soldier, saved from death in the Scutari hospital. "She would speak to one and another," he said, "and nod and smile to many more; but she could not do it to all, you know, for we lay there by hundreds. But we could kiss her shadow as it fell, and lay our heads on the pillow again content."

In time the Nightingale Fund grew to £44,000, and would have reached £50,000 if she had not stopped the flow of subscriptions, declaring that she had enough. While the money flowed in, and while statesmen were discussing peace, she had gone back to the heights of the Crimea, and was nursing the wounded who remained, and the sick men of the army of occupation—constantly visiting the camp hospital in a carriage specially built for service on the uneven Turkish roads. While thus occupied she received from Queen Victoria a beautiful jewel (for which the Prince Consort had made the design) with the following letter:—

WINDSOR CASTLE. *January* 1856.

DEAR MISS NIGHTINGALE,—You are, I know, well aware of the high sense I entertain of the Christian devotion which you have displayed during this great and bloody war, and I need hardly repeat to you how warm my admiration is for your services, which are fully equal to those of my dear and brave soldiers, whose sufferings you have had the *privilege* of relieving in so merciful a manner. I am, however, anxious of marking my feelings in a manner which I trust will be agreeable to you, and therefore send you with this letter a brooch, the form and emblems of which commemorate your great and blessed work, and which I hope you will wear as a mark of the high approbation of your Sovereign!

It will be a very great satisfaction to me, when you return at last to these shores, to make the acquaintance of one who has set so bright an example to our sex. And with every prayer for the preservation of your valuable health, believe me, always yours sincerely,

VICTORIA R.

When at length Florence Nightingale's time had come to return, she took every precaution to avoid a public demonstration. She declined the government's offer to a British man-of-war to bring her home, and travelling privately under an assumed name reached England unrecognized, and proceeded to Lea Hurst, where she arrived on August 8th. Local tradition even asserts that she entered her home by the back door. While the land rang with her praises, she remained quietly with her family, nursing her strength back, that she might next take charge of the great nursing movement on which her heart was set. But this was not to be. The malady from which she suffered increased its hold, and to her bitter disappointment she realized that her life's active work was done.

But the movement went forward, never lacking inspiration in the memory of her good deeds, or words of shrewd and kindly advice from the writing-room in which she lived as a recluse. Books came from her pen—"Notes on Hospitals" in 1859, and in 1860 "Notes on Nursing," of which over 100,000 copies have been sold, and many pamphlets.

Towards the close of her long life, when (we may almost say) she had become too weak to resist, honours were showered on her. She had received the Red Cross from Queen Victoria. On May 12, 1904, as a compliment upon her eighty-fourth birthday, King Edward VII. conferred on her the dignity of a Lady of

Grace of the Order of St. John of Jerusalem. In November 1907 he advanced her to the Order of Merit, of all rewards today the rarest and the most highly prized. Florence Nightingale was the first woman to earn it, and has been the only one. Her true reward, however, lay in the abiding gratitude of a nation. In that, and in the fidelity with which Englishmen who followed the path she had found and carried more and more light to the dark places of human misery—as the Roman vestals tended one fire, never suffering it to die out night or day—turned over to "the Lady of the Lamp" to bless and kindle their beneficent torches. "*The people that walked in darkness have seen a great light: they that dwell in the land of the shadow of death, upon them hath the light shined.*" If such a light shine today in our great cities and in thousands of villages, it has grown and spread from the tiny flame borne by Florence Nightingale from ward to ward along the awful galleries of Scutari.

Walter Reed:

Doctor in Uniform

L. N. WOOD

Until 1900 Yellow Fever was one of the most deadly and mysterious of all diseases. Every year all through the tropics hundreds of thousands of people were struck down by this terrible killer, and although doctors and scientists had been studying the problem for years, they had never been able to determine its cause. The most widely-held theory was that the disease was spread by germs carried in the soiled bedding and clothing (fomites) of Yellow Fever sufferers. Walter Reed, an army doctor whose assignment was to stamp out "yellow jack" in Cuba, didn't believe this. He held a revolutionary theory: that the disease was carried only by mosquitoes. And in a series of dramatic experiments he set out to prove it. They were all heroes—the volunteer subjects who faced death for the sake of science—but it was Dr. Reed whose spirit and dogged faith made this miracle of conquest possible.

The Conquest of Yellow Fever

REED's announcement at the Public Health meeting of his belief that mosquitoes spread yellow fever set no rivers afire —too many claims had been advanced in the past few years, only to be scrapped later. His case was far from established, he knew. One clear demonstration, Kean's, was not enough to break down error entrenched for half a century. It would take the series of experiments, conducted on human subjects, for which Wood had promised funds, to establish this revolutionary theory beyond question.

After consultations with Sternberg, the insect expert Howard, Welch and other Hopkins friends, Reed hurried back to Cuba, where he landed the end of October. He immediately set to work on plans to establish an isolation camp for his experiments. Camp Lazear, it was to be called, in honor of their dead colleague.

On the opposite side of the Calzada Real from Camp Columbia, about a mile from Quemados, was the farm of Dr. Ignacio Rojas. Agramonte thought one of his uncultivated fields would be a good place for the camp. Reed, seeing it, agreed, and they rented it. It was secluded, well drained, and, being almost bare of shrubs and trees, was open to the sun and wind and free from mosquitoes.

Agramonte came to Camp Columbia often to discuss the isolation camp with Reed. Truby and the other young doctors, keenly interested in the coming experiments, followed the plans closely and gave Reed all the help they could, while Kean consulted with him at every step.

There were, Reed explained to them as they sat on the veranda after dinner, to be three phases to the experiments. They would try to infect non-immunes by the bites of mosquitoes which had fed on yellow fever cases in their first stage, by exposure to *fomites,* and by injection of blood taken from yellow fever cases in the first two or three days of illness. In this way he hoped to prove that yellow jack was spread by mosquitoes, that *fomites* were harmless, and that the specific agent of the disease was in the blood. Each experiment was to be carefully controlled, to exclude exposure to any other source of infection than the one directly in question. Each case would be seen by the Havana

Yellow Fever Board, composed of Doctors Finlay, Guiteras, Albertini and Gorgas, so that the diagnosis of yellow fever could not be questioned.

Reed drew up the plans for the camp, and the Hospital Corps erected seven tents, while the Quartermaster's Department started to put up two small wooden buildings that Reed ordered. The work was progressing well when Reed had an unexpected setback.

A violent tropical storm, striking in mid-November with heavy wind and rain, dropped the temperature to the low sixties. *Culex fasciatus,* a delicate insect in spite of its fatal power, cannot survive wind or chill. Most of Reed's laboratory mosquitoes died, and he was greatly alarmed that the sudden cold might put an end to the mosquito season and leave him without insects for the experiments.

The young doctors reassured him: there would still be plenty of warm weather, plenty of mosquitoes to go with it, and plenty of yellow fever. Truby could see, however, that he was still anxious, and wanted mosquitoes, not promises.

"Come on, boys," he suggested after lunch one day. "Let's lay in a supply of mosquito eggs for the major, so he can stop worrying."

He and several of the other doctors set off toward Quemados on a mosquito hunt. As they passed the Quartermaster's dump it occurred to them to investigate there for discarded buckets or utensils holding water. To the deep embarrassment of young Dr. Amador, the post sanitary officer, the dump was a regular mosquito mine, in spite of the mosquito control measures he was enforcing. Most of the utensils had the sanitary inspector's ax hole in the bottom, but enough still held water to make the dump an ideal breeding place. Eagerly scooping up wigglers and eggs to keep Reed in stock indefinitely, they hurried with their find to his laboratory. Reed, Neate and John H. Andrus, a Hospital Corps man who had recently been assigned to the laboratory, joyfully set to work to rear the wigglers and dry the eggs for future use.

The dump was a regular mosquito mine.

Agramonte, meanwhile, was rounding up volunteers among the Spaniards at the immigration station on Havana bay. Selecting only men who were of age, in good health, and without dependents, the board asked them if they would take a bite. Many of them, attracted by the promised money, the prospect of being cared for by the "senoritas Americanas," as they called the nurses, and the reflection that they were likely to get yellow fever anyway, signed contracts with the board consenting to be bitten for the reward.

Reed, oppressed by Lazear's death, and by the heavy responsibility that he and his board were assuming, was dubious, too, about relying on the Spanish immigrants. Their co-operation, he feared, captured by the money involved, might not survive the proof that the "harmless little gnats" which they were paid to let bite them would give them yellow jack.

His anxiety was unexpectedly relieved.

Breakfast at Camp Columbia was at seven, and by eight Reed was at his desk, working on plans for the isolation camp. The knock at the door, so early in the morning, surprised him.

"Come in," he called.

John R. Kissinger and John J. Moran stepped into the room, stepping at the same time, although no one knew it then, into history.

"Good morning, gentlemen," Reed greeted them. "What can I do for you?" He was slightly acquainted with both young men. Kissinger was a private in the Hospital Corps. Moran, who shared quarters with him, also had been in the Hospital Corps until his term of enlistment expired. Now he was a clerk at General Lee's headquarters.

"We heard you wanted volunteers, sir," Moran said, "to submit to some yellow fever experiments. We talked it over, and we thought we'd like to go in for it together."

"It's good of you to offer," Reed said cordially. "I don't know if you understand just what you're getting into. This is the situation." He described the dangers of the experiment to them carefully, emphasizing that he himself had no doubt that mosquitoes spread the disease. "And of course," he concluded, "every volunteer gets a hundred dollars; if he comes down with yellow jack he gets two."

"Well, you see, Major Reed," Kissinger explained, "we're not interested in being paid. The money isn't the point—it's the opportunity," he flushed a little, "to do something for humanity and science." Moran nodded emphatically. "That's right, sir," he said.

Reed, silent with astonishment, stared at them. He saw two young men in their early twenties—two pleasant, intelligent, unremarkable-looking boys about the age of his own son, with the best part of their lives before them. And they were offering to risk those lives not for military glory, not for reward—certainly not for two hundred dollars—but for "humanity and science"! He saw, too, that they meant it. On the verge of explaining that the money was already appropriated, that they might as well take it, he checked himself. Money could never reward this unselfish gesture.

"My dear boys," he said, and they could tell by his voice that the quiet, self-possessed doctor was moved, "I am proud to accept your brave offer."

Greatly cheered by the offer of Kissinger and Moran, Reed no longer feared a shortage of volunteers. American boys, motivated by interest in the experiments themselves, rather than by the prospect of reward, would not back out, no matter what the danger.

"And when everything's running smoothly," he remarked to Truby, "and my personal direction isn't necessary any longer, then I'll take the mosquito test myself."

Truby's face clouded at the announcement. He hoped ardently that Reed could be dissuaded. The major was not robust, and he had to eat sparingly. The strain of preparation and responsibility showed now and then through his usual composure. It would be a dangerous thing for the doctor approaching his half century mark to tempt yellow jack.

Camp Lazear opened the morning of November 20th, without fanfare. Agramonte was busy at the Military Hospital, so Reed selected Ames to take charge of the camp. Dr. Robert P. Cooke, a tall young contract doctor with straight lanky hair and a humorous expression, had volunteered for the *fomites* experiments and was the only other doctor at the camp. A hospital steward, a Hospital Corps private and an ambulance driver, all immune; Moran, Kissinger and six other Hospital Corps privates, all non-immune; and several non-immune Spaniards completed the camp personnel.

The experiments began immediately. At 10:30 on the morning of the 20th, Kissinger rolled up his sleeve and watched with mixed feelings while the mosquito, in the test tube pressed against his arm, took a leisurely bite. He wondered if the fragile little thing would really give him yellow jack. It was funny—he could squash her with a finger tip, and maybe *she* could kill *him* just as easily. As he rolled down his sleeve, he sighed. It was a beautiful day, he realized.

The principal rule of Camp Lazear was simple and rigid: no one could leave or enter without Reed's permission. Only the immunes could go out on such necessary errands as getting supplies from Camp Columbia.

The Spaniards, whose only duty was to gather stones off the ground for a low wall about the camp, could take all the time they wanted to rest, and were mystified and delighted with their life in this strange new world. The soldiers, with nothing to do but keep their quarters neat, passed the time in reading, playing cards and taking naps. Kissinger passed it in waiting for his yellow jack. It did not develop.

Three days later he was bitten again; then, on the 26th and 29th, mosquitoes were held to Moran's willing arm. Still no yellow jack.

"Maybe you're a natural immune, Moran, but I'm going to

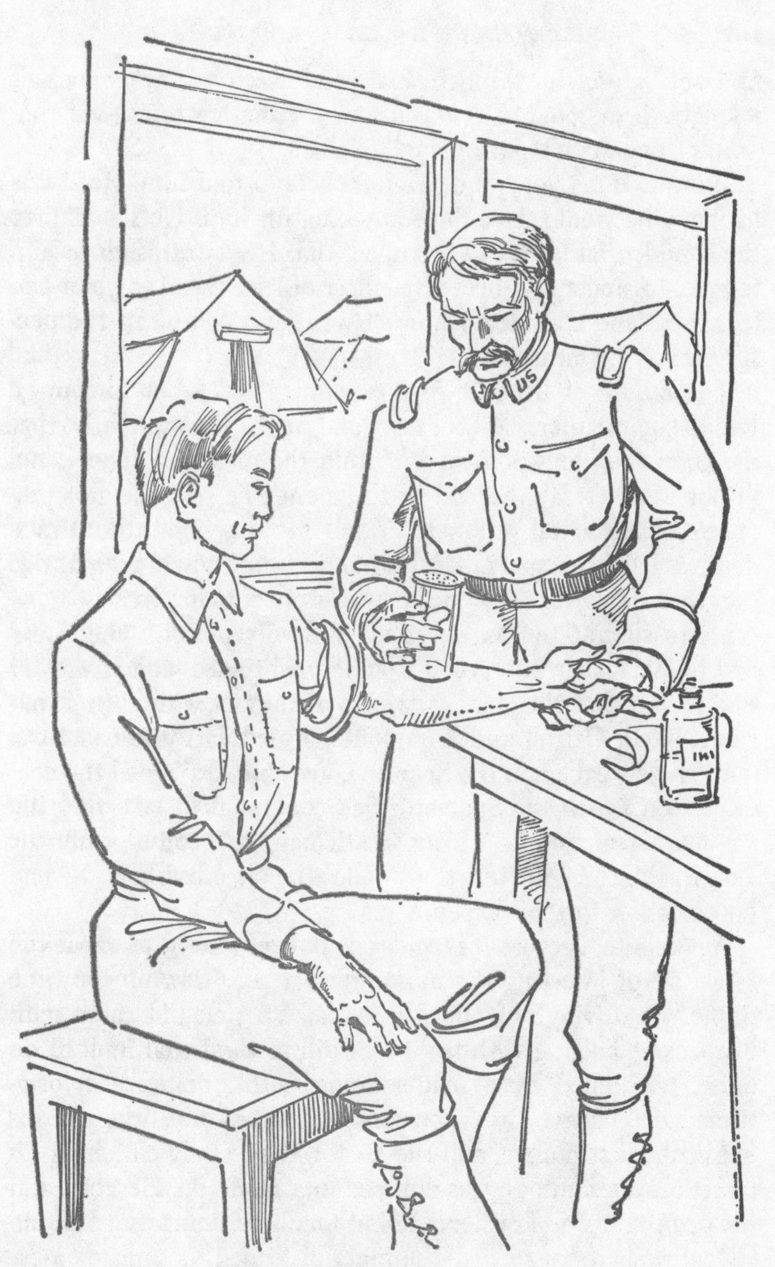

Kissinger rolled up his sleeve.

find out before I'm through with you," Reed warned, only half jokingly. "I'm going to save you now for another test, a very important one. You're still game?"

"For anything you want, Major," Moran told him. Reed was his hero; he would have done anything for him. He slaved over the confidential letters to Sternberg that Reed entrusted to him to type, tossing away sheet after sheet of letter-head to get a perfect copy, and considered himself well rewarded when the doctor praised his neatness.

The failure of his first four experiments did not discourage Reed. The weather was cool now, and he suspected, rightly, that the germ took longer to ripen within the mosquito than it did in hot weather. By the end of the month he still had not produced experimental yellow fever, but life was not without incident. A local newspaper on November 21st loosed a broadside against the heartless Americans who were enticing foreign innocents to submit to the injection of deadly poison. The board had foreseen that some such trouble might arise, and it was for that reason that they had drawn up a contract with each immigrant. Reed, Carroll and Agramonte, armed with the contracts, immediately called on the Spanish consul and explained the conditions on which the Spaniards had consented to take the risk. An intelligent and courteous gentleman, the consul smilingly advised the three doctors that, under the circumstances, he had no objection to their experiments.

Agramonte, because his regular work kept him in Havana, was in charge of infecting the mosquitoes at the Las Animas ward. As he was driving out one day to the experimental camp with his pockets bulging with test tubes full of the lethal insects, his horse, frightened by a road-building outfit, bolted and overturned the buggy. His laboratory assistant, Loud, was pitched out at the first plunge, and the doctor, desperately clutching his infectious mosquitoes, was dumped in a sand pile. He arrived at the camp dusty and disheveled, but loudly rejoicing that his misadventure had not turned a number of loaded mosquitoes loose in the countryside.

The two little wooden buildings, situated at some distance from the tents, were completed by November 30th. Reed had dire and special plans for them. Building Number One, known as the infected bedding and clothing building, was a one-room shack fourteen by twenty feet. The walls were two boards thick, the inner one made of close-fitting tongue-and-groove lumber. Its two windows, both placed in the south wall to prevent through ventilation, were covered with very fine screening, and fitted with wooden shutters to keep out fresh air and sunlight. The building, entered through a double screened vestibule, was constructed in every particular to prevent the accidental entrance of mosquitoes. It was closed tightly in the daytime, and its temperature was kept at about ninety degrees by a coal oil stove, while care was taken to keep the atmosphere humid.

In it was undertaken one of the most revolting experiments to which scientific curiosity and loyalty to his superiors ever persuaded a hero. On November 30th, the day the building was ready, three large boxes containing bedding used by yellow fever patients were carried to it. These articles, foully soiled, had been packed for two weeks in tightly closed boxes.

At six o'clock that Friday evening, Cooke and two privates of the Hospital Corps, Levi E. Folk and Warren G. Jernegan, all non-immunes, entered the hot and stuffy little building and started to unpack the loathsome articles. Reed, with interest and commiseration in his face, watched from outside. The three young men opened the boxes, pulled out and shook several sheets and blankets, as they had been instructed to do, then made an unscheduled bolt for the door. Gulping for air, they stopped.

"Oh, poor fellows!" Reed exclaimed sympathetically.

It was terrible in the little house, but the three volunteers weren't quitting. Shaking their heads and grinning ruefully, Cooke and the two others stubbornly re-entered it, made up their cots with the filthy bedding, and gingerly crawled into them.

The major might be confident that *fomites* were harmless,

but they still could not help feeling that their experiment was not only much more disagreeable, but much more dangerous, than the mosquito test; "everybody knew"—still—that *fomites* carried yellow fever. They spent a bad night between their horrid sheets, disturbed by evil smells and somber and uneasy thoughts. But for science—and the major—they willingly spent nineteen more nights like it.

Kissinger was a determined young man. He had already been bitten twice without result, but he had volunteered for a case of yellow jack, and he intended to get it.

On December 5th, at two in the afternoon, he rolled up his sleeve for the third time and watched the mosquito bite. This was getting monotonous, he thought.

"Do you think she'll take this time, sir?" he asked. "I certainly hope so!"

"I'll tell you in a couple of days," Reed replied, smiling.

By evening three days later, the young volunteer had a headache; the next day, December 9th, he was carried on his bed to the yellow fever ward. Kissinger, at last, had his yellow jack. "In my opinion this exhibition of moral courage has never been surpassed in the annals of the Army of the United States," Reed said.

Reed, his belief in the mosquito as intermediate host of yellow fever finally confirmed, was overjoyed.

"Rejoice with me, sweetheart," he happily wrote his wife that night, "as, aside from the anti-toxin of diphtheria and Koch's discovery of the tubercle bacillus, it will be regarded as the most important piece of work, scientifically, during the 19th century. I do not exaggerate, and I could shout for very joy that heaven has permitted me to establish this wonderful way of propagating yellow fever."

There was no self-satisfaction or personal pride in his modest and generous spirit, only thankfulness. Too excited and happy to sleep, he was up early the next morning and dashed off a note announcing the news to Truby, who had been sent across the island to Rowell Barracks at Cienfuegos as post surgeon. Truby told the news to Lawrence Reed, who was now a second lieutenant and shared quarters with him. Kean, almost beside himself with joy at his friend's conclusive demonstration, carried the tidings to General Wood. The good news was on the wing.

When the volunteers for the *fomites* experiment heard it, the gravity of their bearing disappeared in a rush of uproarious high spirits. They felt as if a death sentence had been lifted. Reed was feeling wonderful. The Havana Yellow Fever Board declared that Kissinger had unmistakable yellow fever—one of its members had earlier declared the mosquito theory "wild and improbable" and reluctantly ate his words—and, to make everything perfect, Kissinger was getting well.

Reed was deeply grateful for his recovery. As a good officer he hated to expose one of his men to a danger he did not share; as a good doctor he hated to gamble with a human life; and as a scientist he feared that the experiments could not continue if one of the cases died. Volunteers would probably be frightened away, and public opinion would force him to stop the work. He desperately hoped that his luck—and his volunteers' luck—would hold.

Within the next week three Spaniards, exposed to mosquito bites just as Kissinger had been, came down with yellow fever. Agramonte, still hopeful of inoculating a laboratory animal, held some of the mosquitoes that had infected them to the abdomen of Jenny, the laboratory's rhesus monkey. Her temperature remained normal, her simian spirits undimmed. The effort to give her yellow jack was a failure.

All the Spaniards recovered. One of them, an engaging young man named Antonio Benigno, whom Reed always called Boniato, Spanish for sweet potato, because of his liking for that vegetable, was overjoyed when he received his reward, which represented huge wealth to him, in ten- and twenty-dollar gold pieces. Several of the Spaniards, however, were convinced by their countrymen's illness that the "little flies" were really dangerous. They forgot, as Reed put it, "their own personal aggrandizement and incontinently severed their connection with Camp Lazear.

Personally," he added, "while lamenting to some extent their departure, I could not but feel that in placing themselves beyond our control they were exercising the soundest judgment." No shadow of doubt as to the guilt of mosquitoes could linger now.

Nor could anyone but a thorough skeptic doubt the harmlessness of *fomites.* On December 19th, after twenty nights passed in the most contaminated surroundings, Cooke and Folk and Jernegan emerged from the infected bedding building in their usual good health. They had even put on a few pounds. Two more non-immunes, James Hanberry and Edward Weatherwalks, took their place as subjects of the revolting but harmless demonstration, and were themselves later relieved by James Hildebrand and Thomas M. England. This line of experimentation, having failed to produce a single case of yellow fever, was finally abandoned after two months.

The seven brave and patient men who underwent this horrible ordeal were at no time in danger of contracting yellow fever, but that comforting fact was something of which they could not be sure until it was all over. It took just as much courage to disprove the virulence of *fomites,* in which the best authorities believed, as it did to prove that of mosquitoes. The practical value of the experiment was immense, since it clearly showed the uselessness of destroying valuable property in an effort to check the spread of yellow fever.

The Havana medical men, abruptly won over by Reed's conclusive results, hurried to do belated honor to their own neglected prophet, Dr. Finlay. They gave him a banquet at Delmonico's in Havana on the night of December 22nd, which was attended by seventy or eighty Havana doctors, Reed's board, Wood, Kean, Gorgas and other military doctors. Dr. Juan Guiteras tactfully distributed the honors to everyone's satisfaction. Dr. Finlay, he said, was like Sir Patrick Manson, who had advanced the theory that mosquitoes carried malaria; and Reed was like Sir Ronald Ross, who proved Manson's theory and gave it practical value.

Finlay, benign and happy, smiled around at the doctors gathered in his honor, doctors who had laughed at him until a few days ago. After twenty years, thanks to the clear, brilliant demonstration of the middle-aged American medical officer, his cherished theory was accepted. They had been long years, and discouraging sometimes, but this—the cheers and applause roared musically in his ears—this wiped out every painful recollection.

Reed, happy as Finlay, was looking ahead—far ahead to a day when his demonstration would bear fruit, when mosquito control measures would wipe the plague from the earth.

Reed was ready for the next step in his demonstration.

"Now we want to show that the difference between an infected and an uninfected house is due only to the presence of loaded mosquitoes. This is the experiment I've been saving you for, Moran," he told his only civilian volunteer.

"Good," Moran said. He was determined, too, like Kissinger. He had bargained for yellow jack, and he meant to get it.

Across a slight depression and eighty yards distant from the infected bedding building, was the second of the small houses that Reed had had built. Building Number Two, or the infected mosquito building, was like Building Number One, except that its windows were placed so as to afford good ventilation, and it was partitioned inside by a very fine wire screen through which mosquitoes could not pass.

Into one of the two rooms formed by the screen partition Reed liberated, on December 21st, fifteen insects which had previously fed on yellow fever cases. Moran, fresh from a bath and in a clean nightshirt—he felt a little like a sacrificial lamb—promptly at noon went into the mosquito-infested room and lay down on a clean cot. The board members, with two non-immune volunteers who were to remain on the mosquitoless side of the partition, watched through the screen.

In a few moments the insects were buzzing close about Moran. Repressing an almost overwhelming impulse to swat them, he winced as they bit him about the face and hands. He lay still for half an hour, while they deliberately settled on him and fed.

"Good boy," Reed commended him. "That should just about do for now. We'll do it again this afternoon and tomorrow. And I think you'll have that yellow jack you've been asking for."

When Moran's three ordeals were over the two non-immunes who had watched the ceremonies with the doctors remained on the other side of the room, separated from the mosquitoes only by the wire screen, but otherwise exposed to exactly the same influences as Moran had been. Moran went back to his tent, took his temperature and pulse every three hours, and waited as patiently as he could for his yellow jack. He felt pretty sure of it this time.

Christmas was warm and cloudy. Reed, unable to get to Camp Lazear in the morning, drove out in the afternoon. He wondered how Moran was feeling. It was about time for him to come down with the fever, he reflected, as he approached the young man's tent. He had already made a stop at the mosquito building, and found the non-immune controls in excellent health and Christmas spirits.

"Merry Christmas, Moran!" Reed said as he entered the volunteer's tent. Moran, lying on his cot, struggled to his feet.

"And to you, sir," he answered.

"Anything new?"

Blinking with headache, Moran pointed to his temperature and pulse chart. Reed glanced quickly at it—fever a hundred and one, pulse fast, he saw—and looked closely at Moran, noting his flushed face and bloodshot eyes.

Concern and jubilation struggled in his face. He had done it again, he had proved his point! Moran was sick, the controls were well—this demonstrated that the mosquito was the essential, the single, factor in making a house infected!

"Get back into bed," he ordered. "Moran," he rubbed his hands gleefully, "this is one of the happiest days of my life!"

Moran, ill as he felt, could not help grinning sympathetically. The major acted as pleased as a young interne—it was almost worth a bout of the fever to see him so elated.

Later that afternoon Stark and his wife, and Kean and Mrs. Kean, who had come with him to Cuba when he returned from sick leave, had a Christmas party for a few of the officers. A guava bush, brightly trimmed, acted as Christmas tree, and all the children under six on the post were invited to receive presents. Reed was the gayest person there.

And the great new discovery in yellow fever was suitably recognized. Dr. Amador, the sanitary officer, was presented with a can of kerosene, fatal to mosquito wigglers, with the jingle:

"Sing a song of kerosene,
Of barrels deep and wide.
Doctors have become so mean
Mosquitoes have to hide.

She thinks she finds a haven
But the doctor's eagle eye
Falls on the poor mosquito
And she will have to die."

For Reed there was a fragile package that seemed to be all ends.

"What a work of art!" he laughingly exclaimed, as he got the wrapper off, and held it up for everyone to see. It was a handsome mosquito, fashioned of a champagne cork and toothpicks, with a formidable stinger, and legs and body realistically striped to resemble *Culex fasciatus*. He read his rhymes out loud:

"Over the plains of Cuba
Roams the mosquito wild.
No one can catch or tame him
For he is Nature's child.

With Yellow Jack he fills himself
And none his pleasure mar
Till Major Reed does capture him
And put him in a jar.

And now, alas for Culex.
He has our sympathy,
For since the Major spotted him
He longs to be a flea!"

It was a happy Christmas, Reed thought as he went to bed, one of the happiest of his life. The guilt was firmly pinned on *Culex fasciatus*, and they knew how to deal with mosquitoes. "With Howard and kerosene," as he wrote the insect expert Dr. Howard, they could practically eliminate the yellow fever mosquito. *Culex* and *anopheles*, what a gay old pair of troublemakers they had been! But now their days were numbered.

Moran slowly emerged from his feverish stupor to realize that the quiet, insistent voice of which he had been faintly aware for sometime was Major Reed's, and that it was speaking to him. He squinted, focusing his aching eyes, and tried to catch the sense of the words.

"Are you in pain, Moran?" the doctor repeated the question.

Moran weighed the form of his answer, whether to nod his bursting head, or speak through the dreadful taste in his mouth.

"Yes," he whispered.

"Can you localize the pain?" Reed persisted, "back, legs, head?"

The sick man noticed that there were other men in the room besides Reed, and his attention wandered briefly to the white side whiskers framing the benevolent face of an old gentleman watching him from the foot of the cot. It was his first glimpse of Finlay.

"No," he answered, a little more clearly, "it's just everywhere."

"You can groan, Moran, or even yell if you want to. It's all right to make a fuss. It may relieve you some," Reed advised him sympathetically. He bent down to catch the mumbled words, ". . . knew what I was getting into . . . not a cry-baby," and straightened, smiling.

Moran, slipping away into stupor again, was still conscious

of the murmur of the doctors' voices, and caught the one clear phrase, "a very pretty case." Pretty! He shut his teeth tight against a groan, and turned his head away.

It might be a pretty case, but that didn't mean Reed liked it. He was terribly anxious. Moran knew the major came to see him early and late, but he never knew how often. It was several days before Reed was sure his volunteer would recover from the experiment through which he had put him. "Thank God!" he thought, "it will be a happy New Year after all."

The Wright Brothers

QUENTIN REYNOLDS

Since the beginning of time men have envied the birds—and have tried to imitate their power of flight. Wilbur and Orville Wright were the first to succeed in this goal, the first to achieve powered flight. In the half century or so that has passed since that day when the Wright boys sent up the first flying machine, we have progressed through the jet age and are approaching an era of rocket flight. Yet the lessons learned by them in their home in Dayton, Ohio, in 1878 and at Kitty Hawk in 1903 hold as true today as they did then. Here Quentin Reynolds, the famous war correspondent and writer, tells how the two boys learn their first principles in the science of flight—and how they later put them to work.

Learning from Mother

SUSAN WRIGHT wasn't like other mothers. She was younger and prettier than most other mothers, and she liked to laugh and she liked to play games with her three youngest children; Wilbur, who was eleven; Orville, who was seven; and Katharine, who was four.

The other mothers would shake their heads and say, "Susan Wright spoils those children; lets 'em do anything they want. No good will come of it."

But Susan Wright only laughed. In the summer she'd pack a picnic lunch and she, the two boys and little Kate (no one ever called her Katharine) would go and spend a day in the woods. Mrs. Wright knew the name of every bird and she could tell a bird by his song. Wilbur and Orville learned to tell birds too.

One day they sat on the banks of a river near Dayton, where they lived. Wilbur and Orville were fishing. Everyone called Wilbur "Will," and of course Orville was "Orv." The fish weren't biting very well. Suddenly a big bird swooped down, stuck his long bill into the river, came out with a tiny fish, and then swooped right up into the sky again.

"What makes a bird fly, Mother?" Wilbur asked.

"Their wings, Will," she said. "You notice they move their wings and that makes them go faster."

"But Mother," Will said, not quite satisfied, "that bird that just swooped down didn't even move his wings. He swooped down, grabbed a fish, and then went right up again. He never moved his wings at all."

"The wind doesn't just blow *toward* you or *away* from you," she said. "It blows *up* and *down,* too. When a current of air blows up, it takes the bird up. His wings support him in the air."

"If we had wings, then we could fly too, couldn't we, Mother?" Wilbur asked.

"But God didn't give us wings." She laughed.

"Maybe we could make wings," Wilbur insisted.

"Maybe," his mother said thoughtfully. "But I don't know. No one ever did make wings that would allow a boy to fly."

"I will some day," Wilbur said, and Orville nodded and said, "I will, too."

"Well, when you're a little older maybe you can try," their mother said.

That was another thing about Susan Wright. Most other mothers would have thought this to be foolish talk. Most other mothers would have said, "Oh, don't be silly, who ever heard of such nonsense!" But not Susan Wright. She knew that even an eleven-year-old boy can have ideas of his own, and just because they happened to come from an eleven-year-old head—well, that didn't make them foolish. She never treated her children as if they were babies, and perhaps that's why they liked to go fishing with her or on picnics with her. And that's why they kept asking her questions. She always gave them sensible answers.

They asked their father questions too, but he was a traveling minister and he was away a lot.

"It's getting chilly," Mrs. Wright said suddenly. "Look at those gray clouds, Will."

Wilbur looked up. "It's going to snow, I bet," he said happily.

"No more picnics until next Spring," his mother said. "Yes, it looks like snow. We'd better be getting home."

As they reached home, the first big white snowflakes started to fall. They kept falling all that night and all the next day. It was the first real snowstorm of the year.

In the morning the wind was blowing so fiercely that Wilbur found it hard to walk to the barn where the wood was stored. The wind was so strong it almost knocked him down. He burst through the kitchen door with an armful of wood for the stove, and he told his mother about the wind.

The wind didn't seem nearly so strong.

"The thing to do is to lean forward into the wind," she said. "Bend over, and that way you get closer to the ground and you get under the wind."

That night when Wilbur had to make the trip for more wood, he tried his mother's idea. To his surprise it worked! When he was bent over, the wind didn't seem nearly so strong.

After a few days the wind stopped, and now the whole countryside was covered with snow. Wilbur and Orville, with little Kate trailing behind, hurried to the Big Hill not far from the house.

Orville's schoolmates were all there with their sleds. It was a good hill to coast down because no roads came anywhere near it, and even if they had, it wouldn't have mattered. This was 1878 and there were no automobiles. Horse-drawn sleighs traveled the roads in winter. The horses had bells fastened to their collars, and as they jogged along the bells rang and you could hear them a mile away.

Most of the boys had their own sleds; not the flexible fliers boys have now, but old-fashioned sleds with two wooden runners. No one ever thought of owning a "bought" sled. In those days a boy's father made a sled for him.

The boys who had sleds of their own let Wilbur and Orville ride down the hill with them. Ed Sines and Chauncey Smith and Johnny Morrow and Al Johnston all owned sleds, but they liked to race one another down the long hill. When this happened Wilbur and Orville just had to stand there and watch. Late that afternoon the boys came home, with little Kate trailing behind, and their mother noticed that they were very quiet. She was wise as well as very pretty, and she soon found out why they were unhappy.

"Why doesn't Father build us a sled?" Wilbur blurted out.

"But Father is away, Will," his mother said gently. "And you know how busy he is when he is at home. He has to write stories for the church paper and he has to write sermons. Now suppose we build a sled together."

Wilbur laughed. "Whoever heard of anyone's mother building a sled?"

"You just wait," his mother said. "We'll build a better sled than Ed Sines has. Now get me a pencil and a piece of paper."

"You goin' to build a sled out of paper?" Orville asked in amazement.

"Just wait," she repeated.

"Get It Right on Paper"

Will and Orv brought their mother a pencil and paper, and she went to the minister's desk and found a ruler. Then she sat down at the kitchen table. "First we'll draw a picture of the sled," she said.

"What good is a picture of a sled?" Orville asked.

"Now Orville, watch Mother." She picked up the ruler in one hand and the pencil in the other.

"We want one like Ed Sines has," Orville said.

"When you go coasting, how many boys will Ed Sines's sled hold?" she asked.

"Two," Wilbur said.

"We'll make this one big enough to hold three," she said. "Maybe you can take Kate along sometimes." The outline of a sled began to appear on the paper. As she drew it she talked. "You see, Ed's sled is about four feet long. I've seen it often enough. We'll make this one five feet long. Now, Ed's sled is about a foot off the ground, isn't it?"

Orville nodded, his eyes never leaving the drawing that was taking shape. It was beginning to look like a sled now, but not like the sleds the other boys had.

"You've made it too low," Will said.

"You want a sled that's faster than Ed's sled, don't you?" His mother smiled. "Well, Ed's sled is at least a foot high. Our sled will be lower—closer to the ground. It won't meet so much wind resistance."

"Wind resistance?" It was the first time Wilbur had ever heard the expression. He looked blankly at his mother.

"Remember the blizzard last week?" she asked. "Remember when you went out to the woodshed and the wind was so strong you could hardly walk to the shed? I told you to lean over, and

The outline of a sled began to appear.

on the next trip to the woodshed you did. When you came back with an armful of wood you laughed and said, 'Mother, I leaned 'way forward and got under the wind.' You were closer to the ground and you were able to lessen the wind resistance. Now, the closer to the ground our sled is the less wind resistance there will be, and the faster it will go."

"Wind resistance . . . wind resistance," Wilbur repeated, and maybe the airplane was born in that moment. Certainly neither Will nor Orville Wright ever forgot that first lesson in speed.

"How do you know about these things, Mother?" Wilbur asked.

"You'd be surprised how much mothers know, Will." She laughed. She didn't tell the boys that when she was a little girl at school her best subject had been arithmetic. It just came naturally to her. It was the same when she went to high school. And when she went to college, algebra and geometry were her best subjects. That was why she knew all about things like "wind resistance."

Finally she finished the drawing. The boys leaned over the table to look at it. This sled was going to be longer than Ed's sled and much narrower. Ed's sled was about three feet wide. This one looked as if it would be only half that wide.

"You made it narrow," Wilbur said shrewdly, "to make it faster. The narrower it is, the less wind resistance."

"That's right." His mother nodded. "Now let's put down the exact length of the runners and the exact width of the sled."

"But that's only a paper sled," Orville protested.

"If you get it right on paper," she said calmly, "it'll be right when you build it. Always remember that."

"'If you get it right on paper, it'll be right when you build it,'" Wilbur repeated, and his mother looked at him sharply. Sometimes Will seemed older than his eleven years. Little Orville was quick to give you an answer to anything, but as often as not he'd forget the answer right away. When Will learned something he never forgot it.

"Mother, you make all your clothes," Wilbur said thoughtfully. "You always make a drawing first."

"We call that the pattern," his mother said. "I draw and then cut out a pattern that's exactly the size of the dress I am going to make. And . . ."

"If the pattern is right, it'll be right when you make the dress," he finished. She nodded.

"Now you two boys get started on your sled." She smiled. "There are plenty of planks out in the barn. Find the very lightest ones. Don't use planks with knots in them. You saw the planks to the right size, Will—don't let Orville touch the saw."

"May we use Father's tools?" Wilbur asked breathlessly.

His mother nodded. "I don't think your father will mind. I know you'll be careful with them. Just follow the drawing exactly," she warned once more.

The two boys, followed by little Kate, hurried out to the barn. Both realized that this was an important occasion. Wilbur always chopped the wood for the stove when his father was away, but he had never been allowed to use the gleaming tools that lay in his father's tool chest.

Three days later their sled was finished. They pulled it out of the barn and asked their mother to inspect it. She had her tape measure with her and she measured it. The runners were exactly the length she had put down in her drawing. In fact, the boys had followed every direction she had given them. The runners gleamed. Orville had polished them with sandpaper until they were as smooth as silk.

"We thought of one other thing, Mother," Will said. "We found some old candles in the woodshed. We rubbed the runners with the candles. See how smooth they are?"

Mrs. Wright nodded. She had forgotten to tell the boys that, but they'd thought it out for themselves. "Now try your sled," she told them.

Followed by Kate, the boys dragged their new sled to the hill only half a mile away where their pals were coasting. They looked at the new sled in amazement. It was long and very narrow. It looked as though it wouldn't hold anyone. The runners were thin compared to those on their own sleds.

"Who made that for you?" Ed Sines asked.

"Mother showed us how," Wilbur said proudly. Some of the boys laughed. Whoever heard of a boy's mother knowing how to make a sled?

"It looks as if it would fall apart if you sat on it," Al Johnston said, and he laughed too.

"Come on, we'll race you down the hill," another cried out.

"All right, two on each sled," Wilbur said. He wasn't a bit afraid. He was sure the drawing had been right, and because he and Orv had followed the drawing, he knew that the sled was right.

They lined the four sleds up. Will and Orv sat on their sled, but it didn't "fall apart." Suddenly Wilbur got an idea.

"Get up, Orv," he said. "Now lie down on the sled . . . that's it . . . spread your legs a bit." Will then flopped down on top of his brother. "Less wind resistance this way," he whispered.

"Give us all a push," Ed Sines yelled.

And then they were off. It was an even start. The four sleds gathered speed, for at the top the slope was steep. Will looked to the right. Then to the left. He brushed the stinging snow out of his eyes but he couldn't see the other sleds. He looked behind. They were straggling along, twenty and now thirty feet in back of him. The new sled skimmed along, the runners singing happily. Both Will and Orv felt a strange thrill of excitement. They approached the bottom of the long hill. The other sleds were far, far behind now.

Usually when the sleds reached the bottom of the hill they slowed down abruptly and stopped. But not this sled. It kept on; its momentum carried it on and on a hundred yards farther than any of the other sleds had ever reached. Finally it stopped.

Shaking with excitement, Will and Orv stood up.

"We flew down the hill, Orv," Will said breathlessly.

"We flew," Orv repeated.

Now Ed and Al and Johnny ran up, excited at what had happened. No sled had gone so far or so fast as the one Will and Orv had built.

"You *flew* down the hill," Ed Sines gasped. "Let me try it?"

Wilbur looked at Orv, and some secret message seemed to pass between them. They had built this sled together, and it was the best sled there was. They'd always work together building things.

"Orv," Will said, "I've got an idea. This sled can do everything but steer. Maybe we can make a rudder for it. Then we can make it go to the right or to the left."

"We'll get Mother to draw one," Orv said.

"We'll draw one, you and I," Wilbur said. "We can't run to Mother every time we want to make something."

By now little Kate had come running down the hill.

"You promised," she panted. "You said you'd take me for a ride."

"Come on, Kate." Will laughed. "The three of us will coast down once. And then you can try it, Ed."

They trudged up the hill, pulling the sled. Two words kept singing in Wilbur's ears. "We flew . . . we flew . . . we flew. . . ."

The Flying Machine

Kitty Hawk hadn't changed much. William Tate was a little older but no busier than he had been on the Wright brothers' first visit. He helped them build a shed to protect their glider and its engine from the storms that occasionally swept over the sand dunes. Then Will and Orv gave him the job of bringing firewood every morning. They paid him a dollar a day for that.

All day long they worked on their glider and their engine. It was a funny-looking thing, and when the men from the life-saving station walked over to look at it they shook their heads.

"You really going to make this thing fly?" one of them asked Wilbur.

"Maybe, maybe," Will said.

"How long you been working on this?" another asked.

"All our lives," Orville said, and that was the truth.

Their first flying machine—the word airplane wasn't used then—didn't have wheels. It had skids (something like skis). Will and Orv built two wooden tracks and laid them out on the sand. They would launch their flying machine from this track. They tested the engine again and again. It made a lot of noise and it shook the whole glider, but it was well fastened to the lower wing and it wouldn't fly off. At least, they hoped it wouldn't.

"I think we can try it today," Will said casually on the morning of December 17, 1903. Will probably didn't realize that forever and ever, boys and girls in school would learn that date. December 17, 1903 is one of the most important dates in history.

"We're as ready as we ever will be," Orv said just as casually.

Outwardly they were calm, but they were human, and you can be sure that they were excited inside. They tossed a coin to decide which one would try the machine first. Orv won.

"I'm going to fly today," Orv whispered to himself. "I'm going to be the first man in the world to fly."

There were only five people out near the lonely sand dune to watch the flying machine try to get into the air, and not one of them thought it could do it. One of the five was a sixteen-year-old boy named Johnny Moore, whose father was a fisherman. They started up the engine. Orv climbed onto the lower wing. Wilbur steadied the glider, which was vibrating terrifically.

"You ready, Orv?" Wilbur shouted.

"All set," Orv yelled back.

"Let her go," Wilbur cried, and Orv released the lever that made the propellers "bite" into the air. The glider started to move along the track slowly . . . a bit quicker . . . and then, just as it reached the end of the track the front of the glider rose up, the rest followed, and the flying machine was in the air. It rose to ten feet. It was flying. It sped along in the air. Wilbur, usually calm, was trembling with joy. Orville was actually flying. The flying machine went a hundred feet and then it glided down gracefully to the sand.

Orville tumbled out of the first machine that had ever really flown.

"We did it, Will," he said, his voice shaky.

"We can fly," Wilbur said with awe. "We can fly."

"How long was I up?" Orv asked.

"Twelve seconds," Will said. "Now let me try it."

Wilbur flew a hundred and seventy-five feet and then let the

Orville was actually flying.

machine come down. Orville tried again and came down after about fifteen seconds.

"Will, see how far you can fly it," Orville suggested when Wilbur took his position to try again. Will nodded. Once again the flying machine was launched. It rose to about twenty feet and then Wilbur leveled it off. Looking down, he saw the sand dunes flying past him. The flying machine kept on and on. This was a real flight. Two startled seagulls flew alongside, screaming shrilly. What new kind of bird was this? When Wilbur had flown eight hundred feet a draft of down air forced the flying machine to land.

"You were up there fifty-nine seconds," Orv shouted as Wilbur climbed down from the lower wing.

"Next time we'll stay up fifty-nine minutes," Wilbur said with a laugh.

"Let's send a telegram to Father," Orv said.

The four men and the sixteen-year-old boy who had watched the first flight of an airplane came running up to shake hands with the two brothers. Even now they could hardly believe their eyes. They had seen a heavy, ungainly looking glider with a heavy engine actually rise from the ground and fly. No one else in history had ever seen anything like this before.

Wilbur and Orville hurried to send a telegram to their father and to Kate. Back home, the bishop and his daughter read the telegram with shining eyes. They ran to the shop to tell Charley Taylor about it. He wasn't a bit excited.

"Knew they'd do it all along," he said calmly.

A week later Wilbur and Orville came home. There was no brass band to meet them. There were no newspapermen at the station. Bishop Wright and Kate were the only ones to welcome them.

"We flew, Kate," Orv said happily.

"They don't believe it," Kate said angrily.

"Who doesn't believe it?" Will asked.

"The newspapers, the people, even the neighbors," Kate said bitterly.

"First they think we're crazy," Orv said. "Now they think we're liars."

"Don't worry, boys," their father said. "I once told you that God had big plans for you two. I was right. No one can interfere with His plans, my sons. He gave you something special that allowed you to be the first two men in history to fly. Let people laugh."

"We'll show them," Orv said grimly.

The Radium Woman: A Life of Marie Curie

ELEANOR DOORLY

The story of Marie Curie is the story of a pure devotion to science. She and her husband, Pierre, a distinguished physicist, were desperately poor most of the time, but they were radiantly happy in the life and work they shared together. The account of their scientific researches into the mystery of radium reads like an exciting tale of true adventure. Even the completely dedicated Pierre Curie was amazed at the superhuman strength and patience that Marie put forth in the four years that she alternately froze or sweltered as she stirred the pitchblende in the miserable shed that served them as a laboratory. Toward the end, after great honors, including the Nobel Prize, had come to Marie, she developed a strange blood condition that puzzled her doctors. It was not until after she had died on July 4, 1934, that it was determined that this gallant woman had died from too much contact with her great discovery, radium.

A Light in the Dark

So the mysterious and radiant stranger had a name, but no one had yet seen its face, not even Pierre and Marie who had given it its name of Radium. It had not, like all respectable and real substances, been touched, seen, put in a bottle, or even weighed. That question of weighing was very important. Weight —"atomic weight"—was to a scientist the very proof of existence. Something existing in the mind of Pierre and Marie, whose atomic weight even they did not know, was not scientifically there at all in the opinion of the scientists. No, Pierre and Marie had to get hold of Radium and weigh it. When they had done that, scientists would believe in it.

"It is in pitchblende," thought the Curies, "and it is too small to be seen; but perhaps if we could get hold of an enormous quantity of pitchblende and extract all the Radium from it, we should have a piece large enough to see."

But how were they to get hold of a really enormous quantity of pitchblende, say a hundred tons? And where could they put it if they had it? And how could they work on it even if they could house it?

The scientist takes one step at a time. First let them get hold of the pitchblende. They knew where great quantities were to be found, because the Bohemians used it in the manufacture of their beautiful glass; but it was expensive and the Curies had no money worth talking about. But the Bohemians did not, of course, make glass of pitchblende itself; they extracted Uranium from it for the manufacture of glass and threw out the useless dust in mighty powdery heaps in the forest of St. Joachimsthal. "Radium and Polonium," said the Curies, "are not in Uranium; so they must be in that waste dust. Perhaps the manufacturers could be persuaded to sell their waste dust cheap."

"Sell?" said the manufacturers kindly. "We'll give it to you if you will pay for taking it away." Even that transport was expensive enough, but the Curies poured out their savings and sent them to Bohemia.

That was settled. The dust would be arriving, whole railway trucks of it. Where in the world would they put it?

Pierre and Marie went round to the great home of Science, the Sorbonne. Surely in that vast set of buildings, some unwanted room could be found for their valuable and exciting dust; but no! They had to go back to their own school of physics and even there nothing satisfactory could be spared them. The only place available was a shed on the other side of the courtyard from their laboratory. And what a shed! The glass roof was broken and the rain would rain through and upset any experiment that had to be kept dry. There was no floor, only a badly tarred surface; there was no furniture, except an old kitchen table or two, a blackboard and an old stove with a rusty iron chimney. In summer the workers would be cooked, because the roof was of glass. In winter, they would freeze when the outside world froze, because the stove gave no heat; or they would be soaked if it happened to rain. Not that that mattered much, for the room was not fitted with a fume cupboard to carry away the poisonous fumes, so that most of their work would have to be done out of doors. Still "Beggars can't be choosers," says an old adage, so the Curies settled down to making the shed do.

The great morning came. The heavy cart horses with their bells and pointed black fur collars, brought their big coal cart to rest outside the school of physics. Perhaps they looked round surprised at the eager pair who rushed out hatless, in science overalls, with exclamations of joy to welcome their load. Not so was coal generally received.

But the load was not coal; it was sacks of brown dust. Marie could not wait for the sacks to be carried in; excitedly, in the street under the horses' solemn eyes, she seized the string with which one was tied and began to tear it undone. This was pitchblende! Her pitchblende! Or rather the part of pitchblende that mattered. Curiosity was in her heart, her eyes, her tingling, working fingers. At last, she was able to plunge both hands into the brown, dull-coloured dust and pine-needles from the Bohemian pine forest. Was Radium, the radiant stranger, really in that? Would she find stars in the dust? Marie was going to get it out, even if she had to boil down mountains of that dingy dust.

The first ton of sacks was carried into the shed and the work

She boiled down the dust.

began, four years' work, the best and happiest and hardest years of Marie's life.

In a great iron cauldron, she boiled down the dust, stirring it perpetually with an iron rod nearly as tall as herself. She stuck to her work all day long, even eating at the shed so as not to interrupt her task. She might have been seen any day, her hair blowing in the wind, her dusty overall flecked and tattered with acids, stirring her ill-tempered mud. She had chosen the man's work of hard manual labour out of doors, while Pierre sat at the table indoors trying to discover the properties of Radium by means of delicate, precise experiments. Sometimes she worked more than forty pounds of dust at a time, filling the shed with great pots of precipitates and liquids. She carried heavy weights, lifted pots to pour their contents into others and stirred and stirred the boiling cauldron.

After an entire day spent at the shed, with such hard work as that, Marie had her nursery work at home. She washed Irène and put her to bed and hoped to be able to go and sit in the study with Pierre. But Irène thought differently. No sooner was Marie's back turned, than a little piteous "Mé" came from the nursery . . . "Mé!" So back went Marie to sit with her baby till she slept. Pierre was not pleased about that; he wanted Marie's time too. But when Irène was asleep husband and wife sat together studying far into the night.

When to-morrow came, they worked again. Where was that Radium? Would they never see it? The days lengthened into months; the months were more than twelve and the second year was slipping into the third, and the third into the fourth. They worked as in a dream, thinking only of one thing, talking only of one thing. "What will it be like when we do see it?" asked Marie one day when she was taking a little time off to pace up and down the courtyard with Pierre.

"I hope it will be a beautiful colour," said Pierre.

In 1900, a French chemist, André Debrierne, came to help them and discovered, before ever they had caught a glimpse of

Radium or Polonium, a "brother" element which he called Actinium.

Time after time, the heavy horses brought more tons of pitch-blende waste to the gate. Every day with her *terrible* patience, Marie was extracting from it a substance in which Radium was more and more concentrated. But still it hid, still it kept itself to itself and preserved its secret.

She had terrible patience, but difficulties were crowding in on the two. She and Pierre had not enough money to live and they had not enough time to work. Pierre had to do a great deal of teaching to earn the £240 on which they lived and that took time from Radium and still was not enough to pay their expenses and those of Irène's nurse. So Pierre tried to get a university post where his work would be more advanced and better paid; where, perhaps, he would have a real laboratory, equipped with electricity for his experiments and where he would not have so many lessons a day and so many wearying corrections at night.

But, unfortunately, posts are not always given to those who do the best work; they often go to the friends of the principal or to those who know the art of praising themselves. When an opportunity came to apply for such a post, Pierre was told that, according to custom, he must go and call on each member of the appointing committee. He hated doing so. Shyly he rang the doorbell, asked for the member, was shown in and sat down, but when the member came, Pierre was so shy that he praised his rival and not himself in the most glowing terms. Naturally, when the day of election came, it was the rival who was elected.

But something had to be done in order to live. Pierre was able to add to his salary by obtaining a humble post of £100 a year as tutor at the *Polytechnique*, one of the two most famous schools of France.

Just as he did this, the University of Geneva offered him his very heart's desire, a lectureship at the university, a beautiful laboratory, all the instruments and equipment he chose to ask for. He accepted and he and Marie went to Geneva. But when they got there, they knew that they could not desert Paris, could not, simply could not, abandon Radium, that child of theirs. However badly Paris treated them, only in Paris could they work at Radium. So with apologies, Pierre abandoned his wonderful post at Geneva and returned to Paris, poverty and Radium.

We next find the two rejoicing because Pierre had obtained a post in the School of Physics, Chemistry and Natural Science and Marie one to teach girls in the Sèvres training school for elementary teachers. They were lucky young women who had Marie Curie to teach them, but it was sad that the world did not realize that the work she was doing on Radium could only be done by her, while many people might have taught Science at Sèvres. Marie prepared her lessons with the greatest care and won much praise, because they were the most original and the most fascinating lessons any of the girls had known. But her long tram rides several times a week tried her and wasted precious hours; so did the preparation of schoolgirl lessons and the weary marking of papers. It was like setting Rembrandt to paint gate-posts. Both Pierre and Marie were wearing themselves out. Would they ever see Radium?

Marie also had forgotten her good resolution to feed well after her marriage. "You scarcely eat, either of you," wrote their doctor to Pierre. "I have more than once seen Madame Curie nibbling two thin rounds of sausage and washing it down with a cup of tea. Do you think that even a strong constitution won't suffer from such starvation? . . . I know what your excuse will be: 'She is not hungry and is old enough to know what is good for her.' She isn't! She's behaving like a baby. I am speaking with all the conviction of my friendship. You don't spend enough time on your meals. . . . You mustn't read while you eat, or talk Physics . . ."

One gets the impression that neither Pierre nor Marie paid the slightest attention to the doctor's good advice. There was that Radium to be brought to life in the shed of the Rue Lhomond and nothing else mattered.

At one moment Pierre suggested that they should devote themselves to a study of the properties of Radium and abandon the effort to see the thing itself, but Marie would not listen.

She was getting nearer. She had ceased to boil down the rough dust. She had obtained from it something which could be kept indoors, something which, in a small space contained all the Radium of the many tons. To work upon it further, she needed delicate instruments, a science room in which there was neither dust nor damp, neither cold nor heat, nothing to upset an accurate experiment. But she had no such room, and dust, heat, cold, wind constantly undid what she did and forced her to waste time and energy doing it again. She had terrible patience.

It was the year 1902. Three years and nine months had passed since Marie had announced the probable existence of Radium. At last she had conquered the radiant stranger. She had seen stars in that dust; she had seen Radium. She had made one decigramme of it. It had weight. It had the atomic weight of 226. Chemists bowed to it.

Marie and Pierre were sitting at home in the evening and Irène had been put to bed. That four year old tyrant had consented to shut her eyes and let Mé go back to Pierre to finish making the tyrant's dress, for Mé made all Irène's clothes. Suddenly Marie put down her work: "Let's go back!" she said.

Pierre needed no asking. They had left their Radium only two hours but they longed to see it again. They wanted it as if it were a new baby. They called to Grandfather Curie that they were going out and then, arm-in-arm, through the crowded streets, past the factories of their unfashionable district, they made their way back to Rue Lhomond and their shed.

"Don't light up," said Marie. "Do you remember the day when you said you would like Radium to have a beautiful colour?"

In the dark of the shed, Radium had something even more lovely than colour. It had light!

"Look! look!" whispered Marie, as she felt her way to a chair and sat gazing round her.

There were tiny points of light in the dark room, like pale blue moonlight dancing on water, specks of light that were never still.

On the table, on the shelves were those strange, mysterious radiances. In its little receptacles there was Radium visible at last, visible by its own light in the dark.

Not for Sale

The whole world was excited! Something entirely new had come into people's everyday life, something that made them change their thoughts about many things. It was not only scientists who talked about Radium: children discussed it on their way home from school; women, who had been disappointed for long, long ages because men had made all the greatest discoveries, rejoiced aloud, that at last it had happened to a woman to discover a new and wonderful thing. But, at first, no one dreamed how wonderful Radium was going to be.

Letters came in packed masses to the two Curies from famous scholars in England, Denmark, Germany and Austria, asking for information about the new discovery. Scientists everywhere took up the study of Radium and found out more about its characteristics and those of its near relations. Two Englishmen, Ramsay and Soddy, found that it threw off from itself tiny quantities of a new gas, which they called Helium. In other words, Radium had the capacity of becoming Helium. That was something very startling. Scientists had been accustomed to laugh at the Medieval Alchemists who believed that they could turn iron into gold. A picture of the alchemist's mysterious smoky cave was a picture of a dream of the impossible. Things, the scientists had said, were themselves, with their own chemical composition and their own atomic weight. Now they had to face the fact that Radium made Helium out of itself, and they wondered what other things might also be occupied with creating new substances. Perhaps the ghosts of the alchemists were laughing at the chemists.

At any rate, to turn iron into gold was no more remarkable a feat than the feats of which this Radium was capable. It looked like dull table salt, but it was two million times more radiant than Uranium. The rays that it gave out could go through every solid metal except lead. It was accompanied by its shadow—a spirit that was so alive and active that even when it was shut up in a glass tube, it destroyed a quarter of itself in a day. It could produce heat of itself, enough heat to melt in an hour a piece of ice of its own weight. If you shut it away from the cold, it would grow hotter than the day. If you shut it in glass, it would turn the glass mauve or violet. If you wrapped it in paper or cotton wool, it ate them. If you had no candle in the dark, it gave you enough light to read by.

One of the most wonderful things about this Radium was that it did not even stick to its own light; it handed it on to everything that came in its way, even though such generosity was often most inconvenient.

It showed a sudden interest in human affairs in that it lent its luminosity to real diamonds, but turned its nose up at paste. Diamond buyers could use it to test the genuineness of their purchases.

Poor Marie found its interference in all her experiments most distracting. Nothing could be left near a tube of Radium without becoming radio-active; it presented its luminosity to the air, the dust, Marie's clothes, her instruments, her notebooks. Those last kept the luminosity they had not been able to refuse, long after she was dead.

Scientists probably enjoy having their ideas upset, so those early years of the baby Radium must have been happy ones for them. Not only did that strange Radium create a new element out of itself, but that new element again made something new, and so on. The radio-elements formed strange faculties in which each member was created by the transformation of the substance of its mother. But the scientists' shocks did not end there. They found that each radio-element lost half of itself in a given time, a time which was always the same, a time so long that we need not worry about finding ourselves bereft of the radio-elements.

Uranium, to lose half of itself, takes a few milliards of years, and a milliard is a million-million. To do the same thing, Radium takes only 1,600 years, while its spirit takes only four days and its spirit's children only a few seconds.

You could look at Radium and see it lying quite still and yet know that, while you were gazing at it, its strange children were being born, were being murdered or committing suicide, or merely colliding with one another.

Then suddenly something altogether new happened to this active stranger as if enough things hadn't happened already. Pierre, exploring still, let it burn him. The skin of his hand became red but didn't hurt. It became redder. On the twentieth day a crust formed as on an ordinary fire burn. Then a sore appeared. On the forty-second day the sore began to heal on the outside edge.

Then Marie, though she had not meant to burn herself, found that her Radium had burnt her, though it was in a glass tube and the tube was in a tin box.

Then their friend Becquerel, going home with a tube of it in his jacket pocket, was quite seriously burnt.

"Your abominable child!" he exclaimed to Marie. "What has it burnt me for? I love the thing, but I've a bone to pick with it." Marie, too, might have had a bone to pick with the thing she loved, because the tips of her fingers hurt horribly and lost their skin.

But soon people began to look kindly on Radium's burns because they healed so well. Doctors became immensely interested in it. They set it to burn away terribly sick skin and, when the burn was healed, the illness had gone too. A wild great hope began for the world. Perhaps Radium could be persuaded to burn away cancer.

At any rate, Radium had been proved to be useful. People were wanting to buy it. Marie, out of eight tons of pitchblende had made one gramme of Radium. It was worth £30,000, but it was not for sale. Marie would treasure it while she lived and leave it to her laboratory as a precious symbol of years of great work and a great triumph.

One Sunday morning as Pierre and Marie were sitting at home in the Boulevard Kellerman, the postman left a letter with an American stamp for Pierre. He read it carefully, folded it, and put it on his desk.

"We'll have to talk," he said, "about this Radium. It is going to be manufactured on a large scale. They have written from Buffalo to ask for information about it."

"Well?" Marie was a little bored.

"Well, we can choose. . . . We can describe quite openly and frankly all our results and methods of making it. . . ."

"Of course," smiled Marie.

"We'll have to talk about this Radium."

"Or," went on Pierre, paying no attention to the interruption, "we can consider ourselves as the owners of our knowledge, the inventors of Radium. If we do that, before we publish our method of extracting Radium from pitchblende, we must take out a patent and draw a profit from the manufacture of Radium in the whole world."

As he spoke, it was quite clear to them both that immense wealth was theirs for the accepting. A patent on the manufacture of Radium would give them enough money to build a great laboratory and to buy Radium for research. What things they could do if they were rich!

Marie thought for a little, and then said: "That is impossible; that would be against the spirit of science."

Pierre agreed, but he told her to think carefully, because the decision once made could not be reconsidered. He reminded her about the laboratory they both wanted and about the future of their daughter. Was she sure she did not want to be rich?

Marie knew the great old custom of the scientists, the custom that people like Pasteur had followed, and she said: "Physicists always publish their researches. It is only by chance that our discovery has a money value. We can't use a chance like that for profit. And Radium is going to help the sick. It seems impossible to me to seek any profit from it."

Marie and Pierre went to gather wild flowers.

Again Pierre agreed that it would be contrary to the scientific spirit to sell their knowledge of Radium. He wrote that very night and gave the Americans all the information they wanted.

So, without a moment's regret, Pierre and Marie turned their backs forever upon the millionaire's faery fortune. Their Radium was not for sale. The scientific spirit had given Radium to them and to the world, and however low the spirit of the world sinks, it still loves the scientific spirit which gives all its knowledge freely to all men without price. Having chosen poverty when they might have chosen fortune, Marie and Pierre took their bicycles and went for their ordinary ride through the summer woods to gather wild flowers for their room.

Plant Wizard:

George Washington Carver

MAY McNEER AND LYND WARD

A LITTLE BOY plodded slowly along a lonely road in Missouri, in the summer of 1874. Over his shoulder swung his belongings, tied in an old shawl, fastened to a stick. He was small and thin, and he did not talk much, for his voice was only a piping squeak. Yet his large eyes moved from side to side and he saw more than most other people did. As his bare feet moved in the dust, the boy felt his shoes bounce against his chest. New shoes should not be ruined by wear, so he had hung them around his neck by the laces. He was tired and rather hungry, but he smiled as he felt the sun and the breeze on his face. Birds sang, all trees were his friends, and every clump of grass and wild flower seemed to nod to him.

This was George Washington Carver, setting out to seek his fortune. It was astonishing that such a small Negro boy should start out alone to the town of Neosho to learn to read and write; yet it was even more surprising that he was alive at all. Many times he had heard his good foster mother tell him of a dreadful night during the Civil War. George was a tiny baby then. He did not remember how his sister had been killed, how his older brother had escaped and hidden, and how he and his mother had been stolen by slave raiders. These slaves belonged to a German farmer and his wife named Carver who were fond of them. Carver had ridden out in pursuit of the thieves and had found tiny, sickly George abandoned by the roadside. His mother had never been heard of again. Carver had given a good horse to the neighbor who had helped him in the search. Sometimes George looked down at his own spindly legs and wondered if he was worth as much as a horse. There was some doubt about it in his mind.

After a few years George's brother, Jim, went away, and George did not see him again. George was not strong enough to do farm work, so Frau Carver taught him to cook and wash clothes. He taught himself about trees and plants, for he loved all growing things.

When George was no taller than the highest weed on the roadside, he made the Carver garden the finest in the neighborhood.

A farmer friend of the Carvers saw how bright he was, and said that he ought to be taught to read. This farmer gave George a book on plants. Although George did not want to leave the Carvers, and they hated to see him go, he knew that he must learn to read. Now George had a dollar in his pocket to pay for his schooling. As for food and shelter—well, he could work hard. He was on his way to the nearest school for Negroes.

George reached Neosho by nightfall and crept into an old barn to sleep in the hay. Next morning he found the one-room school and paid his dollar to enter. For several weeks George slept in the barn beside a stray dog. He earned his food by washing dishes or cutting wood. Then, early one morning, the man who owned the barn came in and saw the little boy curled up beside the dog, and almost hidden under a mound of hay.

"Well, now, what are you doing in my barn?"

George jumped up in a fright, and found it impossible to speak. The young man smiled and said, "You look hungry, boy. Come in the house."

Inside the warm kitchen a young wife was frying bacon and eggs and baking corn bread. She gave George some hot food, and then the Martins sat down to hear his story. When he finished, speaking slowly and politely in his squeaky voice, they looked at each other, nodded, and offered him the shed to sleep in. George stayed there for some months and did odd jobs for the young couple. As he sat in the kitchen in the evenings he heard them talk of the West and of how they might join one of the wagon trains rolling through Missouri. He was not surprised when they decided to go. The day that they left, George sat

"Well, now, what are you doing in my barn?"

down on the steps and wondered what he was going to do now.

He heard a voice. "Boy, get your things and come with me."

George looked up. There stood Aunt Mariah, an elderly Negro woman whom he knew in the town. He jumped up, collected his few clothes and the food left him by the Martins, and went to her little house, where he soon felt very much at home.

George lived with Aunt Mariah and Uncle Andy until he was thirteen and had learned far more than his teacher in the school knew. As soon as he could read, he borrowed every book that he could find and remembered all that he read. The day came when he knew that, to learn more, he must start out alone on the road again. Saying good-by to his friends was hard. He was fortunate in making friends, but always seemed to have to leave them.

George went to Fort Scott, Kansas. There he got work in a hotel and was allowed to sleep on a cot on the back porch. He went to school and found that, even here, he knew more about plants than did the teacher. Since George had very little time to go out into the country, he began to draw trees and flowers. He also got a little paint box, and painted flowers. He joined the art class of his school, and soon became known for his pictures. When he had again learned all that the school could teach him, George was on his way once more. He had grown tall and much stronger, and now his voice was strong, too, though as soft and gentle as ever. He had to earn his living, so he signed up as a laborer on the new railroad that was being built across the western plains, and became a camp cook for a while. Then later, he worked picking fruit or on ranches. Finally he went to Olathe, Kansas, to go to school again.

Here George made more good friends, for everybody liked him. He lived with a Negro couple whom he called Aunt Lucy and Uncle Seymour, and finished high school. Then he went back to visit the Carvers, who urged him to stay with them and farm their land. George was tempted, but somehow he knew that he must do something more. He wanted more learning. He wanted to go to college.

"College?" asked Frau Carver, folding her hands beneath her big white apron. "*Ja*, you should go to college. But how can you?"

George smiled, and nodded. He meant to try. First he applied to Highland College, in Kansas, but was turned down because he was a Negro. Discouraged, he homesteaded land and tried to make a farm of his own for a while, but the earth was very poor, and he gave it up. One day he wandered into a church in Winterset, Iowa, and joined in singing a hymn. As his rich voice rolled forth, the minister noticed him. Next day Parson Milholland looked George up and invited him to his home. Mrs. Milholland was a musician and was so interested in this talented young man that she gave him music lessons. Mr. Milholland said that he would locate a college that would take George. Simpson College, in Iowa, accepted him, and so once again George set out, this time to enter art school.

Making a living was always a problem, but it was not a new one to George Carver. He found a shed, got permission to use it, and started a laundry service for other students. During his second year there, as George pushed the hot iron expertly back and forth over shirts, his thoughts were busy with his future. What did he want to do? He liked painting, but he realized now that he did not want to spend all of his time as an artist. Science interested him far more.

The following year George disappointed his art teacher by leaving Simpson College to go to the Iowa State College in Ames, to study agriculture and botany. And so, at twenty-seven years of age, the tall, gentle Negro began the study of plant life. He was soon known as a remarkable student, and he made many friends. George Carver began to draw attention by his work with plants. After he had been at the State College a few years he was called a "plant wizard," for his long fingers could do more than anyone thought possible. He worked day and night, waiting on table, doing anything to make a simple living. But his happiest hours were spent in the greenhouses with plants and flowers.

George Washington Carver received his degree in 1894, and was asked to teach at the college. Now he could smile when he remembered that he had once wondered whether he was worth as much as a horse! Here, in Ames, Iowa, he had great laboratories to work in and every opportunity to do the things that he could do so well. After a few years George had earned another degree, and was happy in his teaching. It really looked as if this was his place on earth, and his wanderings were over.

Then, one day, up from Alabama came a Negro man whose name was also Washington. This was Booker T. Washington, an educator who was spending his life trying to improve education for his own race. At the end of the Civil War Negroes were free, but most of them were unable to read and write. Many small schools were started for them, but money was scarce, and people had hardly enough to support themselves. Booker T. Washington had bought a piece of washed-out earth in Alabama. Here he had taught a few young men to build a schoolhouse. They built it of bricks that they made themselves from the red clay of the land.

Carver sat quietly and listened as Washington talked to him about the beginning of the school at Tuskegee. He said little, but he nodded every now and then, and sometimes frowned. Washington spoke of the Negro farmers and their wives and children. They had cotton fields and a few other small crops, but could never grow enough both to feed themselves and to sell a surplus to get cash for clothing and supplies. A man who understood farming was desperately needed to teach young men and women to get better crops from their land.

Dr. Carver listened carefully to the big dark man who talked so earnestly about the needs of the Negro people. He made his decision. Quietly, and with a smile, he told Booker Washington that he would come to Tuskegee to do all that he could. This "plant wizard," with such a brilliant future ahead of him at a fine university, would go to live in the poverty-stricken Negro country in Alabama.

Not long after, as he stood and saw the Tuskegee school for the first time, Dr. Carver wondered how he could accomplish anything here at all. The brick building was surrounded by fields overgrown with weeds, washed into gullies by rains. Inside the school he found no laboratory and nothing with which to work. But George Washington Carver had not been a professor all of his busy years. He had worked with hot irons, wash tubs, cook-

Then he planted cowpeas!

stoves, the ax, the hoe, and the plow. In his classes he had only a few young men, with little education and no knowledge beyond the cotton fields. But they knew poverty as well as he did, and they could be trained to make much of very little. He proposed that he help them make their own laboratory.

He led them on expeditions to the dump heaps around the nearest towns. This was a search that became a treasure hunt. The students went through trash piles in alleys, and asked housewives for broken pans, lamps, and kettles. When they had collected a great pile of cast-off utensils, Professor Carver showed them pictures that he had drawn of laboratory equipment. Long hours the boys worked with broken articles—cleaning, mending, making new things from old ones.

And then Dr. Carver got a two-horse plow and went to work himself. Straight furrows stretched out behind him, and students who had thought of farming as ignorant work, not fit for the educated, felt ashamed. Dr. Carver sent them for bucket after bucket of black muck and leaf mold from swamps and woods, and manure from the barns. Then he planted cowpeas! Everybody gasped. Who ever heard of such a thing? Cowpeas were good only for pigs. Cotton was the cash money crop. When the peas were picked, this strange teacher cooked them, and they were so delicious that the students couldn't eat enough.

After that, Dr. Carver planted sweet potatoes, and the earth yielded eighty bushels to the acre. This was unheard of in that country, and now the boys who had not wanted to farm began to speak of being "agriculturists." After a few years of these crops Dr. Carver planted cotton in the enriched fields and showed that crop rotation could help the soil.

Nothing on earth was wasted. That was the belief of this man who seemed to have magic in his fingers. Every day he had a whole handful of new ideas, too. He searched the woods and fields and brought home plants, leaves, and roots. Then he took them to his laboratory and made them into useful products, or medicines, or food. He told his students that they must learn to "see." They must always see something good in nature. They must always look for something that would benefit mankind.

Not even a few handfuls of dirt were too humble to interest Dr. Carver. Yet he wanted almost nothing for himself. He wore old clothes and ancient shoes, and he ate the food prepared for students. He required no luxuries of any kind. His love for flowers was with him, as it had been since he could remember. Instead of painting flowers, Dr. Carver grew them, and he was never seen without a blossom on his coat.

One day the professor's foot slipped as he wandered through a swamp, and he fell into the mud. When he stood up, he saw with surprise that the mud on his hands was blue. He stared at it and then smiled in delight. He brought a pail, collected some mud, and took it back to the school. Not long after that, Dr. Carver told his class that here they had good paint all around them—and had never known it. When the white farmers of a nearby town asked him to speak, Dr. Carver discovered that their new little church was unpainted because of the cost. A few days later he appeared with some students and several buckets of blue paint. The church was soon covered with a handsome blue coating, and the paint stood up in all weathers.

Far and wide people talked about this gentle, hard-working scientist, who could make something out of nothing. His fame spread, and strangers came to see him. The school began to grow, and more students came to it. Yet, as always, money was the problem. Booker T. Washington was often out trying to raise money, lecturing and explaining the needs. Dr. Carver could think of only one way that he could make money for the school. He could play the piano as well as he could paint. A concert tour was arranged, and money came in for new equipment and supplies for the laboratories of Dr. Carver.

There was something else that interested the scientist. He asked himself: How can I reach the poor farmer who needs help, and cannot come to Tuskegee? A thought struck him: If he cannot come here, why can't I go to him?

A wagon was fitted out, and a program arranged. Dr. Carver made talks on crop rotation, on chicken raising, on the difficult problems of the farmers. This was the first movable school for agriculture, and the first demonstration wagon to go out to the people. Farmers' wives were told how to make good pickles and preserves and how to can food well. There was not a single subject that Dr. Carver didn't know, and not one activity that he couldn't actually do himself. Later on, the wagon carried new types of plows and garden tools. And, at one time, the demonstration collection included a live cow.

Farmers as well as students were learning from Tuskegee. Slowly money came in, and Dr. Carver was offered a larger salary. He heard the offer with a smile, and asked, "What will I do with more money?"

He had no interest in money for himself, but his interest in the land and its products grew stronger every year. When the boll weevil, "that little black bug," as the song says, came eastward from Mexico and Texas, Dr. Carver saw the danger in advance. This bug could destroy the very plants of the cotton completely and quickly. He begged farmers to stop planting cotton that year and to plow cotton stalks under to make a belt to stop the weevil. Not understanding, they refused. Dr. Carver urged farmers to spray their cotton fields with poison, and then to plant peanuts. But they refused again, and the boll weevil took over. When the cotton was destroyed, farmers were willing to plant peanuts. But then, because the peanut crop was so large, prices went down.

Dr. Carver set to work in his laboratory. He paid no attention to the things said against him for giving such advice. For many weeks he worked far into the night, and when he called people in to see the results, he showed them cheese, milk, and almost two dozen other products made from the peanut. Later he made other things: face powder, printer's ink, soaps, vinegar, creosote, butter, dyes, and many more. He experimented in the same way with the common sweet potato. Now the farmers had a market for peanuts—and the scientific world was excited. Synthetic products would be valuable. Big business was interested in the fact that useful products could be made from so many things that were formerly thrown out as useless waste.

Dr. Carver was the great pioneer in this field. When Booker T. Washington died, the scientist was offered positions with high salaries at other colleges and in manufacturing plants. He chose to stay at Tuskegee because his interest in helping the poor farmer was as strong as ever. He spent more hours in his laboratory and did less teaching, and in his spare time he painted flowers, worked with them in the greenhouses, played the piano, or made fine tapestries.

When visitors came and asked, "Is that the famous Dr. Carver?" the students thought it a good joke to say, "Yes, and he is still wearing the same suit that he had on when he came to Tuskegee."

Before Dr. Carver died in 1943, he was happy to see a fine new laboratory set up there under his direction. Now he knew that the students could go on to more knowledge under other teachers. He had taught them to see more than others saw, as he did, and he tried to teach them to listen well also. He refused to be discouraged because he was a Negro. George Washington Carver was a man who never looked down on any kind of hard work, and he was one who used his genius to help the people of his own race—those who had so little opportunity. His own love of all things that grow made the work of Dr. Carver an important part of the lives of all people, of all races.

Lindbergh

HERMANN HAGEDORN

For days the clouds make a gray canopy over Long Island, and as dusk creeps in on Thursday, May 19, 1927, rain is dripping on Curtiss Field and beating at intervals against the hangars before the fitful northeast wind. It is no weather for flying, but "Slim" Lindbergh reads the weather reports from Washington and gives up the idea of going to New York to the theater that evening. The Weather Bureau is announcing a high pressure area over the entire North Atlantic, with fogs receding from Nova Scotia and Newfoundland. If the weather *should* clear. . . .

An hour short of midnight the rain is still falling. The young man goes to his hotel in Garden City to get a few hours' rest, but there are too many things still to do to permit of sleep. He is back at the field before daybreak.

A gray smudge is on the horizon. That's dawn. The rain? By George! the rain has stopped. He helps the mechanics run the silvery plane out of the hangar and to lash her to a truck for the trip to Roosevelt Field adjoining. They set her at the field's extreme west end. The "Spirit of St. Louis." She looks like a spirit in the gray morning light.

For a last time he inspects her, calmly, without haste or flurry.

"Well, let's go."

The mechanics began to fill the big tanks of the plane; one hundred gallons, two hundred, three hundred, four hundred forty-eight.

"That's a hundred forty-five more than she's ever lifted before."

"She'll rise to it."

One of the young man's financial backers comes from some-

The mechanics began to fill the big tank.

where with sandwiches. Lindbergh tucks three or four into his pockets. In addition he has army emergency rations in the plane, dried beef, dried eggs, chocolate, hardtack, and four quarts of water; also a fishing line if the worst comes to the worst.

"You're sure you'll have enough to eat and drink?" asks a friend.

"Sure," says the boy with a grin. "If I get to Paris, I won't need any more, and if I don't get there, I won't need any more either."

Someone hands him his fur-lined, one-piece flying suit. With a last searching look at the clouds he steps into the closed cabin. He seems entirely calm and at ease and might be taking off merely to cross Long Island Sound. The thing is, he is prepared. There is nothing haphazard about this enterprise of his, this venture into the terrifying solitude between continent and continent, through the thin upper reaches of the atmosphere. He knows the dangers which confront him, and, so far as a human being may, he has prepared for them, in his plane, in his equipment, in his own training and knowledge. For the rest, there is a spirit which some call Providence and some Fate; and there is an odd and unaccountable joker who hops in and out of situations and goes by the name of Luck. But first, there is courage and resolution and faith and patient work and the steady mind.

He is assured because he has studied the principles which rule his machine and the realm in which it lives.

It is full daylight, but a gray daylight, sunless and chilly. A crowd is on the field drawn together by excited rumors that someone is actually "taking off" on the great hop. They run this way and that across the field with raincoats blowing in the wind.

A mechanic turns over the motor. The young man in the cockpit lets it idle, warming it up until it roars. "How is she?" he calls to one of his men.

"She sounds good to me."

"Well, then we might as well go."

The mechanics pull away the blocks from the wheels. The flier flips his hand at his friends. "So long." That is all.

Down the runway the great plane speeds. The field is wet and heavy. Will she rise? No plane of her size has ever lifted so great a weight. If she does not rise before she reaches the end of the field she is gone and the man inside her is gone. Suppose she strikes a ditch, crumples up, bursts into flame? Those are heartbreaking seconds. Men and women in the crowd with straining eyes and dry throats seem to have forgotten how to breathe.

But suddenly they are breathing again. A joyous sigh marks the relaxation of relief. The plane is off the ground, rising, rising. Then there is a low groan, she settles once more. Barely she clears a tractor on the field. She seems to be diving straight into a web of telephone wires. She clears the wires but has to swerve to avoid a clump of tall trees. Then, at last, she is sweeping upward.

There is a broken cheer, a scurrying this way and that to get a better view.

For a few seconds the plane is outlined dimly against a gray cloud. Then she seems to melt into the cloud.

"Slim" Lindbergh is off for France.

Lindbergh. It is a new name to the American public. For months the newspapers have been talking of a non-stop flight across the Atlantic, but the names which have been mentioned in connection with the adventure have been Byrd and Chamberlin and the Frenchmen, Nungesser and Coli. There have been columns about this man or that, but practically nothing about this fellow Lindbergh. He has come across the country from San Diego in a Ryan monoplane shining like Joan of Arc's armor; an air-mail flier, backed by a group of men in St. Louis. That is all anyone seems to know.

There is indeed not a great deal to tell about Charles Lindbergh. He is just twenty-five and hasn't had a chance to make much history. His father was of sturdy Swedish stock, a lawyer and progressive politician, a Congressman for a while, and candidate for governor of Minnesota on the Farmer Labor ticket when he died in 1924. His mother is partly Irish, partly English and French. Just now she teaches school in Detroit.

It is in Detroit that on February 4, 1902, Charles Augustus Lindbergh is born; but he grows up here, there, and everywhere. In winter he is in Washington, in summer in Little Falls, Minnesota. He goes to a dozen different schools from Washington to California but manages even so to get through high school at sixteen. Schoolmates speak of him as "a peculiar guy." The fact is that he has jumped about so much that he hasn't had a chance to make the attachments natural to boys. Besides, he likes to be alone—alone with his father, alone with his boat, his rifle, or his dog. Does he go in for daydreaming? Is he seeing himself in heroic actions, a knight, a cowboy, a soldier, entering a city of triumph, acclaimed by jubilant crowds? He would not be a boy if he did not. Does it ever occur to him in his dreams that some day the pomp which he sees in Washington now and again around the White House or the Capitol might be mustered to do him honor? What do the flights of airplanes over the Federal city mean to him when he follows them with his eyes for the first time when he is ten?

At eighteen he enters the University of Wisconsin to study engineering. He does not think much of the book work and gets his relaxation tearing about the country on a motorcycle. But no motorcycle covers the ground fast enough for him. He becomes interested in aviation and in the middle of his second year he leaves college and enrolls as a flying student with the Nebraska Aircraft Corporation. The instruction is sketchy, but the young aspirant learns the fundamentals and proves to a skeptical and hard-boiled instructor that he has an uncanny aptitude for flying, an instinctive touch, the thing known as "air sense."

He takes to "barnstorming" with a companion, going from town to town and taking passengers for little spins at five dollars a head. It is not long before mere flying becomes commonplace. Lindbergh learns stunts. Wing-walking is one of them, jumping with a parachute is another. It is all highly entertaining for all concerned. Incidentally, he is accomplishing two things, getting experience and laying by funds to buy a plane of his own. Next spring, when the government is selling off some winged remnants of the war days at an abandoned airport in Georgia, Lindbergh buys a Curtiss "Jennie" for five hundred dollars.

His first solo flight is as desperate an undertaking for him as it is for every young aviator. But it is not long before he becomes accustomed to sitting alone in the cockpit a thousand feet above the earth. He goes "barnstorming" now on his own, up and down the Middle West. He is becoming a flier, but he knows well enough how superficial his knowledge is. In March, 1924, he enrolls in the army training school at Brooks Field outside San Antonio.

It is a stiff course and at the end of six months three-fourths of his classmates have dropped by the wayside. Lindbergh with the remainder moves over to Kelly Field for another half year of training. It is not a type of education adapted to men of faint hearts. There are plenty of close calls in the practice of pursuit tactics, and once there is a crash. A de Haviland machine strikes Lindbergh's, and the ships, locked together, begin to mill around. The other flier is climbing out of his cockpit. All right, if the time has come to give up the ship, very good. Lindbergh climbs out past the edge of the damaged wing, and jumps. Far out he jumps, and falls like a plummet. With the plane falling, too, it is a wise man who assures himself a good head-start. He has fallen several hundred feet, face downward, when he pulls the string which releases the parachute. Instantly, the silken wings bring their support. He lands in a plowed field, uninjured, and within an hour is in the air again in another machine.

When at last graduation day comes, only eighteen remain of the one hundred and four who entered the school at Kelly Field with Lindbergh, but those eighteen are second lieutenants in the air Service Reserve Corps.

When, in the spring of 1926, the Robertson Aircraft Corporation of St. Louis enters into a contract to carry the mail, on the government's new air route between St. Louis and Chicago, Lindbergh becomes its chief flier. For a year through fair weather and foul, he keeps his "appointed round." Twice he is lost in darkness and fog, and, when his fuel gives out, has to jump for his life. It is all a part of the game. In the mail service you don't turn back when the skies are threatening, or a storm breaks, churning the ever restless atmosphere into freakish turbulence; or sleet comes to weigh down the wings. You take the mail according to schedule, learning to handle yourself and your plane in successive crises until it all becomes second nature and you scarcely know where you leave off and your plane begins.

It is on these lonely journeys back and forth that Lindbergh begins to ruminate over the possibility of competing for the $25,000 prize which a wealthy New Yorker named Raymond Orteig is offering to the man who makes the first non-stop flight between New York and Paris. The "hop" can be made, he is certain; and he tells the head of the Robertson Corporation that, given the right plane, he can do it. That gentleman has been watching his chief pilot for a year with growing appreciation. "If anybody can jump the Atlantic and grab the Orteig prize," he says to himself, "Lindbergh can."

He talks the matter over with his friends. Six or eight agree to contribute to a fund to build the ship. Lindbergh himself puts in all his savings, a matter of two thousand dollars, and looks about for a suitable plane. At San Diego the Ryan Airlines Corporation agree to build him what he wants. He supervises the designing, he works with the builders. Seven days in the week, all day and sometimes all night, he works. Every part of the ship feels the touch of his hand. He knows it to the last square inch of canvas and steel.

And long before the ship is ready, he knows also the course he will follow, from San Diego to St. Louis, from St. Louis to New York, from New York to Paris. For months, in a corner of the

The American public has never heard of Charles Augustus Lindbergh.

Ryan shop, he labors over the charts, and checks over the Atlantic route with the nautical tables. Shall he take a navigator with him? A navigator, or thirty extra gallons of gasoline? He decides in favor of the gasoline and the three hundred additional miles of cruising range it will give him.

The great American public knows nothing of all these preparations. It has never heard of Charles Augustus Lindbergh. It begins to hear of him on May 10 when he hops off from San Diego; and takes note of him with some interest on May 11, when he gently comes to earth in St. Louis, fourteen hours later, having broken the record for a single long-distance flight. He makes the hop to New York in seven hours and quietly informs anyone who may be entitled to know that he is about to take off for France.

That, in brief, is the history of the young man whom the raincoated little crowd at Roosevelt Field has watched with dry throats and eyes a little dim disappear into the gray morning.

The young man himself is less excited than the spectators. The haze is clearing. He is over Connecticut, over Rhode Island, over Cape Cod, flying low. Then he is over open water. At noon he is crossing Nova Scotia, noting patches of snow here and there. Beyond, are ice cakes, then open water again, and fishing boats off the Newfoundland coast. He flies low over St. John's. The time is 7:15 P.M. He circles once over the most easterly tip of land on the American continent and sweeps forward into the gathering dusk.

The Weather Bureau has promised clear skies over the Atlantic. The forecast proves false. As night falls, a thin low fog forms through which the icebergs loom, ghostly and clear. Minute by minute the fog thickens and increases in height.

There is no moon and it is very dark and bitter cold. It is lonely over the open Atlantic. Against the body of the plane suddenly beats a gust of sharp crystals. Sleet! The next instant he is in the heart of the storm.

Sleet is nothing new to him and he knows what it means. A plane in flight is kept aloft by the curvature of its wings. Once let these surfaces be flattened by a burden of sleet and the plane will fall like a dead bird.

He can still turn back, make a landing at St. John's, and return to New York for a fresh start under better conditions. But turning back and starting over is not one of the traditions of the air mail. He swoops downward and emerges from the cloudbank scarcely two hundred feet above the black waters. Under the low white roof he speeds eastward, but as he flies he sees the roof press down upon the sea. Lower and lower he flies, and lower and lower presses the thick canopy of fog. The sleet drives down and sweeps over the wings with a gritty sound.

And now the narrow space between cloud and sea is filled and the world is all cloud. Is it lonely, trapped in the fog and sleet of the North Atlantic? If there is any weakness in this boy, any self-pity, now he will break. And that will be the end. His engine will feel it, as a horse feels the spirit of his rider. An engine is a strange, human thing, of which no man knows half that there is to know. She will roar onward for a brave man where she will sputter and go dead for a timid man or one who hesitates.

There is nothing timid, nothing hesitant in the boy whose hand is on these controls. He is filled with a calm confidence in himself, in his motor, and in something greater than both. He had flown beneath the fog bank to escape the sleet. Now that the fog has closed down upon him his only hope is to soar upward to clear air above the fog, taking the chance that he can reach it before the weight of sleet forces him down to defeat.

He climbs upward for two miles and at last, dimly through the mist, he can discern the stars. But even at ten thousand feet elevation he is in a thick haze and now and again finds himself in an upjutting angle of the storm, swept around with sleet. Again and again the weight on his wings forces him to turn back into a clear air and find a way around the storm center. But at last the mists before him clear and the moon rises. At one o'clock, New York time, dawn comes.

Slowly the fog bank descends, and he descends with it. For miles he is flying within a hundred feet of the surface of the water. But a hailstorm drives him upward and soon he is once more in impenetrable fog. He flies high, he flies low; nowhere can he pierce it. He sweeps forward, flying blindly through the white solitude.

Then once more the fog breaks. Patches of sky appear, patches of sea. Slowly the air absorbs the mists, and he is flying through a clear May day with a blue-green ocean beneath him rising to whitecaps.

It is time to be looking out for land. "Come, you Ireland!" He knows what it is going to look like. It will be green, it will be mountainous. He sees a shore line, cliffs, trees, high ridges, valleys. He studies his map. But even as he gazes at the pleasant sight, the vision fades. A mirage, a trick of his imagination. He is on a shoreless ocean again. On his course? Or where?

He comes upon a small fishing boat, then another, and flies low, circling the little vessel. A man's astonished face appears at a cabin window.

The boy closes the throttle and leans out of the cockpit. "Which way is Ireland?" he shouts.

The fisherman is too amazed to reply. The boy sweeps on.

Less than an hour later a rugged coast line appears on the east. Ireland, surely, this time! He swerves toward the nearest point of land to make sure, and consults his map. Dingle Bay—Cape Valentia! Europe! He is across!

He swerves back to his compass course to Paris. The time is twelve-thirty, Saturday afternoon. By three o'clock, he is over southern England, noting English farms and English hedges. Then he is flying across the Channel.

At sunset he is over Cherbourg. At ten in the evening (six o'clock, New York time) he sees the lights of Paris. A few minutes later he is circling the Eiffel Tower looking for the landing field at Le Bourget. Yes, there are the lights. He spirals downward. He can make out the long lines of hangars. Roundabout, the roads are jammed with cars. He wonders why. It has never occurred to him that his arrival might kick up any wide interest. He has expected, in fact, to feel a bit friendless in Paris, and has taken the precaution of arming himself with a few letters of introduction.

How can he, intent on the task, know that, for a day and a half, men all over the world have as it were been holding their breath? News! Lindbergh is over Cape Cod! News! Lindbergh is over Nova Scotia! News! Lindbergh has crossed St. John's! Then silence, suspense!

"Is he still in the air? How far is he now? He's such a kid! And all alone! I bet he makes it! He's going to make it! The kid's going to win! But if anything goes wrong? All alone over the Atlantic!"

Hours, a night of silence. What is his mother thinking, waiting in Detroit? Millions are sharing her anxiety. Saturday comes, morning, noon. . . .

News! Lindbergh is over Ireland. He's crossed the ocean. He wins! The kid wins! *Extra! Extra!* Lindbergh's safe and across!

Lindbergh is over Plymouth! Lindbergh is over northern France!

The American Embassy in Paris is in wild excitement. "Old man" Herrick, the ambassador, is more thrilled than anyone has seen him in years. He is at Le Bourget long before Lindbergh can possibly get there.

Suddenly above the murmur of the crowd comes the far droning of a motor. *C'est lui!* Out of the north, like a noiseless, celestial visitor, a great bird appears, silver-gray in the rays of the beacon.

It flies low over the field once, circles into the wind, and lands; then turns again and "taxis" back to the lights. To the youth in the cockpit, it seems that all the world is surging toward him like a tidal wave. He shouts to the first who reach him to hold the crowd back, but they do not understand and he turns off the motor to keep the propeller from slaughter in that excited mob. He attempts to organize an impromptu guard for his plane, but his words are lost in jubilant shouts of welcome.

He opens the cockpit door and starts to descend. "Well, here

His feet do not touch the ground.

we are," he says, with a shy, friendly smile, to the first face he encounters. "My name is Charles Lindbergh. We—"

His feet do not touch the ground; they do not touch it for half an hour. He is clutched by the exultant crowd and lifted high. As far as he can discern are faces and waving hands and a movement like the movement of the sea. All Paris is out at Le Bourget. Paris which, only this morning, was saying sharp things about war debts and Uncle Shylock, and complaining bitterly because the United States Weather Bureau issued a forecast which, everyone feels, is partially responsible for the loss of the French fliers, Nungesser and Coli—Paris has forgotten its grievances, Paris has forgotten national barriers and, seeing only a brave youth in splendid triumph, is going delirious with joy and pride. Pride? He is not one of theirs. Their fliers are lost in the cold solitudes of that wide ocean which this youth has defied and successfully crossed. And yet, he is their own. What are Frenchmen or Americans in an hour like this? Our kinship is closer than we thought. This youth is the young brother of all mankind.

The Ambassador claims him and spirits him away from the throng which is likely to kill him with its welcome. It is three o'clock in the morning before the crowd outside the embassy and the reporters within will let the young man make his way to a bed.

What is he saying to himself as he lies waiting for sleep? The terrors behind him, the triumph, the welcome! Before him, what?

The world gives him eight hours of sleep, and then it claims him. A crowd is in the street, waiting for him. He appears on the embassy balcony. There is wild cheering and clapping and waving of hats and handkerchiefs. He says nothing. He only bows and smiles. But the bows and the smiles have a shy boyishness in them which captivate the people in the street.

They captivate the bigwigs no less. Heroes, they will tell you, are not rare, but most of them know too well how heroic they are, and topple from their pedestals. This boy does not appear to be thinking about himself at all, or really to feel that the honors are for him. Self does not seem to interest him. "I" is scarcely heard in his talk; it is always "we"—himself plus the machine. He seems, moreover, to have no intention of capitalizing his sudden fame. He receives offers to write this or that, to appear in vaudeville at thousands a night, to enter the movies for fabulous sums. Of course, he will accept? Everybody does.

Lindbergh, it happens, doesn't. France applauds. America, four thousand miles away, gasps and rejoices. In a world largely given, it seems, to grabbing hungrily and spending wildly, here is a young man who is *different.* And his people pronounce judgment on many things in their common life when they say, "Thank God!"

The fact is that Lindbergh is not half so interested in himself or his exploit as he is in aviation; and he tells everyone how much harder was the thing Nungesser and Coli failed in than the thing in which he succeeded.

The President of the French Republic pins a medal on him, the city of Paris, the French Senate, all the great men of France crowd about him, Joffre, Foch, Briand honor him, but it remains for Ambassador Herrick, tender and wise, to give him a larger significance than that of a young hero, and to make clear to the people of France that he is a symbol. The Ambassador has been having a terrible time over the war debt which France owes the United States. The tangle of misunderstanding and suspicion appears to be hopeless. The enthusiasm of the French crowd for Lindbergh gives him his cue. We are all akin, he points out. "The Americans love France, and this young man when he goes back to America will be able to tell Americans, as no other man could, that France really loves the people of the United States."

Lindbergh is no longer just a heroic young man. He is an "ambassador of good will." He fits himself into the rôle, glad for the opportunity it gives him to put the "hero business" in the background a bit. All Europe comes overnight to realize that here is something other than just a gallant young flier. Here is a rare phenomenon—a man, a boy, who can have everything for himself that he wants, personal honors, riches; and he turns aside the honors and quietly rejects the riches, being more interested in a cause than in personal advancement.

It is that phenomenon that statesmen and kings turn out to greet. In Belgium and in England, kings and queens, dukes, princes, and common folk together pay tribute of admiration and affection. From every capital in Europe come invitations, but from his own country comes a more urgent call—and a warship to bring him home.

What is he thinking, "Slim" Lindbergh, air-mail flier, twenty-five last birthday, when he hears of that warship crossing the Atlantic for no other purpose than to bring him home so that the President of the United States may tell him to his face how proud his countrymen are of him? In his boyhood dreams did he ever dare dream anything so romantic as this?

Could any dreams of boyhood equal the tooting of the whistles, as the "Memphis" steams up the Potomac, the ringing of the church bells, the screaming of the fire sirens? Batteries on the warship and batteries on shore exchange salutes; airships wheel overhead. At the Navy Yard, Cabinet officials, admirals, generals are waiting, and a school-teacher from Detroit, invited by the President of the United States.

Through streets lined with cheering crowds, escorted by cavalrymen and marines, with bands playing and flags everywhere, "Slim" Lindbergh comes home. There is handclapping and flag waving, shouting and confetti throwing, in plenty, but there is something else also. There are tears, and sobs barely suppressed and emotion too deep for applause; a sense of exaltation, of wonder, of long-dead dreams remembered, of tremulous satisfaction that for once, in a ruthless, rushing, difficult world, youth and romance are coming to their own.

"Slim" Lindbergh, is it a dream which you are dreaming in the woods near Little Falls, chewing a grass stem, while the birds twitter about you and the insects make music at the river's edge?

The President of the United States, surrounded by the notables of the nation, is speaking. Are these words for "Slim" Lindbergh, for the man on leave of absence from the St. Louis and Chicago air-mail route? "This wholesome, earnest, fearless, courageous product of America." And how the crowd roars its approval and how delightedly the wife of the President applauds! "This young man has returned. He is here. He has brought his unsullied fame home. It is our great privilege. . . ."

Dreams, dreams! Haven't we all dreamed this, lying on our backs, staring at the flies playing geometry on the ceiling?

"It is our great privilege to welcome back to his native land, on behalf of his own people, a Colonel of the United States Officers' Reserve Corps, an illustrious citizen of the Republic. . . ." Those words! What boy has not whispered them? ". . . a conqueror of the air and strengthener of the ties which bind us to our sister nations across the sea. . . ."

A dream, a dream!

No, a reality. No, this thing, this incredible, beautiful, romantic thing, is really happening. The President has spoken his name, "Charles A. Lindbergh." Out across the waving field of faces it floats, and from the slopes round about ten thousand voices roar their cheers.

After this, boys of tomorrow, dare to dream anything!

FROM

The Story of My Life

HELEN KELLER

Helen Keller is one of the truly remarkable women of our times. When she was two years old, an illness left her completely deaf and blind. Yet by the time she was twenty-four, she had been graduated with honors from Radcliffe College. The story of what her companion and teacher, Annie Sullivan, did for Helen Keller, and of her fine spirit and courage, is one of the most inspiring ever written. In this autobiography, written when she was twenty-one, we see Helen at the age of seven as her beloved teacher opens up the world to her.

In the Beginning

I CANNOT recall what happened during the first months after my illness. I only know that I sat in my mother's lap or clung to her dress as she went about her household duties. My hands felt every object and observed every motion, and in this way I learned to know many things. Soon I felt the need of some communication with others and began to make crude signs. A shake of the head meant "No" and a nod, "Yes," a pull meant "Come" and a push, "Go." Was it bread that I wanted? Then I would imitate the acts of cutting slices and buttering them. If I wanted my mother to make ice-cream for dinner I made the sign for working the freezer and shivered, indicating cold. My mother, moreover, succeeded in making me understand a good deal. I always knew when she wished me to bring her something, and I would run upstairs or anywhere else she indicated. Indeed, I owe to her loving wisdom all that was bright and good in my long night.

I do not remember when I first realized that I was different from other people; but I knew it before my teacher came to me. I had noticed that my mother and my friends did not use signs as I did when they wanted anything done, but talked with their mouths. Sometimes I stood between two persons who were conversing and touched their lips. I could not understand, and was vexed.

Meanwhile the desire to express myself grew. The few signs I used became less and less adequate, and my failures to make myself understood were invariably followed by outbursts of passion. I felt as if invisible hands were holding me, and I made frantic efforts to free myself. I struggled—not that struggling helped matters, but the spirit of resistance was strong within me. I generally broke down in tears and physical exhaustion. If my mother happened to be near I crept into her arms, too miserable even to remember the cause of the tempest. After awhile the need of some means of communication became so urgent that these outbursts occurred daily, sometimes hourly.

My parents were deeply grieved and perplexed. We lived a long way from any school for the blind or the deaf, and it seemed unlikely that any one would come to such an out-of-the-way place as Tuscumbia to teach a child who was both deaf and blind. Indeed, my friends and relatives sometimes doubted whether I could be taught. My mother's only ray of hope came from Dickens's "American Notes." She had read his account of Laura Bridgman, and remembered vaguely that she was deaf and blind, yet had been educated. But she also remembered with a hopeless pang that Dr. Howe, who had discovered the way to teach the deaf and blind, had been dead many years. His methods had probably died with him; and if they had not, how was a little girl in a far-off town in Alabama to receive the benefit of them?

When I was about six years old, my father heard of an eminent oculist in Baltimore, who had been successful in many cases that had seemed hopeless. My parents at once determined to take me to Baltimore to see if anything could be done for my eyes.

The journey, which I remember well, was very pleasant. I made friends with many people on the train. One lady gave me a box

I pulled two beads off.

of shells. My father made holes in these so that I could string them, and for a long time they kept me happy and contented. The conductor, too, was kind. Often when he went his rounds I clung to his coat tails while he collected and punched the tickets. His punch, with which he let me play, was a delightful toy. Curled up in a corner of the seat I amused myself for hours making funny little holes in bits of cardboard.

My aunt made me a big doll out of towels. It was the most comical, shapeless thing, this improvised doll, with no nose, mouth, ears or eyes—nothing that even the imagination of a child could convert into a face. Curiously enough, the absence of eyes struck me more than all the other defects put together. I pointed this out to everybody with provoking persistency, but no one seemed equal to the task of providing the doll with eyes. A bright idea, however, shot into my mind, and the problem was solved. I tumbled off the seat and searched under it until I found my aunt's cape, which was trimmed with large beads. I pulled two beads off and indicated to her that I wanted her to sew them on my doll. She raised my hand to her eyes in a questioning way, and I nodded energetically. The beads were sewed in the right place and I could not contain myself for joy; but immediately I lost all interest in the doll. During the whole trip I did not have one fit of temper, there were so many things to keep my mind and fingers busy.

When we arrived in Baltimore, Dr. Chisholm received us kindly: but he could do nothing. He said, however, that I could be educated, and advised my father to consult Dr. Alexander Graham Bell of Washington, who would be able to give him information about school and teachers of deaf or blind children. Acting on the doctor's advice, we went immediately to Washington to see Dr. Bell, my father with a sad heart and many misgivings, I wholly unconscious of his anguish, finding pleasure in the excitement of moving from place to place. Child as I was, I at once felt the tenderness and sympathy which endeared Dr. Bell to so many hearts, as his wonderful achievements enlist their admiration. He held me on his knee while I examined his watch, and he made it strike for me. He understood my signs, and I knew it and loved him at once. But I did not dream that that interview would be the door through which I should pass from darkness into light, from isolation to friendship, companionship, knowledge, love.

Dr. Bell advised my father to write to Mr. Anagnos, director of the Perkins Institution in Boston, the scene of Dr. Howe's great labours for the blind, and ask him if he had a teacher competent to begin my education. This my father did at once, and in a few weeks there came a kind letter from Mr. Anagnos with the comforting assurance that a teacher had been found. This was in the summer of 1886. But Miss Sullivan did not arrive until the following March.

Thus I came up out of Egypt and stood before Sinai, and a power divine touched my spirit and gave it sight, so that I beheld many wonders. And from the sacred mountain I heard a voice which said, "Knowledge is love and light and vision."

First Words

The most important day I remember in all my life is the one on which my teacher, Anne Mansfield Sullivan, came to me. I am filled with wonder when I consider the immeasurable contrasts between the two lives which it connects. It was the third of March, 1887, three months before I was seven years old.

On the afternoon of that eventful day, I stood on the porch, dumb, expectant. I guessed vaguely from my mother's signs and from the hurrying to and fro in the house that something unusual was about to happen, so I went to the door and waited on the steps. The afternoon sun penetrated the mass of honeysuckle that covered the porch, and fell on my upturned face. My fingers lingered almost unconsciously on the familiar leaves and blossoms which had just come forth to greet the sweet southern spring. I did not know what the future held of marvel or surprise for me. Anger and bitterness had preyed upon me continually for weeks and a deep languor had succeeded this passionate struggle.

Have you ever been at sea in a dense fog, when it seemed as if a tangible white darkness shut you in, and the great ship, tense and anxious, groped her way toward the shore with plummet and sounding-line, and you waited with beating heart for something to happen? I was like that ship before my education began, only I was without compass or sounding-line, and had no way of knowing how near the harbour was. "Light! give me light!" was the wordless cry of my soul, and the light of love shone on me in that very hour.

I felt approaching footsteps. I stretched out my hand as I supposed to my mother. Some one took it, and I was caught up and held close in the arms of her who had come to reveal all things to me, and, more than all things else, to love me.

The morning after my teacher came she led me into her room and gave me a doll. The little blind children at the Perkins Institution had sent it and Laura Bridgman had dressed it; but I did not know this until afterward. When I had played with it a little while, Miss Sullivan slowly spelled into my hand the word "d-o-l-l." I was at once interested in this finger play and tried to imitate it. When I finally succeeded in making the letters correctly I was flushed with childish pleasure and pride. Running downstairs to my mother I held up my hand and made the letters for doll. I did not know that I was spelling a word or even that words existed; I was simply making my fingers go in monkey-like imitation. In the days that followed I learned to spell in this uncomprehending way a great many words, among them *pin, hat, cup* and a few verbs like *sit, stand* and *walk*. But my teacher had been with me several weeks before I understood that everything has a name.

One day, while I was playing with my new doll, Miss Sullivan put my big rag doll into my lap also, spelled "d-o-l-l" and tried to make me understand that "d-o-l-l" applied to both. Earlier in the day we had had a tussle over the words "m-u-g" and "w-a-t-e-r." Miss Sullivan had tried to impress it upon me that "m-u-g" is *mug* and that "w-a-t-e-r" is *water*, but I persisted in confounding the two. In despair she had dropped the subject for the time, only to renew it at the first opportunity. I became impatient at her repeated attempts and, seizing the new doll, I dashed it upon the floor. I was keenly delighted when I felt the fragments of the broken doll at my feet. Neither sorrow nor regret followed my passionate outburst. I had not loved the doll. In the still, dark world in which I lived there was no strong sentiment or tenderness. I felt my teacher sweep the fragments to one side of the hearth, and I had a sense of satisfaction that the cause of my discomfort was removed. She brought me my hat, and I knew I was going out into the warm sunshine. This thought, if a wordless sensation may be called a thought, made me hop and skip with pleasure.

We walked down the path to the well-house, attracted by the fragrance of the honeysuckle with which it was covered. Some one was drawing water and my teacher placed my hand under the spout. As the cool stream gushed over one hand she spelled into the other the word *water*, first slowly, then rapidly. I stood still, my whole attention fixed upon the motions of her fingers. Suddenly I felt a misty consciousness as of something forgotten —a thrill of returning thought; and somehow the mystery of language was revealed to me. I knew then that "w-a-t-e-r" meant the wonderful cool something that was flowing over my hand. That living word awakened my soul, gave it light, hope, joy, set it free! There were barriers still, it is true, but barriers that could in time be swept away.

I left the well-house eager to learn. Everything had a name, and each name gave birth to a new thought. As we returned to the house every object which I touched seemed to quiver with life. That was because I saw everything with the strange, new sight that had come to me. On entering the door I remembered the doll I had broken. I felt my way to the hearth and picked up the pieces. I tried vainly to put them together. Then my eyes filled with tears; for I realized what I had done, and for the first time I felt repentance and sorrow.

I learned a great many new words that day. I do not remember what they all were; but I do know that *mother*, *father*, *sister*, *teacher* were among them—words that were to make the world blossom for me, "like Aaron's rod, with flowers." It would have been difficult to find a happier child than I was as I lay in my

She spelled the word water.

crib at the close of that eventful day and lived over the joys it had brought me, and for the first time longed for a new day to come.

Opening World

I had now the key to all language, and I was eager to learn to use it. Children who hear acquire language without any particular effort; the words that fall from others' lips they catch on the wing, as it were, delightedly, while the little deaf child must trap them by a slow and often painful process. But whatever the process, the result is wonderful. Gradually from naming an object we advance step by step until we have traversed the vast distance between our first stammered syllable and the sweep of thought in a line of Shakespeare.

At first, when my teacher told me about a new thing I asked very few questions. My ideas were vague, and my vocabulary was inadequate; but as my knowledge of things grew, and I learned more and more words, my field of inquiry broadened, and I would return again and again to the same subject, eager for further information. Sometimes a new word revived an image that some earlier experience had engraved on my brain.

I remember the morning that I first asked the meaning of the word, "love." This was before I knew many words. I had found a few early violets in the garden and brought them to my teacher. She tried to kiss me: but at that time I did not like to have any one kiss me except my mother. Miss Sullivan put her arm gently round me and spelled into my hand, "I love Helen."

"What is love?" I asked.

She drew me closer to her and said, "It is here," pointing to my heart, whose beats I was conscious of for the first time. Her words puzzled me very much because I did not then understand anything unless I touched it.

I smelt the violets in her hand and asked, half in words, half in signs, a question which meant, "Is love the sweetness of flowers?"

"No," said my teacher.

Again I thought. The warm sun was shining on us.

"Is this not love?" I asked, pointing in the direction from which the heat came. "Is this not love?"

It seemed to me that there could be nothing more beautiful than the sun, whose warmth makes all things grow. But Miss Sullivan shook her head, and I was greatly puzzled and disappointed. I thought it strange that my teacher could not show me love.

A day or two afterward I was stringing beads of different sizes in symmetrical groups—two large beads, three small ones, and so on. I had made many mistakes, and Miss Sullivan had pointed them out again and again with gentle patience. Finally I noticed a very obvious error in the sequence and for an instant I concentrated my attention on the lesson and tried to think how I should have arranged the beads. Miss Sullivan touched my forehead and spelled with decided emphasis, "Think."

In a flash I knew that the word was the name of the process that was going on in my head. This was my first conscious perception of an abstract idea.

For a long time I was still—I was not thinking of the beads in my lap, but trying to find a meaning for "love" in the light of this new idea. The sun had been under a cloud all day, and there had been brief showers; but suddenly the sun broke forth in all its southern splendour.

Again I asked my teacher, "Is this not love?"

"Love is something like the clouds that were in the sky before the sun came out," she replied. Then in the simpler words than these, which at that time I could not have understood, she explained: "You cannot touch the clouds, you know; but you feel the rain and know how glad the flowers and the thirsty earth are to have it after a hot day. You cannot touch love either; but you feel the sweetness that it pours into everything. Without love you would not be happy or want to play."

The beautiful truth burst upon my mind—I felt that there

SPIRIT of St. LOUIS

"The boy closes the throttle and leans out of the cockpit. 'Which way is Ireland?' he shouts."

—Lindbergh

were invisible lines stretched between my spirit and the spirits of others.

From the beginning of my education Miss Sullivan made it a practice to speak to me as she would speak to any hearing child; the only difference was that she spelled the sentences into my hand instead of speaking them. If I did not know the words and idioms necessary to express my thoughts she supplied them, even suggesting conversation when I was unable to keep up my end of the dialogue.

This process was continued for several years; for the deaf child does not learn in a month, or even in two or three years, the numberless idioms and expressions used in the simplest daily intercourse. The little hearing child learns these from constant repetition and imitation. The conversation he hears in his home stimulates his mind and suggests topics and calls forth the spontaneous expression of his own thoughts. This natural exchange of ideas is denied to the deaf child. My teacher, realizing this, determined to supply the kinds of stimulus I lacked. This she did by repeating to me as far as possible, verbatim, what she heard, and by showing me how I could take part in the conversation. But it was a long time before I ventured to take the initiative, and still longer before I could find something appropriate to say at the right time.

The deaf and the blind find it very difficult to acquire the amenities of conversation. How much more this difficulty must be augmented in the case of those who are both deaf and blind! They cannot distinguish the tone of the voice or, without assistance, go up and down the gamut of tones that give significance to words; nor can they watch the expression of the speaker's face, and a look is often the very soul of what one says.

Thus I learned from life itself. At the beginning I was only a little mass of possibilities. It was my teacher who unfolded and developed them. After she came, everything about me breathed of love and joy and was full of meaning.

FROM

Amelia Earhart:

Heroine of the Skies

SHANNON GARST

When she was little, Amelia had an absorbing ambition rather rare for a girl: she wanted to fly a plane. As soon as she could she went to California and learned how to fly. Later, while working at a settlement house in Boston, she spent all her spare time flying. It was while she was there in 1928 that she was invited to make the flight in the Friendship, *as a passenger, and thus became the first woman to cross the Atlantic in a plane. But that was not enough. Amelia wanted to fly the Atlantic by herself, and that is exactly what you see her doing in this chapter. After that she determined to try a round-the-world flight. Her husband, George Putnam, tried to dissuade her. But he remembered what she had written in a poem—"Each time we make a choice, we pay with courage." She had made her choice, and of courage she had plenty. Amelia Earhart disappeared in the Pacific on the last lap of that flight; but she still holds the record as the greatest of all women flyers.*

Lone Atlantic Flight

EARLY in 1932, George Putnam's promise to allow his remarkable wife full freedom was put to its great test.

One evening Amelia announced quietly, "I've decided to fly the Atlantic *alone*."

His heart stopped beating for a moment, then he smiled indulgently as though at a child expressing some fantastic notion, and changed the subject.

"This time *I* intend to do the driving," she went on. "No more of being a back-seat driver or excess luggage. I want to show the world that a woman can accomplish such a feat."

He said nothing either to dissuade or encourage her. It was against their premarital agreement to do the former, and he had no desire to give her encouragement. So the matter rested for some weeks.

Then casually she mentioned the matter from time to time, but her husband steered away from the subject, hoping by his lack of enthusiasm to dissuade her, if he could not actually forbid her going. Soon, however, he realized that her plans were already crystallized. She was going to make the attempt, and neither he nor anyone else could stop her, if they wanted to. Then it was that a sense of elation and pride swept over his spirit, wiping out the dread he had been feeling.

A good friend and mechanic extraordinary as regard to airplanes, Bernt Balchen, was called upon for advice and for getting the plane in shape.

"What do you think about it, Bernt?" she asked soberly. "Is the plane up to it? Am I? I'll leave it up to you. If you say that one or the other isn't equal to it, I'll give it up."

George Putnam held his breath waiting for the momentous reply upon which so much hung.

"Of course you're up to it," the young man cried enthusiastically. "I'll bet on you. And as for the ship—with a little working over, she's equal to it. And I'll see that she gets the right kind of working over."

So the die was cast. Amelia felt a resurgence of her own self-confidence at Bernt's display of confidence in her.

She pledged her husband and Bernt Balchen to secrecy. She wanted no reporters poking around, giving unwanted publicity, upsetting her plans. If anything untoward happened, she wished to feel free to abandon the idea, and she had no wish to have the taunt "publicity stunt" flung at her as it so often was in the case of women flyers. She sometimes said that she flew and dared dangerous missions for the "fun of it" and so she did.

Adventure in the skies was to her the supreme experience. From it she got more than fun; it was indeed sheer ecstasy to accomplish something no woman had ever accomplished before. And, underlying all of her most important achievements, was the very serious object of furthering the feminist cause by proving that a woman could do as much as a man could.

She was quite philosophical about the whole matter. She knew well the terrific risks she was running, but if she succeeded she would accomplish what was, to her, worth all of the hazards. She would immeasurably advance the cause of aviation and of women flyers. If she went down—well, it would be a glorious exit, she thought. Whatever happened, it was worth the cost.

She chartered the plane to Bernt Balchen. It was well known that he was planning a flight to the South Pole. In this manner, no one would anticipate her plans.

Her Lockheed plane was taken to Teterboro Airport, in New Jersey, near Balchen's home. She had flown this plane across the country and here and there for three years. A new engine was installed and the fuselage was strengthened. The cabin was stripped of all nonessentials, in order to equip it with a large fuel tank. Extra fuel tanks were also put beneath the wings.

During the period of waiting, she worked hard to perfect her knowledge of instrument flying, for blind flying is the most difficult sort, as in darkness or fog, with nothing to guide the eye, it is impossible to know whether one is flying upside down or is climbing or descending. The flyer must depend entirely on his instruments in such cases, and this sort of flying demands sure knowledge and considerable practice.

Bernt Balchen, however, kept bolstering her self-confidence by declaring that he was certain she could do it. G.P., too, had put his shoulder stanchly to the wheel, now that her decision was made, and was doing everything in his power to assist her.

The plane was rapidly being put into shape and the plans were all made—even to the clothes and food to take along. These were astonishingly simple. She would wear her usual well-tailored jodhpurs, simple silk blouse, and leather flying jacket. Nothing else. She would not even take a nightie. She would merely tuck a comb and toothbrush into a pocket. Her food supply was a small thermos jug of soup and a can of tomato juice with a straw to sip it.

Now that everything was in readiness, came the nerve-racking wait for proper weather conditions.

She pestered her friend of the Weather Bureau, Doc Kimball, daily for weather reports. He must have suspected her plans, but wisely said nothing, since she did not choose to take him into her confidence.

The Atlantic is a difficult ocean to fly. In the north, where the distance is shortest, the climate creates a severe weather hazard. In the south, where a gentler climate prevails, a greater distance forms the obstacle. Amelia elected to fly the northern route.

It was May 20th when she decided that conditions were favorable. She drove her car to Rye and changed into her flying outfit, seizing her maps, scarf, soup and juice and hurrying back to Teterboro she was ready for the take-off at three o'clock in the afternoon for St. John, New Brunswick. Bernt Balchen with Gorski, the mechanic, were to fly the plane to St. John, so that she would be fresh for her lonely flight over the Atlantic.

She was to leave from Harbor Grace in Newfoundland. There she went to sleep while Balchen and Gorski tuned up the engine. The telegrams from New York indicated favorable weather, but not perfect.

"I'm going to take off," she said. "Probably the weather will never be better. It's seldom absolutely perfect."

She shook hands with the two men, who wished her the best of fortune.

She smiled as she climbed into the cockpit.

She smiled as she climbed into the cockpit and waved to them.

With a rush and a roar, at fifteen minutes past seven, the red plane was in the air, headed toward England, with over a thousand miles of deep, cold water to cross.

The setting sun painted the clouds a glorious hue, as if to furnish a fitting setting for such an epic adventure. As she flew into the clouds with nothing but the empty sea below her, such an elation filled her soul that it was almost pain.

"Even if I don't succeed," she told herself, "it will be worth it, simply to feel like this even for a brief moment."

She looked down at the dazzling sea trimmed with giddy white ripples. Toy boats bobbed in the water off shore. Children's play houses dotted the land she was leaving behind.

The blue dome of the sky arched over her, and in front lay an immensity of distance. It was as if the whole world opened up before her. She drew in her breath exultantly as the excitement of this great adventure rushed through her veins like fire.

Then the wind took her plane and bounced it like a kite. She took a firmer grip on the controls. The wind, like the hand of fate, was always the unpredictable factor in flying. It might help greatly or bring disaster to a flight. It could bear its weight against one wing and so push the plane off its course. If the wind blew head on, it could make the flight a hard battle, waste fuel and time. On the other hand, it could lend a helping hand by pushing at the rear, giving the flyer fuel and daylight to spare.

"Please, wind, be my friend," Amelia prayed silently.

The dark closed in like a soft, smothering veil and, for a moment, the combination of blackness and loneliness caught her heart in a grip of terror, but she shook it off.

"This is what you wanted to do, Amelia," she told herself. "You asked for this; now make the most of it."

The fear dissolved, but not the loneliness. She had never been so completely alone in her life. When she flew across the Atlantic before, she had had companions. When she flew alone over land, there was always the knowledge that there were people below. If she crashed someone would find her—or at least the pieces. But now there was no one below. If she went down, it would be to the most complete oblivion. It was a thought that brought desolation to her soul.

Then the moon came over a cloud bank and silvered the world with beauty, and again her heart took wings. Far below, the silver-edged waves danced in loveliness.

"No one else in the world has ever done just what I am doing now," she told herself with awe. "No one else in the world has ever felt just the way I feel now. How wonderful it is to be alive. What a lucky person I am."

Then suddenly she was to have another unique experience. One not so pleasant. Her altimeter failed. This had never happened to her before, and a feeling of panic gripped her spirit as she saw the needles standing motionless and useless. There was no way to gauge her height. She might be high in the heavens or dangerously close to a watery grave. The moon had disappeared. The plane was dipping and swaying in the strong wind that was doubtless blowing up a storm.

Then jagged spears of lightning split the sky, and the wind tossed the plane like a ship in a heavy sea.

One thought gripped her mind. She must climb, climb. Perhaps she could rise above the storm. At any rate, she would not be in danger of diving into the sea. It was almost impossible to hold the course in that lashing wind; in fact, she was blown off it at this time.

Finally she realized by the decreased speed of the ascent that the wings were picking up ice. There was only one thing to do in this case; descend into warmer air in the hope that the ice would melt. She dove, then, until a moonlit path through the parted clouds showed the waves lapping dangerously close, and she must again climb a bit out of their greedy reach.

A wonderful sense of peace and relief seized her as the plane bored its way through the clouds. She saw one very bright star lighting the clouds, and she thought it quite the loveliest sight

The moon had disappeared.

she had ever seen. She felt so close that she could almost reach out and touch it.

Then her brief time of comfort was abruptly ended when she saw a streak of blue flame with ugly red tongues darting from a broken weld in the manifold ring of the engine. A sense of hopelessness gripped her. There wasn't anything she could do about this—merely sit glued to the seat, and hope that the metal would prove thick and strong enough to hold the flame in check until she reached land.

She sat tense as she sped through the night. The flames might take a long time to eat through; they might do it quickly, aided by the vibration of the engine.

At last the night began to dissolve into the pearl gray shades of dawn—then became rose-tinted by the sun. And with the coming of daylight her spirits rose, for the flames looked less ugly and terrifying and did not seem to be making too dangerous headway.

She had forgotten about food, but now she drank the tomato juice.

Later she found the gauge of one of the reserve tanks of gasoline leaking. Her destination was England. Now her only thought was to land as soon as possible. She changed her course due east and headed for Ireland determined to land in the first likely place she found.

She strained her eyes, staring into the distance for a sight of land. Ahead was something like the shadow of a cloud perhaps. Or was she imagining things? No. Gradually the shadow began to take solid shape and assume color, distinct from the gray ocean. It *was* land. A wave of relief and joy flooded over her.

The grayish mass slowly became green. She flew low over the land until she saw a toy town below her. Londonderry it was, although she did not know it then. She dipped low several times, trying to find a landing place. At last she chose a cow pasture and came to a stop in a level meadow.

A cow looked at her with startled, shocked eyes, not knowing that hers was the honor of gazing at the first woman to fly across the Atlantic Ocean alone.

FROM

The Story of Albert Schweitzer

JO MANTON

Albert Schweitzer is a quiet sort of hero, but a great and courageous man none the less. He was thirty years old and already famous as a concert organist when he decided to study medicine. For a long time he had been thinking of the miserable lot of the natives of Africa, with no medical help at all. He plunged into the new life he had chosen—as a doctor in the worst poverty-ridden, fever-infested jungles of French Equatorial Africa. Since that time, nearly 50 years ago, he has seldom left his hospital at Lambaréné, but through his writings has become one of the most influential thinkers in the world today, and was awarded the Nobel Peace Prize. Schweitzer's philosophy is a profound and simple one, based on respect for all living things—"a reverence for life." At 83 years old, the "jungle doctor" still puts in a full day's work in his African hospital, and has interested many other doctors and institutions in spreading his good work throughout the once dark continent.

The Chicken-House Hospital

THE mission station was built on three small hills above the river, where a narrow strip of land had been cleared from the forest and planted with coffee bushes and lemon and orange

He would find them waiting for him.

trees. Twenty yards from the houses the forest rose in a sheer wall. There was nowhere to walk in the evenings or on Sundays, but up and down the narrow clearing, where not a breath of air stirred the heavy palm fronds.

"If we could only cut down a corner of the forest, we might get a breeze from the river," said the missionary, "but we haven't the money or the men for that."

To the Schweitzers at first it felt like living in a prison, though they loved the view from the veranda of their four-room wooden house. "It is entrancing," wrote Schweitzer; "below us is the stream, which widens here and there into a lake; all around is forest, in the distance a stretch of the main stream, and in the background a range of blue hills." They did not have much time to look at it. News had spread through the forest that a doctor had come to Lambaréné, and even before their packing cases of drugs and instruments arrived on the river-steamer, patients began to crowd around the house. Schweitzer could not send them away; without drugs or equipment he still had to see them and do what he could to help.

Every morning, when he stepped out on to the veranda, he would find them waiting for him, thirty or forty Negroes squatting on the ground in the shadow of his house. These were not the educated Africans of the coast, but wild nomads from the forest. They watched him, rolling the whites of their eyes in their black faces, as hopeless and uncomplaining as animals in their suffering. One old leper held out the stump of an arm, wrapped in filthy rags; his wife had paddled their canoe more than two hundred miles when they heard that a doctor was coming. A woman rocked a crying baby in her arms; it looked as though it had been dipped in red jam, the whole of its body raw and smeared with blood. He saw the tall, graceful Galoa women, with their swaying cotton skirts, hollow-eyed and shaking with malaria fever. The savage Pahouin from deep in the forest were stunted and lined with hunger, their faces blank with despair and the fear of a thousand torturing superstitions. There were children from the famine district, on the N'Gomje river, who scratched up the earth and crammed it into their mouths. Their arms and legs were as thin as sticks, their stomachs bloated and swollen.

"Here among us everybody is sick, everybody is ill," said a young man; and an old chief nodded his gray head sadly. "Yes, our land devours its own children." All their faces were turned toward Schweitzer for comfort; he was the only man for hundreds of miles who could help them, he was alone, and he had not even his drugs or instruments.

At last, during the night, he heard the whistle of the steamer, and learned next day that his seventy packing cases of stores had been unloaded by the main river, as the captain could not bring his ship up the shallow side stream leading to the mission. Next

They carried all the cases uphill from the river bank.

morning Schweitzer and the missionaries set out with all their African servants and helpers in a fleet of canoes, and paddled the baggage safely back to the little bay, shaded by a spreading mango tree, which served as their harbor. The next job was to carry all the cases uphill from the river bank to the hospital. "Each case suddenly got a crowd of black legs underneath it, and two rows of woolly heads apparently growing out of the sides," wrote Schweitzer, "and so, with shouting and shrieking, it crept up the hill."

It was difficult to unpack the cases, because there was nowhere to put the stores. Schweitzer had been promised a corrugated-iron hut as a hospital, but the Negroes who should have put it up had all found better-paid jobs as lumbermen in the forest. For the time being he had to put the most necessary drugs on shelves in his sitting room and treat his patients in the open air. Whenever the drenching tropical rainstorms began, he had to snatch up medicines and bandages and run into the house, where he could not take the sick people for fear of spreading infection. This clearly could not go on and he began to search for a temporary building.

The only free building was a tumble-down shed in which an earlier mission had kept chickens.

"Good. I'll promote the old fowl-house to the rank of hospital," said Schweitzer, and set to work. He got some shelves fixed on the walls, covered the worst of the dirt with whitewash and moved in an old camp-bed. It was horribly stuffy and close, and so much heat came through the holes in the palm-leaf tiles of the roof that he had to wear a sun-helmet indoors, but at least it kept off most of the rain. When he heard the storm rattling on the roof, he went calmly on with his bandaging, and looking around the squalid little hut, said to himself, "How fortunate I am!"

He was determined to see the beauty of Africa and the cheerful side of everything, but there must have been days when he despaired. What could one man do against a whole world of suffering and misery? "The need is terrible," he wrote to his friends.

He could never have come through the first six months without his wife to help and support him. Try as he might he could not get used to the sight of so much despair. When he tormented himself, as he always did, with worry about the patients who were seriously ill, she alone could understand his feelings and calm his fears. She worked as hard as he did. She had to run the house, weigh out the stores, and supervise the African servants, who were too unreliable to work without her eye upon them. Then at ten in the morning she left her housework to go over to the fowl-house. There she cleaned the surgical instruments—no easy job in a climate where the dampness blunts and rusts every piece of metal. She prepared everything for the doctor's operations, and gave anesthetics on operating days. She also took charge of the hospital's washing, since none of the Africans could understand that dirty and infected linen must be thoroughly boiled.

Even with his wife's help, Schweitzer could not carry on his work without an interpreter to translate for him. The African mission schoolteacher who had promised to help failed to turn up, because he had become entangled in some interminable tribal lawsuit in his own village. Schweitzer was in despair, and the missionaries said to him with a smile: "Ah, Dr. Schweitzer, now your education is beginning. Never rely on our tribesmen for anything; time means nothing to them."

Then one day, among the patients, a tall, very intelligent-looking Galoa turned up. He spoke to the doctor in fluent French.

"Where did you learn to speak French so well?" Schweitzer asked him.

"I used to be a cook to a white man, but now I want to change my job," answered the Negro. Schweitzer noticed that all his movements were deft, and the smile on his dark face very kindly.

"Would you like to come to me as cook, and also to help me in the hospital?" he asked. The man's face lit up with pride and pleasure. "Yes, Doctor," he said, "I will help you with everything."

That was the beginning of Joseph, who stayed faithfully with the doctor for many years. He was a remarkable man in many ways. He could speak eight Negro dialects as well as French, and although he could not read or write he never made a mistake when it came to taking down a bottle of medicine from the dispensary shelf.

"How do you know which one to take?" Schweitzer asked him. "The bottles are nearly all the same."

"I remember the look of the words on the label," explained Joseph simply.

He was not afraid, as so many of the Negroes were, of blood or pus, and soon learned to bandage sores, and even to help, under Madame Schweitzer's supervision, at operations.

Joseph had one peculiarity; he had learned his anatomy, as well as his French, in the white man's kitchen, and when he described the cases to the doctor, it was in terms of cookery. "This man's leg of mutton hurts him," he would say with pride, or, pushing a patient gently forward, "Look, Doctor, this woman has a pain in the loin, and the left upper-cutlet!"

It was Joseph who explained the ways of Africa to his employer. Schweitzer was angry and hurt when someone stole his precious copy of Bach's *St. Matthew Passion* from the piano; but Joseph said, with a flash of white teeth, "You forgot to lock it up, Doctor, so of course it went for a walk."

It needed calmness and courage to live in the tropical forest. Lambaréné is big-game country, and the windows of their little house were barred against marauding leopards. Poisonous snakes nested in the undergrowth, and crocodiles basked half-hidden in the sandbanks of the river. A missionary who trod on one, mistaking it for a log, had great strips of flesh torn out of his leg. The lovely, basketlike nests of the weaverbirds in the palms before the house were robbed by birds of prey. Yet the large creatures were not as deadly as the small. Mosquito-nets had to be constantly mended, for night-flying mosquitoes carry the germs of malaria. By day the tsetse fly, which looks like a common house-fly, can pierce through the thickest cloth and implant the germ of sleeping sickness.

One night, at the end of the rainy season, the Schweitzers were awakened by the clucking of frightened chickens from the fowl-house. "What was that? Traveler ants! Take the bugle from the wall and blow three blasts to warn the other houses," he shouted, running out to the shed. A quivering black mass covered the whole of the fowl-house floor. It was a column of traveler ants on the march, close-packed and murderous. Already they were beginning to suffocate the hens by swarming in their mouths and nostrils. "No living thing could survive in that," said Schweitzer grimly. "If we leave them they'll pick every chicken to the bone."

Already the ants were beginning to swarm over them. As they tried to brush them away, the strong jaws remained embedded in their flesh, to be picked out painfully later in the surgery. The chickens were saved by the servants from the mission, who came running with buckets of lysol and water. Schweitzer poured these on the mud floor and the moving mass broke into particles as the ants scurried away into safety, leaving their dead in the puddles. Tired but triumphant the Schweitzers went back to bed. The traveler ants were regular visitors at the beginning and end of the rainy season, and in one week they had to drive off four night attacks.

During the first months of ceaseless work and worry, Schweitzer did not allow himself any recreation. He had brought with him to Lambaréné as a farewell present from the Paris Bach Society a magnificent piano, with pedals like an organ, specially built for the tropics in a zinc-lined case. The Africans at the mission had paddled it up the stream for him in a canoe hollowed from a gigantic tree trunk, and had carried it up the hill to his house. Now it stood in the crowded little sitting room, which was also study and pharmacy, as a reminder of all that he had loved and renounced. He had not the heart to play on it.

"No, don't ask me to play," he would say to his wife in the evenings. "Coming to Africa means the end of my life as a musician. It will be easier to bear if I allow my fingers and feet to get rusty."

One evening he was sadly turning over the pages of a Bach organ fugue, when he thought suddenly: "After all, why shouldn't I practice? Here I don't have to worry about concerts—I can take my time. I'll learn pieces one by one, deeply and thoroughly, even if it takes me months to get one by heart."

Outside was thick darkness, faint starlight on the water and the stealthy rustle of wild creatures in the forest. Suddenly from the small house by the river clear, triumphant music rang out into the night. Every evening, from that day onward, the voice of music spoke in the forest.

The Hospital Established

By the autumn the Paris Missionary Society was able to let Schweitzer have his promised hospital building. It was no more than a shed of corrugated iron on the bank above the river, divided into two rooms, one of which he used for examining patients and the other for operations. Hélène Schweitzer set up her dispensary and sterilizing room in a lean-to shed at the side. The Negroes on the station helped to build a large hut of raffia leaves, so that at last there would be somewhere for patients who needed prolonged treatment to sleep. Until now they had been sheltered in a boathouse.

Schweitzer looked around the large, dark hut, and, taking a sharp-pointed stick, drew sixteen squares on the mud floor. "These are the sleeping places," he said to the little crowd which stood watching. "Here are axes; find wood and make beds by nightfall." He thought that the friends and relations who came with each patient should do some useful work instead of chattering or lying under the palm trees all day. They went away, laughing and pointing in all directions. All day the canoes went up and down the river; the sound of the choppers rang out, and women and children were sent into the forest to bring back ropes of twisted creeper. By evening the beds were finished. Each was made of four forked posts, which supported side poles and shorter poles laid crosswise. The whole was firmly bound together with creeper stalks. Dried grass was heaped up for a mattress. There was a sigh of satisfaction with their work. "Ah! Good sleeping places!"

At six o'clock, when the darkness came swiftly and suddenly down, as it does all the year round at Lambaréné, the first patients were laid on their beds. When Schweitzer came on his last round at night, he found several sick people lying on the floor, while their friends enjoyed the new experience of a night in a real bed. He woke them and turned them out. "Nobody is to have a bed while a sick person lies on the floor," he said, and smiled wryly to himself at the memory of the spotless and orderly hospital in Strasbourg, where he had walked the wards as a student.

In this hut hospital, men and women camped with their friends and all their belongings. They were supposed to bring their own food, but those who had none lined up outside the house each day for Madame Schweitzer to give them the hospital ration of bananas, which they ate green and boiled, and long sticks of bread made from the starchy roots of manioc. Each family made its own little fire on the ground outside the hut, and cooked separately.

Now that the hospital was well established a daily routine had grown up. At dawn, when the weaverbirds began to chatter in the palms, canoes came gliding across the water to moor under the shade of the great mango tree in the hospital's little bay. At half-past eight the patients and all their friends were squatting in a circle outside the doctor's house. Joseph now appeared, dignified in a European sun-helmet.

"I am Dr. Schweitzer's first medical assistant," he announced. "Listen, everyone! These are the doctor's standing orders:

"1) Spitting near the doctor's house is strictly forbidden.
"2) Those who are waiting must not talk to each other loudly.

"3) Patients and their friends must bring enough food for one day, as they cannot all be seen early in the day.

"4) Anyone who spends the night on the station without the doctor's permission will be sent away without any medicine.

"5) All bottles and tin boxes in which medicines are given must be returned.

"6) In the middle of the month, when the steamer has gone up the river, none but urgent cases can be seen till the steamer has gone down again, as the doctor is then writing to Europe to get more of his valuable medicines.

"May the doctor's words be made known through all the villages, both on the river and on the lakes!"

At each sentence the black heads nodded, and they grunted to show that they had understood.

The morning wore on while the ground, sodden with the last night's rain, steamed in the fierce heat of the sun. Wreaths of mist shifted and trailed across the shining river. One after another, Joseph showed the waiting patients into the iron shed, and stood by, ready to translate.

"What is your name?"

"M'Buru."

A bare black arm waved vaguely toward the river. "Many days' journey."

"How old are you, M'Buru?"

"Ninety years old."

Schweitzer looked at him in surprise; the man was thin and lined, but not past middle age.

"He counts each rainy and dry season as one year," explained Joseph. "Why do you come to the doctor, M'Buru?"

"Worm, worm in my head." He shook his head wearily from side to side. All pain and disease, to the primitive tribesman, is caused by a worm in the body.

"Do you sleep well?"

"Many nights not sleeping. Then always tired and sleeping by day. Now cold, cold." He wrapped his thin arms around his body and shuddered in spite of the blazing sun outside. Schweitzer laid a practiced hand against his neck; the man had fever.

"Find him a place in the sleeping hut, Joseph." He would have to spend a whole morning tied to his microscope searching for the trypanosomes of sleeping sickness in the patient's blood, while outside there were still thirty patients waiting to be seen, dressings to be changed, teeth to be drawn, medicines made up and water disinfected.

"I must somehow put up a special hut for the sleeping-sickness cases, across the river, well away from the other buildings." He sighed, and brushed his hand wearily across his face to wipe off the sweat. "Next, please."

The next patient was a little girl with one leg encased in rags. The mother put her on his table, where she lay limply, too exhausted even to cry. He unwrapped the leg with a sinking heart, knowing already what he would find. The whole surface of the foot was one single sore, in which the sinews and bones showed like white islands. A sickening smell of decay rose from the rags.

"I know what happened," he said sternly to the mother. "The child had a sore on the foot; you put a paste of earth on it, so the pus could not escape, and now it has spread. Is that true?" She nodded, her eyes fixed on him.

"The child must stay here at the hospital, until I have cleaned the sore right down to the sound flesh. It will be weeks, perhaps months. Can you stay with her?" She nodded again.

"What happened to cases like this before we came?" he asked Joseph.

"People cannot bear the smell. They put them in a hut away from the village, bring them food. In the end they die," explained Joseph simply.

"Weeks and months," thought Schweitzer, "we shall have to keep them, and feed them both, all that time. It will use up half a case of bandages, and even then she will always limp. But what a joy when we see her step into the canoe, well enough to go home!" But to Joseph he only said: "Next, please, Joseph."

The morning went on—malaria, scabies, coughs and colds. "I

The child must stay here at the hospital.

might as well be in church at Günsback on New Year's Eve," thought Schweitzer, listening to their sneezes. At last he looked at his watch. A rest at midday is essential in the tropics. "It's half-past twelve. I think that's all for this morning, Joseph. Tell them I'll come back at two o'clock."

Joseph announced: "The doctor is going to have his lunch"; and the crowd scattered under the trees to light their own cooking fires and eat their bananas. At two, Schweitzer came back, and worked through the afternoon until at six darkness fell. Often there were still patients waiting to be seen. At first Schweitzer had wanted to carry on by lantern light.

"Impossible," said the missionaries. "Light brings mosquitoes; mosquitoes bring fever." So Schweitzer had to go back to his own house in the evenings, until it was time for his last round of the hut.

"If only I knew what they did with the medicines!" he said to his wife. "Joseph tells them, over and over again, and it is written on the bottles in case anyone in their village can read, but I am never sure they don't drink the whole bottle at one time, or eat the ointment! And that reminds me; we need more bottles. Cardboard boxes simply fall to pieces in this damp. We must keep a list of every bottle that goes out of the hospital and insist on having them all back."

At first it was a problem to know how to keep records of the patients, in case they came back for further treatment. Finally Schweitzer entered all his notes in a register under numbers and gave each patient his own number on a disk when he left the hospital. He noticed that they kept these disks very carefully, usually on a string around their necks.

"They believe the disks are magic, powerful magic," explained Joseph. In fact the patients had no idea of medicine except as a kind of witchcraft, and Schweitzer found that he was regarded, up and down the river, as a powerful witch-doctor. The name the Africans gave him was Oganga, which means the great fetishman, for the things he could do seemed to them magical.

"Truly he is a great fetishman," said an old woman, with a

heart complaint, to Joseph. "He knows I can hardly breathe at night, and that I often have swollen feet, yet I didn't tell him, and he never even looked at my feet!"

They were most impressed of all by his anesthetics. "Since Oganga has been here, we have seen wonderful things," said a little girl. "First he kills the sick people, then he cures them and then he wakes them up again."

Sometimes the monotony of the days at the hospital was broken by a journey up the river, when Schweitzer was called to a case at one of the other stations of the Paris Missionary Society.

They always set off in the misty morning, two hours before dawn, since it would take twelve hours to paddle a journey of thirty-five miles against the current. Schweitzer sat on a folding chair in the bow of the canoe, with his tin trunk and the day's ration of banana for the crew piled up amidships. The six pairs of rowers plunged their paddles into the water, singing a rhythmic chant, in which they complained how early the heartless doctor had made them start work. As they swung out of the side-stream into the main river, the singers stopped instantly. "Hippopotamus," shouted the leading rowers, pointing to some dark shapes moving through the water. In silence they edged the canoe over to the bank and crept upstream under the overhanging trees, until they were safely past. An angry hippopotamus can dive under a canoe and hurl it into the air.

The sun came up, and the surface of the river began to shimmer and flash with light. "It's like being shot at with fiery arrows," thought Schweitzer, closing his aching eyes. At midday they stopped at a native village, where the crew lit a fire and roasted their bananas. Then they set off again. Gaudy-colored birds squawked overhead and flew with a clap of wings from tree to tree. A crocodile lay sleeping with half-open eyes on a tree stump in the water.

"Shoot?" asked the leader of the rowers, but Schweitzer only shook his head and left his rifle lying across his knee. "You never even touch your shooter!" said the rowers reproachfully, but he did not answer them. He was remembering the time when one of the missionaries had shot at a monkey, and searching in the undergrowth they had found a little baby monkey clinging with piteous cries to the body of its dying mother.

On these journeys, he had decided, he would never use his rifle except in self-defense.

Between work at the hospital and journeys on the river, the seasons passed.

After nine months, Schweitzer was able to write to his friends in Europe that he had treated more than two thousand people. He had seen sleeping sickness, leprosy, malaria, tropical dysentery, diseased bones and joints and endless skin diseases. Looking back, the things he remembered more vividly than anything else were the emergency operations, particularly for strangulated hernia, which seemed to be common among the Negroes. A man was brought by his friends in a canoe and carried up the hill, writhing with pain.

"More than once I've seen a man like this, rolling on the floor of his hut and howling in agony until death came to release him," said one of the older missionaries.

"Now I am here—the only man for hundreds of miles around who can save him," thought Schweitzer, and could not put his feelings into words.

He went over to the stretcher, where the man lay moaning.

"Don't be afraid," he said, laying his hand gently on the black forehead. "In less than an hour's time you will go to sleep, and when you wake up, you won't feel any more pain."

He went to the house to fetch his wife, and calmly, as if they were in a clean, well-equipped European hospital, she made everything ready in the operating theater. She gave the anesthetic herself, and gave quiet directions to Joseph, who stood by, wearing a long pair of rubber gloves, to act as the doctor's assistant, handing him the instruments and mopping the sweat off his face with a towel.

When the operation was over, Schweitzer sat by the sick man's side in the dark hut, waiting for him to wake. Slowly he stirred, sighed, rolled his head on the pillow and came back to consciousness. Suddenly his eyes opened wide.

"I've no more pain!"

He stared about him, fixed his eyes on the doctor and repeated as if he could not believe it, "No more pain! No more pain!" His hand felt for Schweitzer's, gripped it tightly and would not let it go. "I've no more pain!"

The African sun shone through the coffee bushes into the dark shed, where they sat side by side. "Now we know," wrote Schweitzer, "the meaning of the words, 'All ye are brothers.'"